Value Economics

M. R. Griffiths • J. R. Lucas

Value Economics

The Ethical Implications of Value for New Economic Thinking

M. R. Griffiths
Governor, British Institute of Florence
Florence, Italy

J. R. Lucas
Fellow, Merton College, Oxford
Somerset, United Kingdom

ISBN 978-1-137-54186-4 (hardcover)   ISBN 978-1-137-54187-1   (eBook)
ISBN 978-1-349-95898-6 (softcover)
DOI 10.1057/978-1-137-54187-1

Library of Congress Control Number: 2016956422

Cover illustration: © Fanatic Studio / Alamy Stock Photo

Printed on acid-free paper

This Palgrave Macmillan imprint is published by Springer Nature
The registered company is Macmillan Publishers Ltd.
The registered company address is: The Campus, 4 Crinan Street, London, N1 9XW, United Kingdom

Preface

The last financial crisis revealed a gap between business practice and ethics. *Value Economics* examines some of the reasons for this "ethical" gap, the resulting loss of confidence and trust in the financial system, and the ability or otherwise of the regulatory authorities and economic planners to forecast and control the economic factors which led to the crisis. One of the reasons has been hazy or inadequate thinking about how we "value" the outcomes of economics and business practice, and relate the compensation of business and financial executives to the creation of economic value, as opposed to monetary wealth. We believe that the creation of economic value and business ethics are closely linked, and propose that economic value should become the basic criterion and metric for evaluating economic performance, and that businessmen as economic operators should be accountable for answering the question: "What is the economic value you are creating not only for the shareholders but for all stakeholders in your business enterprise?"

The book examines the rationality of a number of philosophical principles for business practice, all of which relate to the objective and task of creating economic value. This leads us to reconsider how all stakeholders participate in the economic value of companies, and how we distinguish between total shareholder return (TSR) and value (TSV). We also look at the possibility of greater employee participation in decision making and ownership, not through nationalization, but through the allocation of shares in the companies for whom they work. We also propose that the concept of economic value be applied to public enterprises in evaluating both their social and capital efficiency in providing public services. The result of this kind of economic thinking is to see business, both private and public, as primarily a non-privative, participative and sharing activity, with an important component of philanthropic giving—a concept of business which will lead to a redefinition of "Economic Man" as both a social contributor and profit maximizer.

With this emphasis on business as a participative "shared value" activity, the principle of profit maximization is conditioned and modified in light of the different "self-interests" of all parties involved, and of how economic value is to be shared between all of the stakeholders. If this kind of economic thinking is accepted, it has implications for seeing economics as a moral as well as an econometric science, the arguments for which the book opens, and also for revisiting or revising the philosophy of economics and business ethics with which the book ends in calling for a closer working relationship between the "practical" businessman and the "theoretical" expert—whether economist, financial advisor or regulator. The book, written by a businessman and a political philosopher, hopes to make a contribution to new economic thinking on the part of the "experts" in a way which will engage and convince the businessman in looking at ways for making business a more participative and sharing activity in terms of its organization, management and remuneration.

In the end the book's success has to be judged by whether or not it makes a contribution to recreating that confidence and trust on the part of business in the financial system within which it operates, and also of the general public, epitomized by the man on the Clapham Omnibus, of which he is an inseparable part. In looking at the implications of value for business ethics, the book seeks ways in which codes of business ethics can enter into the DNA of a business organization, and avoid the risk of such codes becoming a list of "motherhood" statements to which only "lip service" is paid. The challenge is how the ethical principles of honesty, fairness, transparency and accountability are to be incorporated into business practice. For this reason we look at the "greed is good" mentality, and the tendency that we are not always honest, if given the opportunity not to be so. In this context we look at what we mean by business "excellence", which can be seen as the "virtue" of a businessman in creating economic value, which in the end determines how successful business is going to be in achieving economic justice—which remains the "end" of all economic activity.

M. R. Griffiths
Florence, Italy

J. R. Lucas
Oxford, UK

Contents

Contents

List of Tables

List of Tables

1

Introduction

Abstract This book is a sequel to *Ethical Economics*, published by Macmillan Press and St Martin's Press in 1996, which investigated rational philosophical principles for economic activities and business behaviour. As a sequel it looks at the validity of these principles following the last financial crisis, but with the additional objective of taking a new look at how we define and measure economic value, and how the creation of value relates to business ethics. In this Introduction we set the scene for *Value Economics* by summarizing those principles for business we examined in *Ethical Economics*, and how they relate to some of the unanswered questions facing modern capitalism today. Finally, we describe the structure and contents of the book, and suggest how it can be read as a Compendium for new economic thinking. We have tried to write the book in a way which will engage the interest of businessmen, as well as economists, regulators, financial advisors and students of business in general.

One key theme of *Value Economics* is to take a new look at how we value the results of economic activity. The complexity of doing this is well expressed in a remark attributed to Einstein when he said: "Everything which can be counted does not necessarily count; everything that counts

© The Editor(s) (if applicable) and The Author(s) 2016   **1**
M.R. Griffiths, J.R. Lucas, *Value Economics*,
DOI 10.1057/978-1-137-54187-1_1

cannot necessarily be counted." The relation between price and value remains a key issue for economics. In the words of Warren Buffett, "Price is what you pay: Value is what you get" a phrase which echoes Oscar Wilde's famous definition of the cynic as "a man who knows the price of everything and the value of nothing".

1.1   Rational Principles

It was the aim of *Ethical Economics* to think out the nature of business and economic activity from first principles, and to see how these relate to other forms of social interaction, and to draw fine distinctions about selfishness and self-interest, morality and values, cooperation and conflict, and rights and responsibilities, as they relate to business decision making. Our purpose was to gain a clearer appreciation of the nature of business, and to avoid the danger of identifying profit with selfishness, and prudence with immorality, so that those who are engaged in taking business decisions can work out for themselves the ethical considerations they should take into account when defining the policies which determine those decisions. The key conclusions to emerge from this investigation challenged those false images which see "Economic Man" solely as a self-interested profit maximizer with scant regard for the requisites of corporate social responsibility.

A key conclusion of Ethical Economics was that it is rational to see business as a "non-privative", as opposed to a "privative", activity, where the rational principles of business management are cooperation, not conflict, and service, not exploitation. It is rational to see business in terms of the Prisoner's Dilemma as a "non-zero-sum game" activity, where we have to take into account the needs and interests of the other parties involved in a business transaction. The cardinal principle is one of "alteritas" (consideration of the "Other"), which supports the rationality of regarding business as a non-privative activity, where, by its very nature, we need to "empathize" with the interests and values of all those involved in that activity—shareholders as well as all the other stakeholders. Another important conclusion was to see money not as an inert amoral substance but rather as "encapsulated" freedom of choice, which allows "consumer preferences" to be realized in the multivarious world of market economics. Encapsulated choice is a prerequisite for economic freedom, but the exercise of that freedom has to take account of the moral imperative of "alteritas", where the individual freedom of choice of the "other person" is the criterion for the organization of markets, but within the context of a "level playing field", which assists, regulates and controls the freedom of market choice. The "alteritas" principle involves letting people "do as they like" but within the constraints of "what other people also want to do", and the broader dictates of society where human welfare and well-being are the purpose and end (telos) of economic activity. The individual member of society is, as Aristotle put it, a social as well as a political animal, which means that the dictares of self-interest have to adjust to the self-interest of the other. How do we reconcile conflicts between two different "self-interests"?

The ends of economic activity have to be judged in terms of the economic justice they are achieving or impeding, and how successful they are in satisfying the needs of human welfare in removing the inequalities of wealth, poverty, health, discrimination and conflict. If business is to gain the respect of the general public for the legitimacy of what it is doing then the businessman, as "Economic Man", has to demonstrate that he is a rational moral being, with a clearly defined and understood social role, and not just an economic manipulator of resources. Profit maximization is not irrational or immoral when it encompasses not only "shareholder return" but also the return for all stakeholders, which leads to the concept of "shared value" in economic affairs. The interest in looking at the rationality of economic activity in this way, and the moral issues involved, was widespread in the reactions to *Ethical Economics*, but, as a result of the last economic crisis, people were asking what we need to do to improve the institutional and self-regulatory controls of economic activity, and the procedures for conducting business in terms of the creation of economic value and the ethics of business in general. These procedures need to address the increasingly complex nature of risk management, and systems for the prediction and control of free markets, which take into account the normative (ought) aspects of economics, and the ethics of business behaviour in a global environment. As one graduate economics researcher from the European University Institute in Florence put it: "As economists we are mainly concerned with economic predictive modeling systems paying little or no attention to the ethical issues regarding economic activity."

This kind of reaction, and our belief that in *Ethical Economics* we may have underplayed the importance of practical codes of business ethics in setting business objectives, has led us to reaffirm Keynes's belief that economics is a moral, as well as a mathematical, science. Moral considerations inevitably play a part in business decision making, and a businessman should take responsibility for the ethical implications of what he is doing. Ethical codes are important, but of themselves they will not change behaviour unless they become part of the DNA of a business organization in terms of "this is how we do business", which is clear to all those both within and outside a firm. We hoped that by discussing the rationality of business in terms of its ethical as well as its "profit" responsibilities, *Ethical Economics* may have contributed to strengthening the legitimacy of business in the eyes of the general public and society at large. The "healthy" sales of *Ethical Economics* indicate that we may indeed have succeeded to some extent in doing this. However, following the recent financial and economic crisis, and patent examples of malpractice in business, pace Enron, there has been a crisis of confidence and trust in business leadership, and indeed in the ability of the modern capitalist system to protect the interests of the "poorer" members of society in terms of employment and economic well-being. People have asked why the "experts" were unable to regulate and control the economic activities and debt levels of individual nation states within a global environment, which has been manifested in the boom and bust experiences that have occurred over the past twenty years. Why were the lending policies of individual national banking systems not controlled in allowing the risks involved in such things as subprime mortgages, which led to the solvency crisis of major financial institutions when, as Alan Greenspan said, "an infectious greed seemed to grip much of our business community"? And why was it possible for banking compensation systems to become so misaligned between the creation of short-term and long-term value?

As a result of these and similar questions, *Value Economics* seeks to take a new look at the way we measure and control the "economic value" which business is creating, and how the creation of wealth should be rewarded. What are the implications for "value" accounting and control, and for relating value to business ethics? Another of the purposes of *Value*

Economics is to look at how we relate the creation of monetary wealth to economic value, and to propose that "economic value" become the basic metric for measuring business performance, and for evaluating the over- or undervaluing of market share prices in relation to economic value. As Alan Greenspan put it, "how do we know when irrational exuberance has unduly escalated asset values?" We propose that one way could be to have mechanisms which compare market share prices with the economic (or intrinsic) value of those shares. As there are many ways of defining value in economic terms, which *Value Economics* considers in detail, we propose that "economic value", defined as operating profit after tax (NOPAT) less the cost of capital (COC), should become the first measure for establishing whether or not an economic enterprise is creating value. This has implications for economics as a moral, as well as a mathematical predictive science, since the concept of "value" has moral implications, which manifest themselves today in such things as the increasing inequalities now emerging in the distribution of incomes. New concepts of economic value are now emerging in the form of welfare and environmental economics, and "Triple Bottom Line Accounting," which measures not only the profitability "value" of the traditional statutory accounts, but also the social and environmental "values" of economic activity.

Value Economics also proposes a number of philosophical principles for economics, which can be linked to "value creation" and codes of business ethics related to the specific functional job descriptions of any business organization. Every job has an impact on the creation of "economic value", in terms of productivity, cost efficiency and departmental effectiveness and profitability. In this way the "value" of what each person is doing becomes the criterion for setting objectives and measuring performance, so that "value orientation" becomes part of a company's business philosophy, and the creation of "economic value" the motivating force for economic and business decision making.

1.2 Modern Capitalism

Since 1996 the debate between two principal undercurrents of economic theory, Keynesian "aggregate demand" and Friedmanite "monetarism", has continued leading in the aftermath of the last financial crisis to a dispute between the supporters of austerity or not, as the key for resolving the problems of the most recent economic crisis, and for achieving acceptable levels of public debt. But, as we said in 1996, the debate is between those who are primarily egalitarian in their desire to achieve a fairer distribution of wealth in reducing the economic inequality of incomes, and those who insist that the maximization of profits has to be the prime purpose of business in creating the economic wealth to be distributed, and that income differentials will and must always exist. But an unresolved problem for modern capitalism is how to reduce the increasing difference in compensation between the top and bottom levels of company remuneration, where the difference has now been estimated to be about 300 times—compared with 20 times in 1965. This economic discussion is further complicated by the different opinions of those who see public debt as a suffocating load on the private economy and those who see debt as an investment in the future. In the UK this became an argument between Gordon Brown, as Labour Chancellor of the Exchequer and then Prime Minister, whose plans for public investment, and rash claim that the days of boom and bust were over, were rudely shaken by the last global crisis (the reasons for which are set out in his book *Beyond the Crash*), and the Conservative Chancellor of the Exchequer, George Osborne, who accused Brown of being an irresponsible public debt creator, and who championed the cause of rigorous public debt reduction and a balanced budget. And in the USA economists like Paul Krugman are looking at public debt in another light where they believe that austerity is not the answer, since it penalizes above all the lower paid members of society in terms of unemployment.

The debate, however, suffers from a lack of analysis and definition of the economic values at stake, and particularly the economic value being created by public investment in social services such as the NHS, and what the expenditure on these services should be in relation to other commitments such as defence and overseas aid. This raises the need for the introduction of new economic thinking about the whole question of the appropriate relationship between the private and the public sectors, and the issue of how to reassess the "private good, public bad" mentality, which still remains a largely unresolved question for modern western capitalism. In most economic debates the word "value" is curiously absent, and even the Labour Shadow Chancellor in the UK, John McDonnell, in calling for an expansion of the Bank of England's mandate from "inflation targeting" to include "growth, employment and earnings", made no reference to the "economic value" of what all these factors should be creating and protecting. Modern capitalism is thus often being conducted without a thorough economic analysis of the costs and benefits of the private and public sectors where one side is singing the song of "private good and State bad", and the other that of "State good and private selfish bad". So, the debate risks becoming a populist ballgame, with each side trying to outplay the other, which makes a serious debate about issues like these difficult, if not impossible. For example, way back in 1968, the London *Times* (28 September 1968) had a leading article entitled "Spreading the Wealth" in which it proposed that "more of the nationalized industries should be denationalized by a general distribution of shares", which raised indignation that "the State is a separate entity from its citizens and has no right to distribute its assets to its citizens, even if it is not argued that the State has no right to tax the citizens' assets". "Spreading the wealth" is just as lively an issue today as it was then, and is a subject which *Value Economics* considers in terms of discussing how remuneration could be related to the creation of economic value.

In July 1975, *TIME* magazine published an article called "Can Capitalism Survive?", which still remains a good vade mecum on the subject, and which also considered the issue of wealth inequality. The article proposed that the argument between capitalism and authoritarian economic systems boils down to two questions: Which system can make the most efficient use of manpower, materials and money to create the greatest opportunities for free choice, personal development and material well-being for the greatest number of people? And which system is more just and satisfying in human terms? This was written twenty years before the fall of the Berlin Wall, leading to the development of Russia's form of communist capitalism, which today is trying to combine state capitalism and free markets in an attempt to reduce the disparity of wealth between the rich and poor. The outlook is not encouraging, however, given the arrival of the new Russian plutocrats. The article was also published before China surprised the world with its new form of state capitalism underpinned by the Tao Yin Yang philosophy of duality forming a whole. Across the water we find the Japanese form of capitalism with its interlocking share ownerships, and network of cross-shareholdings, which is today struggling with the effects of stagflation (high inflation, low interest rates and low levels of economic growth) after the golden years of its economic growth and outstanding product and managerial (JIT) innovation. So, today western capitalism, with its emphasis on production privately owned, private property and deregulated markets, is competing with a number of variations on the private/public theme. The debate continues. More recently, we have had Anatole Kaletsky's article "How to Save Capitalism" in Prospect magazine (August 2010), proposing that the boundaries between State and market will be redrawn, and warning that the "NHS has become an incubus, sucking the life out of all other public services, which have to be starved of funds to meet its insatiable demands", which has undertones of the "State not good" mentality referred to above. How are we to evaluate its insatiable demands if we have no idea about the NHS's economic value, and, like any business, its investment needs as an "ongoing" business in the future? Is it unreasonable to ask the question, "What is the economic value of the NHS?", which puts on the table the fundamental economic philosophical question of what is the "value" relationship between the private and public in economics.

New economic thinking about capitalism is taking place in a number of different ways. For example, in a recent article "The Rise of Anticapitalism" (*INYT*, 3 March 2015), Anthony Rifkin looks at the new infrastructure of technology—the so-called Internet of Things—in possibly pushing much of economic life to near zero marginal cost over the next two decades, and the increasing importance of non-profit organizations. Thomas Piketty's bestselling book *Capital in the 21st Century* discusses what might be done to tackle the rising inequality problems evident in modern capitalism, and how to "spread the wealth". The debate also encompasses the future of work, which Charles Handy was looking at more than twenty years ago in books such as *The Empty Raincoat* (1994), well before the full impact of the Internet revolution, discussed by Anthony Rifkin, reached us. In the 1990s many thinkers became excited about the concept of the Third Way with books such as those by Tony Blair *The Third Way: New Politics for the New Century* (1998) and Anthony Giddens, *The Third Way: the Renewal of Social Democracy* (1998), but interest in it for economics and business never really took off. Anthony Giddens's theory of structuration, and reference to the endemic conflict between capital and labour, lacked detailed analysis and proposals for what the Third Way means for economic philosophy and business management. The concept was not taken up and fully worked out in terms of management theory either by the CBI or unions in the UK, although its potential for greater participation had already been considered in the Cadbury Report which led to new standards for corporate governance in the UK, and it was further developed by organizations like the International Organisation for Standardisation (ISO) with its ISO 26000 proposals for the development of corporate social responsibility (CSR). It is not the purpose of *Value Economics* to enter into a long discussion on the future of capitalism, but to flag some of the "economic value" issues for new economic thinking and for the way in which business is organized, managed and controlled, now that "Triple Bottom Line Accounting" has arrived looking at the social and environmental, as well as the economic, results of business enterprises. And within this context Samuel Brittan's *Capitalism with a Human Face* (1995) remains as relevant today as it did then in looking at the connection between economics and ethics, and in particular at the concept of wider ownership in "spreading the wealth" among those who create the "cooperators' surplus", or, in other words, "economic value", which remains a key challenge for modern capitalism and its legitimacy as a creator not only of monetary wealth, but also of economic justice. Debate and books about the causes of the last financial crisis abound, and many books, including *Masters of Nothing* by Hancock and Zahawi, *Going off the Rails* by John Plender, *The Financial Crisis: Who is to Blame?* by Howard Davies, *Boomerang* by Michael Lewis, *The Price of Civilisation: Economics and Ethics after the Fall* by Jeffrey Sachs, and *The Entrepreneurial State* by M. Mazzucato have all contributed to the writing of *Value Economics* in giving a new emphasis to the creation of economic value, and how it could be distributed between all contributors to the "cooperators' surplus" of a business.

1.3 Structure of the Book

Chapter 2 presents a case for seeing economics as a moral science, which, in combination with the statistical disciplines of econometric modelling, analyses consumer preferences, rational decision theory and the indeterminate nature of the outcomes of economic activity. **Chapter 3** considers cooperation and facilitation as rational principles for economic activity as a "non-zero sum" game, based on the recognition of the self-interests of the "Other" (the "alteritas" principle), which requires procedures for cooperation with all the stakeholders in a business enterprise. **Chapter 4** emphasizes the need to recognize the "slippery" and "sticky" nature of money as an instrument for conferring freedom of choice in satisfying consumer preferences and considers its potential for greed and self-aggrandizement, or for altruism and philanthropy, in the way it is used. **Chapter 5** considers the characteristics of a moneyed society in its social setting when meeting the demands of money for consumption, savings and investments in the private and public sectors of the economy. It looks at measures for calculating the economic and social value of a moneyed society, such as GDP, and quality of life measures such as the Human Development Index (HDI). It suggests ways in which businessmen as economic operators could be more involved in the setting of assumptions for economic modelling, in order to strengthen the relationship between the economist and the businessman in the management of a moneyed society. **Chapter 6** examines the "bubble" conditions which occur during business cycles, with examples from over the past twenty-five years, and calls for an analysis of how individual companies have been affected by these "economic bubbles" and responded to them. **Chapter 7** looks at the problems of unemployment and increasing inequalities of incomes, and the demand of employees for greater participation in decision making and profitability arising from improved productivity. We also look at how the "future of work" may change the nature of traditional employment.

All of these chapters discuss the economic factors which contribute to the creation of monetary wealth and the economic value of business enterprises. **Chapter 8** is a central theme of the book, proposing that we need to clarify and agree how to measure the economic value of business enterprises. We discuss the many concepts of value which exist today, and the concept of shareholder value expressed both in terms of Total Shareholder Return (TSR) and Total Shareholder Value (TSV), which has to be modified in light of "value" for the other stakeholders. Today value accounting in terms of the traditional statutory accounts is moving into the area of "Triple Bottom Line Accounting" covering economic, social and environmental results. As a start, we propose that economic value (defined as NOPAT less the cost of capital), become the basic metric for measuring the value being created by an economic enterprise, which can also be combined with the analysis of free cash flows. Such a metric could also be used for comparing economic value with market share prices to see whether "market exuberance", to use Alan Greenspan's phrase, is over- or undervaluing the economic value of a company, which, we argue, is a valid and comprehensible measure of a company's worth at any one moment in time. Economic Value in this sense can also become the measure for setting the objectives of value based management. The last financial crisis revealed a mismatch between performance compensation and the creation of short- as opposed to long-term value. **Chapter 9** looks at the current state of the art for performance-related compensation, including stock options and other instruments for participation in the performance and ownership of a business enterprise, and makes suggestions for using economic value as the basic measure for relating compensation to the creation of value.

Chapter 10 looks at the needs of regulation and control from a "businessman's" point of view, and calls for the use of "economic value" in regulatory reporting and control to get the balance right between economic value and solvency. **Chapter 11** considers the concept of "Triple Bottom Line Accounting" for social Accounting in terms of social and environmental results, and the use of the Social Balance Sheet, or Sustainability Report, for providing economic and social information for all stakeholders and how it can be used for their economic education. It also looks at how these reports can be structured, including Codes for Business Ethics and Rules of Conduct. **Chapter 12** presents some principles for a definition of economic philosophy, and how they can be incorporated into practical codes of business ethics. It proposes that the creation of economic value is an essential component of economic philosophy, and how this can be related to what we mean by "management excellence" in setting objectives and measuring performance. In discussing economic philosophy and theory we make a call to avoid the danger of "econospeak" in communicating with the businessman, and to involve him or her more in the setting of assumptions for econometric modelling which take account of the experience and needs of the different sectors in any economy. The final chapter, **Chap. 13**, summarizes the key conclusions of the book in looking at the principles of economic justice on which codes of business ethics could be based. It also proposes a number of questions for further study to analyse the financial crises of the past twenty years and the effects which they had on the economic value of specific economic sectors and individual companies within those sectors, which could possibly be conducted by the Bank of England, in conjunction with the London School of Economics and the newly founded Institute for New Economic Thinking in Oxford. The purpose of this would be to answer a set of five strategic questions for new economic thinking with the aim of deciding how economic value and economic justice can be combined to strengthen the basic concept of *Value Economics* which sees business as a participative, non-privative, and "shared value" activity within the wider social framework of "Triple Bottom Line Accounting".

How to use the book To ease the reading of the book each chapter is preceded by a short abstract, and an overview of each chapter, before the chapter itself. The purpose of this is to provide a quick read through the abstracts, or a slightly longer first read through the chapter overviews, which are about 15 percent of the main text. The chapters are also written on a "stand-alone" basis, so that the book can be used as a "Compendium" for looking at the ethical implications of value for new economic thinking.

References

Beinhocker E. The origin of wealth. London: Random House; 2011.
Blair T. The third way, new politics for the new century. London: Fabian Society; 1998.
Brittan S. Capitalism with a human face. London: Edward Elgar; 1995.
Brown G. Beyond the crash. London: Simon and Schuster; 2011.
Can capitalism survive? TIME, July 1975.
Davies H. The financial crisis: who is to blame. Cambridge: Polity; 2010.
Giddens A. The third way: the renewal of social democracy. Cambridge: Polity; 1998.
Griffiths MR, Lucas JR. Ethical economics. London: Macmillan; 1996.

Hampden-Turner C, Trompenaars F. The seven cultures of capitalism. Judy Piatkus, 1994.

Hancock M, Zahawi N. Masters of nothing. London: Biteback; 2011.

Handy C. The empty raincoat. London: Hutchinson; 1994.

Hutton W. The state we're in. London: Vintage; 1996.

ISO 26000 Social Responsibility Paper.

Kaletsky A. How to save capitalism. Prospect, August 2010.

Lewis M. Boomerang. London: Allen Lane; 2011.

Mazzucato M. The enterpreneurial state. Lodon: Anthem; 2014.

Piketty T. Capital in the 21st century. Cambridge: Belknap; 2014.

Plender J. Going off the rails. Chichester: Wiley; 2003.

Plender J. Capitalism. London: Biteback; 2015.

Rifkin A. The rise of anticapitalism. INYT, 3 Mar 2015.

Sachs J. The price of civilisation: economics and ethics after the fall. London: Bodley; 2011.

Sowell T. Basic economics. New York: Basic; 2011.

Spreading the wealth. London Times Leader, 28 Sept 1968.

Turner A. Just capital. London: Macmillan; 2001.

2

Economics as a Moral Science

Abstract The purpose of this chapter is to reaffirm economics as a moral science, which, in combination with the mathematical disciplines of statistical analysis and econometric modelling, analyses economic activity in a way which takes account of consumer preferences, rational decision theory, and the inherent variability and indeterminacy of human behaviour. It considers the moral dimension of economics in the Kantian sense that we should act in a way that treats people never merely as a means, but always also as ends in themselves, and looks at the relationship between the moral and the natural sciences, believing that the two can "bed down" together in the quest for verifiable truth and justice in human affairs. It also looks at the human dimension of economics in terms of Adam Smith's concepts of sympathy and virtue discussed in *The Theory of Moral Sentiments*, but always in the light of the principles of uncertainty and unpredictability contained in Heisenberg's uncertainty principle and Gödel's "Incompleteness Theorem".

© The Editor(s) (if applicable) and The Author(s) 2016   **15**
M.R. Griffiths, J.R. Lucas, *Value Economics*,
DOI 10.1057/978-1-137-54187-1_2

2.1   Chapter Overview

If economics is concerned with human affairs, it cannot just be limited to the statistical analysis of macro- and microeconomic events, but needs to understand the human motives which influence economic behaviour and determine consumer preferences. The axiom of classical economics that "Economic Man" is concerned solely with the maximization of profit needs to be reviewed with regard to the responsibility he has towards other people and society in general, which introduces a moral dimension into the study of economics in the Kantian sense that "we should act in a way that treats humanity never as a means but as an end". Economics cannot ignore the normative question of "what ought to be" which results from the statistical analysis of "what is", and the moral implications of economic conclusions. This gap between economics and ethics has been summed up by Amartya Sen when he says, "Economics has been substantially impoverished by the distance which has grown up between economics and ethics".

The natural sciences have great prestige and the moral sciences are sometimes considered to be inferior because they do not conform to the strict principles of the "scientific method". But a comparison of the two disciplines can be useful in highlighting the differences between the scientific rationality of strict uniformity and causality, and the rationality of the moral sciences which has to be adaptable to the non-uniformity and random causality of human beings. This requires an empathy, or "verstehen," of human insight when investigating the rationality or irrationality of human behaviour. Some thinkers believe the two disciplines to be incompatible, others feel that they can be compatible if there is a "synthesis" between the fixed knowable laws of Newtonian physics, and the less fixed moral laws of cause and effect. Kant's theory of the "categorical imperative" asserts that moral law is a principle of reason itself whose motive is the "worthiness of being happy". Even if neuroscience may hope one day to demonstrate scientifically the nature of happiness, it is a subject which hitherto has remained outside the province of natural science, and been left to the study of philosophy, although the concept of "happiness" is inherent in the study of welfare economics and utility maximization.

So, the natural and moral sciences have an opportunity to bed down together, with the natural sciences examining the reality of the universe and its structure, and the moral sciences the reality of being a human being in terms of psychology and "Free Will" in decision making. Both the natural and moral sciences look for a "certainty" that their axioms and conclusions are right. Moral certainty is characterized by that high degree of uncertainty and randomness we find in Chaos Theory, which studies the behaviour of dynamic systems highly sensitive to the "initial conditions" which determine their nature in the first place, and where one small change or error (the so-called "butterfly effect") can lead to a totally unexpected future event. Moral science has to accept that people make mistakes, and the same principle applies to econometrics where small changes or errors in the initial assumptions can invalidate the certainty economists seek in predicting the future nature of economic events and outcomes.

The last financial crisis has also called for new economic thinking, which led to the creation of the Institute for Economic Thinking (INET), financed by the billionaire investor George Soros. We need to widen the study of economics to include the other human sciences which look at the motivations of human behaviour. The Classical Economics axiom that profit maximization is paramount in economic decision making is "skewed", if it ignores the human dimension of that decision-making process. There are indications that we are moving away from the idea that economics is a "hard value-free science" as neuroeconomics and welfare economics tackle the questions of how human beings take decisions and how economics contributes to the "well-being" of society. Economic Sociology attempts to investigate ways in which Weber's "disenchantment" can be resolved in bridging the gap between economics as a mathematical science and a human science.

It is useful to look again at the implications of Adam Smith's *The Theory of Moral Sentiments*, which discusses the importance of sympathy and virtue as we engage in the task of creating the "wealth of nations". The neglect of such human motivations has led, in the words of Amartya Sen, among other things to a neglect of the "connection between ethics and economics". But defining a new paradigm for economics in terms of cooperation and facilitation between all the stakeholders in an economic enterprise, and of "empathy" in economic relationships, does not demean the importance of the econometric analytical techniques which seek to give a scientific objectivity to the predictive modelling of present and future economic scenarios. A new paradigm for economics in these terms can only increase the legitimacy of business in the eyes of the general public, and contribute to showing that economic justice is based on rational principles where people as economic agents are treated as ends and not just means.

2.2   Moral Dimension of Economics

In 1861 the University of Cambridge's Moral Sciences Tripos was reconstructed and set up in parallel with the Natural Sciences Tripos. The latter still survives, giving undergraduates who want to be scientists a grounding in many different sciences, before specializing in any particular one. With the Moral Sciences, however, which originally included History and Law, the different disciplines successively decamped to be studied in isolation, such as Economics, Philosophy, Politics, Psychology and Sociology. Although there are advantages in separation and specialization, there are also disadvantages in failing to take into account the wider picture and the relationship with other disciplines. One reason for talking about the Moral Sciences is to focus attention on common themes and methods of argument, which distinguish disciplines concerned with human affairs, such as economics, behavioural science, politics, sociology, psychology and philosophy, from those concerned with natural phenomena. It was Hume who, in his "Enquiry concerning the Principles of Morals", looked for a systematic study of human nature and relationships, which could establish "a science of human nature" based upon empirical phenomena, and excluding all that does not arise from observation.

In his paper "An introduction to Economics as a Moral Science" (2000), James Alvey traces the debate between economics as a technical or as a moral science, or as a combination of both, from the time of Adam Smith and Ricardo, to John Stuart Mill, who introduced the notion of "Economic Man"; to Marshall, who saw economics as a mathematical and also a moral science; up to the times of Keynes and Friedman, and economists, like Frisch, who see economics as the study of econometric models with no place for its study as a moral science, and, more recently, the work of Amartya Sen, who regrets that "economics has been substantially impoverished by the distance that has grown up between economics and ethics".

If Economics is concerned with human affairs, it cannot be limited to mathematical and statistical analysis of micro- and macroeconomic events. In order to understand fully the nature of Economies, we need to be able to exercise a humane insight into men's motives, as we do when we seek to understand the motives of historical agents. A man may be designated as "Economic Man", but he also has a network of family, colleagues, friends, commitments, interests and beliefs, which circumscribe his options and influence his behaviour. To understand economics properly, we should not study it in isolation, but as an aspect of human activity, interpenetrating and interacting with all the other aspects of human behaviour which influence human decisions.

These considerations are crucially important. Traditional economics has abstracted from the messy complexity of human affairs some crucial features about how markets behave, such as the theory that free markets are able to regulate themselves through Adam Smith's "invisible hand", which moves them towards equilibrium without outside State intervention; or the theory of rational choice, where individuals and firms maximize their utility in terms of prices and profits, without necessarily concerning themselves with the moral issues of maximization, provided it does not breach the legal framework within which business has to operate. As a result, economics has developed rigorous analytical systems, deducing from the basic axiom that in economics consumer preferences relate to a choice of alternatives based on the degree of utility, satisfaction or happiness which those alternatives can provide. From the results of these analytical systems economists draw a range of conclusions regarding how markets operate in macro- and microeconomic terms. Unfortunately, though the economic reasoning may be rigorous, the premises and conclusions may not be true—for example, it is often untrue that people will buy in the cheapest market or sell in the dearest markets, which classical economists purport to be true in conditions of perfect economic equilibrium.

Economics has to explain why econometric predictions are sometimes found to be inadequate in terms of explaining the future. It is necessary to take a wider view of how and why economic preferences come into being, and to re-examine very carefully our perceptions of who and what "Economic Man" is, and to challenge the philosophical rationality of the axioms of classical economics, such as, market equilibrium, utility maximization, perfect competition, free markets and monetary control. How sacrosanct is the maximization of profit in a social environment where there is an increasing interest in corporate social responsibility, and in the future sustainability of economic activities, which may contaminate and destroy the natural environment, as occurred in the industrial disasters of Bhopal and Chernobyl, and, more recently, the environmental disaster surrounding the DeepWater Horizon oilrig?

The profitable exploitation of resources is now being conditioned by a new set of social and environmental obligations, which means that the economist can no longer study his subject in isolation from its wider context in human affairs. Each aspect of human behaviour, which determines the way in which the consumer defines his preferences, needs to be studied, if economics is to become the kind of science which Marshall proposed in his *Principles of Economics*. His aim was to combine the objectivity of mathematical analytical techniques with the more subjective and open-ended techniques, which analyse the random nature of human behaviour, and which is the province of the moral sciences. This need to study the human aspects of economic activity means that we need to revive the concept of economics as a "moral science". We use the word "moral" in a wider sense of the word than that derived from the Latin "mores", meaning customs or habits, to cover the underlying principles which inspire our patterns of behaviour. It goes beyond the concept of expediency or prudence as the motivators of our behaviour to the wider Kantian sense that "we should act in a way that always treats humanity never simply as a means but as an end". We need to ask the question: how can the interested and expedient behaviour of some economic agents be brought to account in moral terms?

This introduces a moral dimension to economic activity where economists need to specify very carefully the axioms, which will influence the assumptions, or hypotheses, on which their econometric models and predictions will be based. To paraphrase G.B. Shaw, it is the assumptions on which people habitually act that reveal the beliefs they hold, and it is a requirement of any predictive modelling system to demonstrate at the outset the validity and rationality of the assumptions on which those predictions are based. If we acknowledge the moral dimension of economics, we can reaffirm Keynes's belief that economics needs to protect itself from mathematical abstractions which of themselves do not focus on the social consequences of economic activity in terms of such things as full employment or not. Although his concepts and reasoning can be questioned in terms of identifying the correct balance between the private and public sectors in a "mixed economy", Keynes did much to rescue economics from just being a science of mathematical predictive techniques, and opened up the debate between the non-interventionists of "laissez faire" and the interventionists, themselves divided between proponents of his "demand-side" theory (which stresses the importance of investment as the dynamic factor for fostering full employment) and the monetarists (whose strict money supply principles for containing inflation can lead to recession and unemployment). The trade-off between inflation and full employment remains a key focus of economic study and raises the normative question of "what ought to be" as opposed to "what is" when modeling and predicting economic activity.

2.3   Natural and Moral Sciences

At this point it may be useful to compare the disciplines of the natural and the moral sciences. We shall see that they are not easy bedfellows, but that there are opportunities for cooperation between the two disciplines where the strict principles of objective empiricism and the verifiability of the scientific method can contribute to a more scientific approach to the study of moral questions, as is indicated by recent work in neuroscience and economic sociology. On the other side, the more subjective and less deterministic approach of the moral sciences can provide a "sounding board" for the way in which the natural sciences have to face the "uncertainty" factor in the scientific study of indeterminate systems, such as quantum mechanics, and the nature of stochastic systems whose behaviour is intrinsically non-deterministic and random. The success of the natural sciences has engendered a widespread belief that they can explain everything, and leave no room for any other understanding of human nature that is not based on empirical investigation and verification. The debate on these questions is still open particularly when we enter the field of Free Will and whether it is nature or nurture, or a combination of both, which determine the moral choices of human behaviour. Are the disciplines of the scientific method compatible with the more open ended and relativistic disciplines which investigate moral issues, and the question of Free Will?

The Natural Sciences have great prestige, and the Moral Sciences are often thought to be inferior because they do not conform to the Natural Sciences principles of uniformity and causality. The difficulty in countering this is that rationality does require some principle of uniformity, or "universability" as it was termed by Kant with his proposition of the "categorical imperative", but the uniformity presupposed by the Natural Sciences is a more rigid one than that invoked in the Moral Sciences, which has to be adaptable to the infinite variety, and non-uniformity, of human beings. The less rigid requirement of rationality required in the Moral Sciences is made up for by empathy, or "verstehen" (human insight), which enables us to get inside the skin of other human agents to gain an insight into why they behave as they do, whereas one cannot see things from the point of view of an electron, or molecule of sulphuric acid or an amoeba.

But many thinkers believe that the two sciences are not incompatible, and have adopted what might be described as a "two-pocket" approach. Kant, for example, sought to resolve the dispute between the empiricists and the rationalists by proposing that our experience of the phenomenal world is conveyed by our senses and shaped by our mind, and that the scientific concepts of space and time are not derived by experience but exist as preconditions (a priori) which the mind shapes in understanding that experience. Thus, there is a "synthesis" between the objective order of nature (the fixed knowable laws of Newtonian physics) and the subjective experience of the moral laws of cause and effect, which led Kant to his theory of the "categorical imperative", which should determine our behaviour in moral terms, and his belief that moral law is a principle of reason itself, whose motive he described as the "worthiness of being happy".

Happiness is a moral imperative which lies outside the study of natural science, but its study falls within the "remit" of the Moral Sciences, which per se links them closely with the more recent disciplines of "behavioural and welfare economics". We can find another example of the "two-pocket" approach in the work of Peter Strawson, who believed that scientific determinism is compatible with human freedom and Free Will, rejecting the idea that explanation of our thoughts, feelings and mental life has now been superseded by neuroscience. However much we believe in the scientific method, he asserted, people will never give up talking and feeling about moral responsibility, praise and blame, guilt and pride, crime and punishment, gratitude, resentment and forgiveness, which are "the province of Shakespeare, Tolstoy, Proust and Henry James", and not just the results of what some materialists would call the unscientific psychology of "folk lore".

When using scientific method (the empirical verification of observable phenomena) we assume the uniformity and complete causality of nature, but when examining human nature, although the disciplines of psychology, cognitive science and anthropology may provide observable factual data, we have to empathize with human behaviour accepting that human beings can act both rationally and irrationally. Empathy concerns the capacity to recognize and understand the mental and emotional states of other sentient beings, and in recent years it has entered the field of neuroscience with the attempt to understand the cognitive aspects of empathy through the use of MRI (magnetic resonance imaging), but we are still in the early days of understanding the moral and ethical implications of empathy in the way we interact with other people, for example, in the often confrontational nature of business transactions. In his book *Wired to Care* (2009) Dev Paitnik found there to be a lack of empathy in many large corporations, but he coined the term "Open Empathy Organisations" to describe companies such as Nike, Harley Davidson and IBM, where there is a recognition of the importance of developing empathy skills in the way their businesses are managed.

Some natural scientists claim that human beings are material objects whose behaviour is determined by their nature and by the environment in which they have been raised, and that our intimations of Free Will are an illusion. If natural phenomena are governed completely by natural laws, then there is no possibility of human actions, regarded as natural phenomena being other than they are. However, there are two arguments against this view that arise from the theory of Gödel's Incompleteness Theorem, and the indeterminate randomness of Quantum Mechanics, both of which indicate the difficulty of regarding human beings as being deterministically predictable in the way they make decisions and accept responsibility for what they do. However, natural phenomena are not governed entirely by natural laws. The fundamental laws of physics are probabilistic, rather than deterministic. They assign different probabilities to different outcomes. We cannot, as Laplace has supposed, trace out the exact course of development of the universe, given complete information of its state at any one time. We can make predictions, but not about everything. We can, to a high level of accuracy, predict the future positions of planets round the Sun, but not about everything that goes on within them. In spite of the indeterminism of particle physics we can still make predictions if we shift the focus of attention, and concentrate on the wood rather than the trees. We cannot predict the kinetic energy of each particular molecule of a gas, for example, but we can predict the kinetic energy of very many molecules. It is rather like a turbulent stream—we cannot predict what any bit of water will do, but can safely say that there will be eddies. In a similar way, we cannot predict what an individual may do, but we can predict the likely outcome of the way social groups may behave when caught up in the kind of economic and social environments which produced the French and Russian revolutions. These kinds of environment are subjects for economic study and analysis, but after the mathematics of such analysis, whose province is it to comment on the rights and wrongs of the way human beings behave in these environments?

Both the natural and the moral sciences are concerned with the "certainty" of their conclusions. The Heisenberg principle of uncertainty confutes the deterministic certainties of natural science, and introduces the concept of indeterminacy in explaining the behaviour of matter we find, for example, in quantum mechanics, where it is impossible to determine accurately both the position, direction and speed of a particle at the same instant. Moral certainty does not have the degree of mathematical certainty, and we have to be content, as Aristotle proposed in the *Nicomachean Ethics*, with the kind of certainty which is appropriate to different persons, cultures and circumstances, so that in taking decisions we can never hope to expect the certainty of mathematics. In other words, we can never be absolutely certain that people will interpret and actualize Kant's "categorical imperative" in the same way.

Where do economists stand when it comes to understanding the uncertainty of economic outcomes, and defining the hypotheses on which the models they use for predicting the future are based? The definition of economic hypotheses cannot ignore the historical results of the past, which can help us to explain why and how economic events occur. For example, if we look at the antecedent human decisions which lay behind the Depression of the 1930s, we shall be led back to the reparation conditions imposed on Germany by the Treaty of Versailles in 1919, a response so different from the conditions of the Marshall Plan to rebuild the European economy after the Second World War. The causality of such events is a legitimate subject for economic enquiry, and if that is the case we introduce a moral dimension to the enquiry as to why those economic events of the 1920s and 1930s took place. Mathematical modelling techniques are necessary for understanding the technical characteristics of those economic events, but in themselves they will not be sufficient to explain the moral, or amoral, motivations which lay behind the human decisions which determined the economic policies in those two decades. Close argument establishes, using Gödel's Incompleteness Theorem, that no Turing machine (an idealized version of a mechanism programmed like a computer) can be an adequate representation of an ideal human mind, for a human brain can always do something the Turing machine cannot in weighing the arguments for and against a set of alternatives for action, and then deciding which action to take.

Despite appearances and different analytical techniques, the natural and moral sciences can bed down together, each bringing its own perspective on the world without undermining the other; the natural sciences can propose what is the reality of the universe and its structure, and the moral sciences can propose what is the reality of being a human being in terms of psychology and the exercise of Free Will in decision making. Although, as we have seen, there can be a compatibility between the two approaches, they also have significant differences. The natural sciences are based on the uniformity of the natural world. Natural scientists presuppose some principle of limited variability which entitles them to draw definite conclusions from available evidence. Human affairs, by contrast, are, like human beings, complex and often contradictory. We can characterize them, but cannot count on completely characterizing them in any limited number of features: however far we go there is always the possibility of a new factor entirely altering the situation, as it does in Gödel's Incompleteness Theorem.

We can generalize, therefore, but not absolutely. In thinking about human affairs we can imagine ourselves in the position of agents, and consider how we might have been inclined to act had we been in that situation. In the moral sciences we can empathize in Aristotle's sense of identifying with the agent we are witnessing on the stage, which we cannot do in the natural sciences. Of course, we may empathize wrongly: our experience or knowledge may be too limited, our depth of understanding and interpretation too shallow, for us to enter into the motivations and behaviour of another man whose culture and history differs totally from ours. So we cannot necessarily be infallible—and nor for that matter can natural scientists who, at one time, believed the world to be flat. But each in its own sphere can provide some understanding and illumination of the physical and human world in which we live. Deciding what to do is one of the primary tasks of a rational human being. We have to size up the situation and reach a decision in the time available, which may be short, giving us no opportunity for lengthy deliberation. On second thoughts we may want to change those decisions, and come to the conclusion that our judgement of what ought to have been done was incorrect.

Thus, the logic of the moral sciences is both holistic (natural systems and their properties should be viewed as a wholes rather than as a collection of parts) and tentative (open to the fact that a decision or a system may be incorrect in that particular time and circumstance), while the logic of natural science is monotonic (seeking to preserve the given order on the basis of an agreed set of premises), and conclusive (definitive at the time on the basis of all the evidence available). The logic of moral science is one of proposals and counterproposals, of suggestions, objections and rebuttals of objections, of weighing the pros and cons, and trying to balance them and arrive at tentative conclusions, which are accepted "other things being equal" (ceteris paribus) but still open to reconsideration in the light of further factors. Moral certainty is less certain than the absolute certainty of the mathematician and the physical certainty of the natural scientist, and is characterized by a high degree of uncertainty and randomness. But in that it has much in common with the entropy (the tendency from order to disorder) we find in isolated systems, and in the dissipation or degradation of natural resources, which is inherent in that syndrome of growth and decay, creation and destruction that we observe in the life cycles of the natural world. And where does that leave "certainty" as a field of study for economics and business in general?

Econometrics hopes to establish economics as a science by formulating empirical economic models whose conclusions can be verified as true or false. This may give us greater confidence in the validity of those economic models, but still leaves open the question of how certain we can be that they are right. This leads economics back into the field of Chaos Theory, which studies the behaviour of dynamic systems that are highly sensitive to the "initial conditions" which determine them in the first place. What are the "initial conditions" implicit in any economic model, and how do we evaluate the "butterfly effect" that a small error in setting those conditions may result in widely diverging outcomes? This means we need to bring into those equations the likelihood of not being right in the long term, the control of which requires economic models to be monitored continually in terms of their initial assumptions, or conditions, and their nature as dynamical rather than static models. What was the nature, and what were the potential risks, of those "initial conditions" of reparation in 1919, which led to the creation of national socialism and to the rise of Hitler? Did anyone in 1919 evaluate the "butterfly effect" of possible changes in those initial conditions, which created economic and social chaos in Germany, and led to the "hurricane" of the Second World War and the deaths of nearly 50 million people?

Moral science accepts that people may make mistakes, be mistaken, and change their minds, which means we cannot obtain a conclusive absolute assurance about what was right or wrong at a particular time or circumstance, and nor should we seek it. Instead of cast-iron certainty, we should be content with as much certainty as the amount of subject matter or economic data we possess. Different disciplines have special rules of procedure and special standards of cogency, in the sense that although they may not be verifiable in terms of formal logic they are nevertheless weighty and should carry conviction. For example, lawyers may cut short arguments of expediency or morality with a curt "That is not the law", or historians in their attempt to reconstruct and interpret the past must describe and analyse the numerous historical antecedents, or accidents, which lie behind historical events, if their conclusions are to carry conviction. Were there cogent arguments behind the Allies' insistence to require "unconditional surrender" during the final year of the Second World War, or to bomb Dresden when German resistance was starting to crumble? There is a trade-off between a firm decision-procedure giving definite answers within a required time span, and full sensitivity to all the relevant factors, which can open up a rift between well-established conclusions of recognized procedures of economic analysis, and our intuitive sense of what is really right or true. And however scientific economics may be in terms of econometric procedures, it is falling short of economic analysis in the fullest sense, if it ignores the moral implications of economic decision making.

In conclusion, the moral sciences differ from the natural sciences in terms of the mode of understanding and the schemata of explanation. Whereas the natural scientist deals with uniformities and causality, as the economist does when constructing and analysing his economic models, the moral scientist seeks to understand an action by projecting himself into the agent's shoes and trying to see things from the agent's point of view. In terms of economics this requires an analysis, for example, of economic history as it moves through the days of "laissez faire" and free trade, as the basic theories of economic activity, to the more interventionist approaches of Keynesian demand and supply theory, and Friedmanite monetarism, to today's interest in sovereign debt levels, globalization, corporate social responsibility and the valuation of intangible assets in business enterprises. After the collapse of the Marxist economic system and its aim to eliminate private ownership, and the recent crises of western capitalism, the need has emerged for new economic thinking, which balances the needs of classical capitalism (let the market decide) with those of better regulation and control of financial markets and products, based on a new paradigm of what we mean by the creation of economic value, not just monetary wealth.

The creation of the Institute for New Economic Thinking (INET), launched by George Soros, has been an important initiative in this direction. The challenges for new economic thinking are complex and extensive, and cannot avoid the moral implications for economics of the social problems of poverty, health, education and the inequalities in these areas between the world's developed, developing and underdeveloped economies. There are moral implications here for the future study of economics which take it beyond the technical contributions of econometrics into the moral issues implicit in what we mean by economic justice in terms of its distributive, commutative and fiscal components, which remain—as always—the basic challenges for Economic Man in developing a rational philosophy for what he is doing.

2.4   Human Dimension of Economics

If we accept the arguments in the previous paragraphs, there is a case for widening the study of economics beyond the analysis of economic data and econometrics, and the resulting conclusions of econometric analysis, to an interpretation of why those economic events took place, including the moral motivations which lie behind the decisions taken in the past, and on which the hypotheses for modelling future economic scenarios are based. In this area the economist can have much in common with the historian. Historians read the records of their predecessors, but they write their own work differently, bringing new insights that had not appeared to earlier generations—as can be seen, for example, in Fernand Braudel's *The Mediterranean and the Mediterranean world in the Age of Philip the Second*, or Niall Ferguson's *The Pity of War*.

The economist has a rich history which describes the long debate between the maximum freedom of "laissez faire" to the more interventionist theories of recent times, as the pendulum swings between the advocacy of different degrees of freedom and control. This widening of the discipline of economics to include the study of the other human sciences, such as history, sociology, law, behavioural science, industrial psychology and organizational theory, can help economists to see beyond the confines of their analytical mathematical techniques into the more uncertain and human world of the moral sciences. Academics need to be generalists as well as specialists. Although it is good to know all there is to know about some specific subject, insights into the theories of other disciplines can provide us with new information for challenging or revisiting the axioms of our own discipline, in the way that Gödel challenged the certainties of established mathematical theories.

The study of economics can benefit too. Economic transactions, like legal transactions, do not take place in a vacuum, but in a social and moral context as occurred, for example, in propounding theories for national income policies in the UK in the 1960s. Although arguments for the autonomy of law and economics can be adduced and need to be met, the obvious fact is that those engaged in economic or legal transactions are human beings with a "mindset" of motivations and aspirations which determine how they react to the particularity of the time and circumstances in which they find themselves. Classical economists see "Economic Man" as a profit maximizer, possessing perfect information, and buying in the cheapest and selling in the dearest market; in other words, a pragmatic manipulator of the resources at his disposal where considerations of business ethics and economic justice (outside the legal framework of business law in which he has to operate) have to take second place to his main priority of running a profitable and sustainable enterprise. However, this concept is skewed, as it does not fully accept the cogency of the social environment in which he operates, which today, for example, calls for greater attention to be paid to the corporate responsibility of business, and to the trade-off between the economic and social responsibilities of business. It is not so long ago that practices of child labour and dumping toxic waste into rivers were common place, as it still is in some developing economies.

So, classical "Economic Man" is forced to change his Scrooge-like self-interested image to one of "social economic man" (or, perhaps more accurately, "ethical economic man"), where the businessman is cognisant and proud of his role as an economic and social contributor to society at large. As Dubček in Czechoslovakia in 1968 had called for the introduction of

"Socialism with a Human Face", so capitalism still has to convince people at large that it is not motivated primarily by greed and what it can get away with (as the recent financial crisis showed in terms of remuneration), and that it has a human face in the way it responds to the demands for economic growth, education, poverty, health and protection of the environment, all of which have an overriding human dimension in the way in which the social investments in each area are set and prioritized. The fact that economics may be changing, and re-emphasizing its human dimension, can be seen in the developments in the field of behavioural economics with its more recent explorations in what is now called neuroeconomics (studying economic decision making in terms of risk and uncertainty, and loss aversion, and how neuroscientific discoveries can contribute to economic modelling); and welfare economics (studying the social well-being which results from the allocation of resources in an economy, and the costs and benefits involved in such allocations). Welfare economics has moved into ecology economics, which challenges the concept that economics is a hard value-free science as being unrealistic, if it ignores the "well-being" implications of what it is doing. Since any economy is embedded in an environmental system, economics has to concern itself with the value and cost of maintaining and protecting the environment for the benefit of "human welfare".

So, we now have classical economics moving into Ecological Economics and Energy Economics, both of which have strong human undertones. Economic Sociology has been around since Jevons coined the phrase in the 1870s, and its belief that economics has to be embedded in social institutions, if the "disenchantment" between economics and religion described by Weber in *The Protestant Ethic and the Spirit of Capitalism* (1905) is to be resolved. Economic Sociology contributed much to the Marxist theory which focuses on the social implications of capitalism and its preoccupation with "commodity fetishism". Although Marxist economic theory has been found to be "wanting", because of its excessive State control and repression of individual freedom, the human implications of economics for the place of the individual in society remain the same. We now have the Global Academy of Economic Sociology and Political Economy (ES/PE), and the Society for the Advancement of Socio-Economics (SASE) contributing to the debate between classical economics and new economic thinking in the areas of behavioural economics and welfare economics.

The key question still remains: "How is classical economics going to address the issue of the trade-off between income distribution and the maximization of social welfare?" In contributing to the debate as to what is the correct relationship between the private (the individual) and the public (the State), economics has a fundamental role to play in providing the hard facts of economic analysis in deciding how society can get the balance right between the needs of economic and social justice. The human implications of the Pareto efficiency axiom (where no individual can be made better off without making someone else worse off) just will not go away. How do we achieve a distribution of wealth where some people can be made better off without other people becoming worse off? In considering the human dimension of economics, it can be useful to recall that Adam Smith's *An Inquiry into the Nature and Causes of the Wealth of Nations* was preceded by *The Theory of Moral Sentiments*, which opens with a discussion of the moral sentiment of sympathy in human affairs, and goes on to look at the character of virtue. Where does one find a discussion of sympathy and virtue in economic theory? Amartya Sen, in his introduction to the Penguin edition of *The Moral Sentiments*, expresses this well when he says that the ideas in *The Wealth of Nations* have been interpreted without reference to the thought developed in the *The Moral Sentiments* with the result that the understanding of this book "has been constrained, to the detriment of economics as a subject. The neglect applies, among other issues, to the appreciation of the demands of rationality, the need for recognizing the plurality of human motivations, the connection between ethics and economics, and the co-dependent—rather than free-standing—role of institutions in general and free markets in particular in the functioning of the economy."

It was one of the purposes of *Ethical Economics* (1996), in looking at the legitimacy of business, to explore the philosophical rationality of economic activity, and to propose that the axioms of profit maximization at all costs, and of business as a purely privative activity, are not rational principles of economic behaviour. In that book we asserted that we need to give equal importance to the recognition of the "Other" (alteritas) in economic activity, an approach that introduces the concept of business as a non-privative activity. We used the word "alteritas" (derived from the Latin word for "Other" in the sense of someone or something else) to stress the rationality of understanding the interests and values of the "Others" involved in business (stakeholders as well as shareholders). In the wider social context of business, the rational principles, or axioms, of economic behaviour are "other oriented"; these include activities such as respect for consumer preferences (freedom of choice), cooperation (not confrontation), facilitation (customer service), and the creation of economic value for all the stakeholders in an economic enterprise, which is not just the privative property of the shareholders.

The creation of economic value depends on using money as the means for enabling the expression of "encapsulated choice" on the part of the individual or the State, whose "preferences" may differ substantially, and are often conflictual in terms of end use and priorities. So, in setting the assumptions for econometric modelling, economics is involved with the study of consumer preferences and the normative issues of what is right or wrong in terms of rational economic behaviour. Economic assumptions have to make a careful distinction between "needs and wants" in economic decision making, whether it is buying luxury goods, investing in a major new pharmaceutical plant, purchasing audio-visual entertainment products, investing in a house or the stock market, or supporting a local cancer hospice. All of these divergent preferences, which arise from this complex nexus of "needs and wants", are related to human behaviour. This is already taking classical economics into the area of behavioural economics, which studies the social, cognitive and emotional factors in economic decision making, and which shows that people often make decisions on a "rule of thumb" (heuristic) basis, whether it is rational or not. All of these considerations argue strongly for widening the study of economics to take account of its human dimension.

But that does not diminish in any way the importance of economics' strong and rigorous mathematical analytical techniques of predictive modelling, optimization, game theory, statistics, hypothesis testing and econometrics, which remain fundamental to its discipline as it seeks justification as an empirical science. However, as a mathematical science, economics is inseparably linked with the human implications of what it is doing in identifying solutions for the creation and distribution of wealth, and whether those solutions are contributing to greater economic justice in the world or not.

Economics needs to show that it is not a "dismal science", but that it in fact has a "human face" which sees people not simply as statistical units, but as unique individuals whose potential for rational and responsible behaviour is difficult to predict. The economist cannot abrogate to the social scientist, or philosopher, the task of studying human behaviour, but needs to recognize that economics has an important contribution to make to the study of the whys and wherefores of human behaviour in exercising "encapsulated choice" in deciding how money is to be obtained and used. The role of money in economics, which might be described as the prime material of economic activity, will be investigated in Chap. 4 of this book. But before we talk more about money, in the next chapter we investigate the importance of cooperation and facilitation as rational principles of economic activity, which play an important role in rationalizing the legitimacy of business, and its contribution to the realization of economic justice.

References

Economic and Moral Considerations

Alvey J. An introduction to economics as a moral science. Int J Soc Econ. 2000;27(12):1231–52.

Hume D. A treatise of human nature. London: Penguin; 1985.

Kant I. The metaphysics of morals. Cambridge: Cambridge University Press; 1996.

Kant I. Critique of pure reason. London: Penguin; 2007.

Keynes JM. Economic possibilities for our grandchildren. In: Pecchi L, Piga G, editors. Revisiting Keynes: economic possibilities for our grandchildren. Cambridge, MA: Massachusetts Institute of Technology; 1930a (2008).

Keynes JM. The general theory of employment, interest and money. Palgrave Macmillans 1936.

Keynes JM. Treatise on money. New York: Cosimo; 1930c (2006).

Marshall A. Principles of economics. Basingstoke: Palgrave Macmillan; 2013.

Mill JS. Utilitarianism. Indianapolis, IN: Hackett; 2001.

Mill JS. Principles of political economy. Oxford: Oxford World's Classics; 2008.

Milton F. Capitalism and freedom. Chicago, IL: University of Chicago Press; 2002.

Paitnik D. Wired to care: how companies prosper when they create widespread empathy. Upper Saddle River, NJ: FT Press; 2009.

Scruton R. Kant: a very short introduction. Oxford: Oxford University Press; 2001.

Smith, A. The Wealth of Nations. Book II: Of the Nature, Accumulation, and Employment of Stock, and Book IV: Of Systems of Political Economy.

Smith A. The theory of moral sentiments. New York: Penguin; 2010. Introduction by Amartya Sen.

Strawson P. Individuals: an essay in descriptive metaphysics. Abingdon: Taylor & Francis; 1959 (1964).

Swedberg R. Principles of economic sociology. Princeton, NJ: Princeton University Press; 2003.

Turing AM. Intelligent machinery. In: Evans CR, Robertson ADJ, editors. Cybernetics: key papers. Baltimore, MD: University Park Press; 1948 (1968).

Weber M. The protestant ethic and the spirit of capitalism. Mineola, NY: Dover; 1905 (2003).

Econometrics and Probability

Arrow K. The work of Ragnar Frisch, econometrician. Econometrica. 1960;28(2):175–92.

Gleick J. Chaos: making a new science. London: Vintage; 1988.

Gödel K. On formally undecidable propositions of principia mathematica and related systems. Monatshefte für Mathematik und Physik. 1931;38:173–98.

Heisenberg W. The physical principles of the quantum theory. Chicago, IL: Dover; 1931 (1998).

Laplace PS. Memoir on the probability of causes of events. Mémoires de Mathématique et de Physique, Tome Sixième. Stat Sci. 1774;1(19):364–78. English translation by S. M. Stigler 1986.

Economic History

Braudel F. The Mediterranean and the Mediterranean world in the age of Philip II. New York: Harper & Row; 1972.

Braudel F. Civilization and capitalism, 15th–18th century. New York: Harper & Row; 1981.

Court WHB. A concise economic history of Britain: from 1750 to recent times. Cambridge: Cambridge University Press; 1954.

Ferguson N. The ascent of money: a financial history of the world. London: Penguin; 2008.

Ferguson N. The pity of war. London: Penguin; 2009.

Sowell T. Basic economics: a common sense guide to the economy. New York: Basic; 2015.

3

Cooperation and Facilitation

Abstract This chapter looks at cooperation and facilitation as rational principles of economic activity and business organization, considering the need to reconcile the different self-interests of all the parties concerned in a business transaction. It discusses the Theory of Games to demonstrate that all parties are better off if they take account of the self-interests of the "other", which we call the "alteritas" principle of economics, and which is an essential component of any theory of economic justice. Finally, facilitation is seen as part of the cooperation between business and its customers, where the International Customer Service Institute (ICSI) and the Society for Customer Service Professionals in Europe (SOCAPE) provide advice and service on systems for customer service management.

3.1 Chapter Overview

Business is primarily a cooperative activity where the Theory of Games demonstrates that the motivations of self-interest are modified in light of the needs and wants of the "other" cooperators, or stakeholders, in a business enterprise, all of whom have particular "self-interests", which we

© The Editor(s) (if applicable) and The Author(s) 2016   **37**
M.R. Griffiths, J.R. Lucas, *Value Economics*,
DOI 10.1057/978-1-137-54187-1_3

are required to take account of in any business transaction or relationship. Thus, cooperation, based on a consideration of the "other" in business, becomes a rational principle of economics, which we call the "alteritas" principle, arguing that it is an essential component of economic justice. As J.C. Penney put it, "The keystone of successful business is cooperation. Friction retards progress."

However, economic justice in any given situation is often indeterminate in its outcomes, because it depends on the specific conditions of individual businesses, which vary according to the economic environment and economic viability of a business at any particular moment in time. This calls for a clear definition of how businesses intend to cooperate with their stakeholders. For example, what should be the policy guidelines for cooperation with employees (industrial relations) and customers (product offering and customer service)? The legal and normative requirements which set guidelines for the conduct of a business may be seen as deterministic, but they are unable to predetermine individual business outcomes, which vary according to the economic possibilities and negotiating strengths of the parties involved. It is this indeterminate nature of business which calls for the establishment of clear cooperation procedures between all the parties involved in realizing the product or service offering which a business offers to its "customer stakeholders".

Any business transaction has implications for the economic justice of that transaction, and raises the question of how people participate in business transactions. For example, if employees, as cooperators in a business enterprise, contribute to the creation of the "cooperators' surplus" (profits), how do they participate in that process and share in the economic results of an enterprise? Answers to these questions will depend on whether or not we accept the principle of seeing business as a non-privative, rather than solely a privative activity, for which we argue is a national principle of economic activity. The acceptance of seeing business as a non-privative activity requires a new look at the organization and procedures we need for cooperation and facilitation in managing the relationships with all of the stakeholders. These questions also have implications for the cooperative relationship with the State as a stakeholder who receives economic benefits from business as a corporate taxpayer in the form of fiscal and social contributions. In Chap. 5 we look at the relationship between the public and private in a moneyed society and the implications this has for cooperation and facilitation between the private and public sectors of the economy, in terms of new economic thinking which we discuss in Chap. 13. This raises important issues of cooperativeness in economics discussed in "Cooperative Enterprise" (Stefano and Vera Zamagni), and how cooperatives can work with the "owner-capital" models of economic organisation.

The Theory of Games demonstrates that business is not a "zero-sum game", but that everyone is better off if they take account of the self-interests of the other parties in agreeing to a business transaction. This means that cooperation and facilitation are fundamental components of business management, the principles of which need to be reflected in the business model of any economic enterprise.

Finally, the chapter discusses customer service in terms of facilitation, where the "International Customer Service Institute" (ICSI) and the "Society for Customer Service Professionals in Europe" (SOCAPE) provide advice and service for customer service management.

All of these considerations mean that we need to revisit the classical definition of "Economic Man," whose self-interest of profit maximization needs to be modified in light of the self-interests of all of the stakeholders in an economic enterprise. In this context the principles of cooperation and facilitation become essential parts of any rational theory of business management and organization, since they contribute to the creation of those intangible assets of business, such as employee motivation and morale, customer loyalty and the reputation of a particular business in the eyes of the outside world, which are the hall marks of any cooperative enterprise.

3.2   Self-Interest and Cooperation

Business transactions are primarily a matter of cooperation, and take place because we can do better if we cooperate than if we do not. We are not always selfish, even if Adam Smith stressed the importance of self-interest in economic relations: "It is not from the benevolence of the butcher, the brewer, or the baker that we expect our dinner, but from their regard to their own interest. We address ourselves, not to their humanity but to their self-interest, and never talk to them of our own necessities but of their own advantage." This is a view which has often led people to regard business negatively as a selfish activity determined primarily by self-interest, but that is a mistaken view which fails to recognise the importance of cooperation in business transactions. Cooperativeness, rather than being a matter of altruistic benevolence, is in fact a necessity.

This is demonstrated by the Prisoners' Dilemma in the Theory of Games (see Appendix at the end of the chapter), which shows that if each party pursues his own interest regardless of the other, they end up worse off than if each took the other's interest into account. You and I do better if we both consider what would be the best for both of us than if I considered only what is best for me for me, and you considered only what is best for you. We each need to move from the first person singular (I) to the first person plural (We). When we speak of Aristotle describing man as being a "political animal", the translation is misleading because it ignores the other meaning of "social", which is inherent in the original Greek word "politikos". Social relationships require us to modify our motivations of self-interest in the face of the needs and wants of other people.

In that sense we might describe "Economic Man" as being not only a political animal, but also, by force of social circumstance, a "cooperative animal". This view means that we should widen our view of "Economic Man" as an economic manipulator to one that sees him also as a cooperator in the efficient management of economic resources. When we cooperate we bring about a new state of affairs with different outcomes for the "cooperators". But not all outcomes of cooperation will be of equal value to everyone concerned, and outcomes have different pay-offs for different people. In economic relationships a definition of what the pay-offs are for the different cooperators is essential, if there is to be any "buy-in" to the benefits which business transactions provide to those who participate in those transactions. The extent to which we are prepared to cooperate will depend on how much we share values and have common interests. In effect, a business is an entity, or enterprise, of cooperation which requires a clear understanding of what are the values and interests of those who participate in the enterprise. Mission statements should specify what are the underlying values, or guiding principles, of a business which determine the way in which it is to be managed and organized. This means that organizational theory has to address the question of cooperation and define the operating procedures for implementing cooperation within an organization. Job descriptions—in addition to a definition of functions, responsibilities, and reporting relationships—also need to define with whom specific jobs are expected to cooperate and how. In this way cooperation becomes one of the operating "values" for setting objectives and measuring "job performance".

3.3   The Theory of Games

The Theory of Games (see Appendix) is useful for showing how the powerful motivations of "self-interest" have to adapt themselves to the "interests" of the "other" in business decisions. We can construct a decision matrix, in which, for each decision maker and participant in the "game" of business, the available alternatives and expected outcomes are listed for each category of stakeholder, which enables us to define the trade-offs between one set of objectives and another. Services are rendered, goods are handed over, employment provided, as a result of which the stakeholders involved are better off than they were before.

Thus, business is a "non-zero-sum-game", where it is not a question of "the winner takes all", but a negotiation of interests between different groups of stakeholders. There are admittedly adversarial, if not conflictual, sides to business transactions, but they all have to take place within the wider framework of "give and take" cooperation, which forces the interested parties to modify their "self-interest" in light of the "self-interest" of the other. This requires business to develop effective negotiating procedures for all areas of negotiation, for example, customer management and industrial relations, which specify the procedures for negotiation and resolving the conflicts of interest which may arise.

3.4   Consideration of the "Other" and Economic Justice

But we still need to face the question of partiality in business decisions and transactions where it is the responsibility of the other party to decide whether the transaction is good as far as his values and interests are concerned. In the words of Wicksteed's *The Common Sense of Political Economy*, a business transaction is "non-tuistic" (second person singular), that is to say it is concerned not with the right or wrong of the other person's personal and individual values or interests, but with the fact that in cooperating we have to recognize the generality of other people's values and interests in the "vous-istic" (second person plural) sense, which will influence the ease or not of finalizing a business transaction.

In other words, we are not concerned with a person's gender orientation or beliefs, but with his appartenance to an organization, such as a labour union, which may have a different set of values and interests to those of management, where "we beg to differ", but seek in negotiation to reconcile divergent interests. This kind of cooperation requires a set of negotiation procedures and skills on the part of all the parties involved, which in a process of "give and take" can assist in reaching the compromises often necessary in agreeing "trade-offs" between the parties involved. The history of industrial relations is full of examples of successful and unsuccessful cooperation in reaching final decisions where all parties in the end agreed, willingly or otherwise, to contractual obligations covering wages and employment conditions. Once I recognize that I cannot rationally invite you to do business with me simply on the grounds that I want to profit by it, but must, rather, hold myself as being willing to serve your wants, I have introduced the notion of "concern for the other" (alteritas), which is the foundation of justice. Justice, therefore, is of prime importance in business and economics. It seeks to provide the criteria and standards by which different people can work together without feeling that one party has been exploited or done down by the other.

But we do also talk of hard bargains being struck and stigmatize some contracts as being unfair, which means that business has to resolve the disputes which arise, particularly in wage negotiations where employees are seeking what, in their opinion, should be the just wage, or recompense, for their services. However, economic justice is indeterminate in the sense that, for example, wages will be determined by the time, place and circumstances in which negotiations take place for establishing what those wages should be. Minimum wage rates will be taken into account, but the number of jobs available will be determined by the ability of an enterprise to pay those minimum statutory rates. As economic environments differ in terms of market conditions (growth or recession), economic justice needs to be filled out in the context of market conditions at any one time. This means that economic justice cannot be worked out according to a set of standards which predetermine what the just price or wage should be (even if guidelines for a minimum wage have been legislated), but is the result of a complex process of negotiating what those prices or wages should be in a given situation, and also the related levels of employment. This process can put considerable strain on the willingness to cooperate on the part of those concerned, which calls for a high level of competence not only in negotiating, but also in providing and understanding the economic information required for informed decision making in agreeing prices and wages. Economic education on the part of all concerned is essential for deciding whether price and wage decisions are economically just or not.

We need criteria to decide what is feasible for the business conditions at any specific time, as the final agreements on wage levels and the related outcomes of employment will be indeterminate, rather than predetermined, in their final outcome. National wage agreements have to be flexible in responding to different local environments, which vary in terms of their efficiency and productivity, both of which are determining factors in providing employment and the possibility of bonus compensation related to increased productivity. Employee compensation systems and levels of remuneration need to be related to the economic value of the business concerned, an argument we address further in Chap. 9.

In saying that economic justice is indeterminate we are not asserting that it is "relative" in the modern sense in which moral values are said to be relative. Although justice is often relative to the particular situation and context concerned, it must take account of the jurisdictions and conventions of the countries or markets in which it operates, and which determine the legal and economic framework within which it operates. This does not contradict the indeterminacy of economic justice, which depends on the economic viability of each enterprise to provide employment. However subject individual firms may be to national sectoral wage contracts to pay agreed levels of wages, the number of people they are able to employ will depend on the relative size and efficiency of the individual firm concerned. And as individual firms are made up of individuals whose contributions and rewards vary according to skills, experience and productivity, economic justice will depend on the extent to which the individual firm is able to negotiate agreements with a unique group of individuals whose willingness to cooperate will vary according to their interests, needs, wants and qualifications. In that sense, whether the individual firm is unionized or not, the final agreement on pay, conditions and levels of employment cannot be predetermined, but will depend on the particularity of the firm concerned in terms of what it can offer economically or not.

The management of this kind of indeterminate negotiating process requires specific skills and clear procedures for cooperation, if employees are to "buy in" to agreements as informed cooperators in the business enterprise, rather than being unwilling acceptors of decisions forced upon them. The development of negotiating skills (see Karras 1993) needs to become a "sine qua non" of business management training whether provided by business schools or by internal employee training programmes.

3.5   Facilitation and Service

If businesses are primarily cooperative activities, they are also facilitators in providing goods and services to their customers, with clear responsibilities in terms of quality, performance and respect for the terms and conditions of sale. Customers should not be misled and exploited; rather, they should be helped to make a rational choice in accordance with their needs and values. It is up to the seller to provide goods and services which meet the quality and transparency standards of the goods and services being offered. As the importance of consumer protection has increased, the principle of "caveat emptor" (the customer is responsible for his decision to buy even he is being sold a "lemon") has been complemented by the principle of "caveat vendor", where it is the responsibility of the vendor to see that the customer gets what he really wants.

For example, in 1977 the Unfair Contract Terms Act was passed in the UK, and a later Sales of Goods Act in 1979 was extended in 1982 to cover services as well as goods, in response to a demand for greater customer protection. Customer service management today encompasses an extensive range of functions, covering sales, customer support and education, after-sales service, complaints management, customer feedback surveys, and measurement of customer satisfaction and loyalty.

Facilitation and brainstorming procedures can also be used where the use of an outside facilitator assists in evaluating the level of customer satisfaction, and identifying opportunities for improvement (see Verhoef 2003).

The International Customer Service Institute (ICSI) publishes standards covering aspects such as performance improvement, customer service conduct, customer complaints and resolution of disputes. It also has a model for measuring customer satisfaction, retention and loyalty, and employee commitment to customer service. The Society for Customer Service Professionals in Europe (SOCAPE) offers services and conferences to promote effective customer service management. All of these developments in the field of facilitation and customer service confirm the cooperative nature of business, and the need to see the businessman as a service "facilitator" in managing the relationships not only between company and customer, but also between the other stakeholders, each of which has specific "service" needs. If we take into account all of these considerations we need to extend the traditional concept of "Economic Man,' as a maximizer of efficiency and profit, to seeing him also as an economic cooperator or facilitator where "service" as well as "profit" are the joint motivators of his behaviour[1].

---

[1] Richard Sennett's book Together: the Rituals, Pleasures and Politics of Cooperation (2012) is an interesting contribution to the cooperation debate, particularly with regard to the way he looks at what he calls the "cooperative frame of mind", and how social relations become embittered at work when, as he puts it, the "social triangle" or earned authority, mutual respect and cooperation break down. He looks at the making and repairing of the workshop where the work unit is small and related to a craft or particular skill set, in stark contrast to the Charlie Chaplin production line. He touches on the theme we referred to in Chap. 2 of Dev Paitnik's book Wired to Care in discussing how companies prosper when they create empathy. Empathy also relates to the development of that sense of belonging to a work group or community of which one is a recognized contributor in the Japanese culture of "gratitude" for employment, similar to the Chinese "guanxi" principle of being able to criticize and advise on work practices and conditions. But in his book Sennett does not discuss the importance of ownership and shared value (neither of which words occur in the book's index) as motivators for cooperation, which we discuss in Chaps. 8 and 9. When we have a sense of ownership in what we are doing and a sense that we participate in the economic success of our enterprise, cooperation becomes a more likely outcome of the way we behave and act.

The trauma of the UK Miners' strike was that conflict took over from cooperation in trying to find an equitable solution for a radical downsizing of the mining industry, which became all the more bitter because of the break-up of local communities which had existed for generations. Cooperation in such an explosive social setting required not only negotiating skills of the highest order assisted by facilitation and arbitration, but also a "new deal" approach to finding a solution which the aggrieved parties, the miners facing unemployment, could accept without the entrenched bad feelings of us against you. The UK miners' strike should become a textbook example of what happens when conflict takes over from cooperation.

Appendix[2]: The Theory of Games

Summary

The Theory of Games helps us understand our reasoning when we make decisions involving more than one person. It shows why I need to take account of other people's decision making as well as my own, why what has happened in the past is relevant as well as what may happen in the future, and why my values need to develop to encompass our common good and not just my own individual good. In this appendix, we present four examples of the Theory at work in practice in decision making between parties with different intentions and points of view:

1. *The Rule of the Road*, showing the importance of conventions.
2. *The Battle of the Sexes*, balancing different preferences.
3. *The Prisoner's Dilemma*, compromising one's preferred outcome.
4. *The Altruist's Dilemma*, adjusting one's preferences in light of the other's.

In the Theory of Games each decision maker, or "player", has a number of choices, yielding a large number of "outcomes" according to the choices made by himself and other players. Thus, if there are four players each with three possible courses of action, there will be 81 (i.e. $3 \times 3 \times 3 \times 3$) possible outcomes. Each outcome is evaluated by each player according to his system of values, and the value he assigns to it is called his "pay-off". The pay-off is normally expressed in numerical terms, with the suggestion that we are dealing with the cardinal, interpersonal utilities that utilitarians believe in, but there is no need to assume that they are always cardinal and interpersonal; for most purposes it is enough that each player can decide his order of priorities as between the various outcomes that may result from his and others' choices.

The outcomes are evaluated differently by the different players whose actions brought them about. The Theory of Games enables us to

[2] Reprinted from M. R. Griffiths and J. R. Lucas, 'Appendix A The Theory of Games' in *Ethical Economics*, 1996, Macmillan Press Ltd, pp. 222–9. Reproduced with permission of Palgrave Macmillan.

characterize cooperative activities as opposed to purely competitive ones. In a competition there are necessarily losers as well as winners. They are "zero-sum games" since my gain is your loss. In cooperative activities, however, there need be no losers, since by collaborating we both do better than we would have done on our own. These are "Non-zero Sum Games". Many are of a simple unproblematic sort: there is one outcome which is better from every player's point of view, and so each has a good reason of choosing to act so as to bring it about. But some pose problems for those who construe rationality in terms of maximizing one's own pay-off. In this discussion we differentiate between the point of view of the **utilitarian**, who judges outcomes in terms of his maximum happiness, and the **consequentialist**, who judges only by consideration of what future outcomes will be. In the tables which summarize the satisfaction of the outcomes of the four examples, the numbers refer to the level of satisfaction for each party—from zero for no satisfaction to ten for maximum satisfaction. In looking at the Theory of Games we come face to face with the conflict between **deontology** (obligation or duty to adhere to a set of rules), and **solipsism** (the individualism of someone who believes that only his beliefs or mind set are to be taken into account).

For a fuller description of the Theory of Games, see The Theory of Games and Economic Behaviour by von Neumann and Mortgenstern, (Princeton, 2004).

1. Rule of the Road

The Rule of the Road shows the importance of conventions, "Coordination Norms" in enabling players in a many-person game to concert their decisions so as to secure outcomes that they all prefer. In driving, in communicating, in dancing and in many other social activities, we need to coordinate our actions with one another, so as to concert our efforts and avoid collisions. Schematically we represent two motorists, Mr Knight and M. Chevalier approaching each other, and needing to move over in order not to run into each other, by the matrix (with Mr Knight's pay-off in top right of each outcome, and M. Chevalier's in bottom left):

Note: The ratings in each of the boxes indicate the degree of satisfaction or dissatisfaction of the parties involved.

Table 3.1 Theory of Games "Rule of the Road"

The rule of the road: the importance of conventions		
	Mr Knight goes right	Mr Knight goes left
M. Chevalier va à droite	5 each passes other safely 5	0 collision 0
M.Chevalier va à gauche	0 collision 0	5 each passes other safely 5

Provided both go right, or both go left, they will pass each other safely: what is essential is that they do not each decide what he, on his own, thinks best, but both abide by some convention, or rule, or law, or mutual agreement. That is to say, I should not attempt to do whatever seems to me to be productive of the best consequences, but should reliably act in the way that other people expect me to act. I should drive on the left and not cut corners, give way when the other driver has the right of way, so that other drivers know where they are with me, and can plan their own movements accordingly. There is a necessary imperfection of information about the future actions of free agents in the absence of publicly avowed rules: norm-observance deontology is the key to coordination. A simple maximizing strategy is impossible, and each player must keep in step with others, usually by means of their all abiding by some relevant convention. Whatever the apparent attractions of consequentialism for the single operator, they are shown to be illusory, even by consequentialist standards, once the agent sees himself to be not a solipsistic loner, but one person among many, each needing to recognize others as initiators of action with minds of their own whose decisions can be anticipated only if they adhere to well-known rules.

2. Battle of the Sexes

In the Battle of the Sexes He and She want to spend their holiday together, but He would prefer to go mountaineering in the Alps, whereas She would rather they both spent it sunbathing by the sea. The matrix is:

Table 3.2 Theory of Games "Battle of the Sexes"

The battle of the sexes: balancing different preferences		
	She goes to Alps	She goes to the sea
He goes to Alps	8 lovely for him: good for her 10	4 "wish you were here too" 4
He goes to sea	0 beastly for him: beastly for her 0	0 good for him: lovely for her 8

Since for either of them the second best is so much better than the third or fourth alternatives, it would pay either to settle for that if the very best appeared unattainable. And therefore it would pay the other to make it seem so. If She can throw a fit of hysterics and say she cannot abide the Alps and will not go there at any price, then He, if he is reasonable, will abandon his hopes of an Alpine holiday, and settle for the sea, which he would like twice as much as solitary mountaineering. But equally He may see that the moment has come to take a firm masculine line, and let the little woman face up to the realities of the situation, and either come along with him or go her separate way. And if once it becomes clear that this is the choice, She will have no option but to cave in, and buy a knapsack instead of a new bikini. It is thus irrational to be guided only by the pay-offs of the outcomes that are available at any one time, because that enables the other to manipulate one's choices. If I am to retain my autonomy, I cannot be altogether a direct consequentialist. Once you know that I am guided by consequences alone, you can induce me to do whatever you want by rigging the situation in such a way that by the time I come to make a decision the least bad outcome available to me is to fall in with your plans. Rationality, rather, requires that we extend our consideration over time as well as person. The Battle of the Sexes shows the importance not of other persons but of other times. If we are to avoid being manipulated by unscrupulous fixers, we need long-term assessments, and a guarantee of not discounting the past as being merely water under the bridge. We cannot alter the past, but we can still assess it and take it into account, and thus free ourselves from being at the mercy of anyone who can rig the outcomes at one particular time. In the Theory of Games it is often an advantage to be able to bind oneself absolutely, or equivalently to rule out certain options absolutely. The strategy of Mutually Assured Destruction only worked provided both sides believed that the other was not governed solely by consequentialist considerations, and really would retaliate if attacked, even though there would be then no advantage in doing so. In order to reinforce this expectation, mechanical devices were constructed which in the event of a nuclear attack would operate automatically without the possibility of being switched off by any consequentialist survivors. In a less grisly way the whole logic of making and keeping promises is to ensure that some actions of an agent need not be altered simply by reason of factors which had been future becoming, by the exclusion of time, past. If we discount all past considerations we not only lay ourselves open to manipulation, but give only a partial account of the context in which our decisions are made, and from which they obtain their significance. I cannot be coherently oriented towards the future alone once I recognize that all my futures will one day be past. If it were not for existence of some transferable token of value, economic transactions would mostly be instances of the Battle of the Sexes: most of the benefit would accrue to one of the parties, and the other would have the choice of either cutting off his nose to spite the other's face or of letting the other get away with the lion's share of the cooperative cake. If, however, there are not just two stark alternatives but an almost continuous range of intermediate courses of action, the claim by the one party that his offer is the only one available, and that the other must either take it or leave it, becomes implausible, and the other can counter with an offer which is more plausible as a final offer, and which the first party would be evidently foolish to turn down out of hand. Bargaining becomes possible, and a refusal to bargain unacceptable.

3. The Prisoners' Dilemma

The Prisoners' Dilemma was first discerned by Protagoras, and greatly impressed Plato, and later Hobbes, who made it the cornerstone of his argument for Leviathan. In its modern form it is due to A. W. Tucker. He considers two prisoners, Bill Sykes and Kevin Slob, held incommunicado, who have jointly committed a serious crime. The prosecution, however, does not have sufficient evidence to convict either of them, and they know it. But it does have evidence to convict each of them of a less serious crime, say tax evasion, for which the penalty is six months' imprisonment. The prosecution then suggests some plea bargaining to each: if he will confess to the major crime, and give evidence so as to secure the conviction of the other, he will be pardoned for both the major and the minor crime. If he confesses, and the other confesses too, both will receive a suitably reduced sentence for having pleaded guilty, say five years. If he does not confess, but is convicted on the evidence of the other, then he will receive the full sentence of ten years. The prosecution lets each prisoner know that it has made the same proposition to the other. Each prisoner then has a strong incentive to confess: for if the other confesses too, he would get ten years unless he did, while if the other does not confess, he will get off scot-free, instead of doing six months for the minor offence. So, if they act according to their individual scale of values, they will both confess. But by so doing they will both end up worse off than if they both kept silent. If they both kept silent, they would each receive only six months for the minor offence; but by both confessing, they receive the five years for having pleaded guilty to the major crime. The matrix is given the table below. There are many Prisoners' Dilemmas in real life: tax evasion, fare dodging, stealing, are all familiar instances, where, other things being equal,

Table 3.3 Theory of Games "The Prisoners' Dilemma"

The prisoners' dilemma: compromising one's preferred outcome		
	Sykes keeps silent	Sykes confesses
Slob keeps silent	−1 Both jailed for tax −1	0 Sykes let off: maximum jail for Slob −10
Slob confesses	−10 Slob let off: with maximum jail for Sykes 0	−5 Both jailed reduced sentences −5

it would seem like a good idea oneself to do them, but a very bad idea to have other people doing them too. Hence the need for laws backed by the sanctions of a State wielding coercive power. The importance of the Prisoners' Dilemma, however, lies not only in its showing the need for the State, but in its revealing the inadequacy of static ascriptions of values to individuals.

For there is a sense it which it is obviously in the prisoners' interests not to confess, and this rationality the static schema employed by the Theory of Games occludes. This point is often missed, because the prisoners are supposed wrongdoers, and hence presumed to be selfish. If only people were unselfish, and put others before self, then, so the argument runs, all would be well: the prisoners would not confess, the taxpayer would pay his taxes, the traveller buy his ticket, and nobody would ever wrong his neighbour.

4. The Altruist's Dilemma

That all would not be well, however, is evident once we consider the dilemma of the altruistic couple where He tries to maximize Her pay-off, and She His, with the result they both end up with something they neither want. Thus He might be keen on cars, and She on food. If He mends the car and She cooks, they have a good lunch, followed by a drive in the country. If He helps Her cook, instead of messing about in the garage,

Table 3.4 Theory of Games "The Altruist's Dilemma"

The altruists' dilemma: adjusting one's preferences		
	She cooks	She helps Him mend the car
He mends the car	5 good lunch, followed by pleasant drive 5	0 record journey, with meal in Transport Cafe 10
He helps her cook	10 super lunch, but no drive 0	1 indifferent lunch, followed by mediocre drive 1

they have an absolutely super lunch, though no drive in the country. If, on the other hand, She helps Him mend the car, the car will go like greased lightning, but they will have to eat in a Transport Café. But if they each insist on doing what the other wants, He will try His hand in the kitchen, while She will wriggle under the car, and the result will be an indifferent lunch followed by a mediocre drive, much worse for both of them than if each had acted non-altruistically.

The Altruists' Dilemma is the mirror image of the Prisoners' Dilemma, and shows that the trouble lies not in one's being concerned to maximize one's own pay-off, but in being tied to just one pay-off throughout. In practice we are able to resolve or surmount the Prisoners' Dilemma because we modify our original preferences in the light of what we come to know about others', and are not conned to a single occasion. I conjugate over persons, and knowing what you want, see that we shall both be better off if we follow a cooperative strategy, and for that reason come to want it. Although, other things being equal, I want to get off scot-free, and prefer a short prison sentence to a longer one, I do not want to let down my confederate. I identify with him, and begin to take his interests to heart, and consider what is best for us jointly, rather than for just me individually. I may not do so completely, and make his interests mine, as the utilitarians urge, but I do so enough to alter the balance of advantage so as to favour the cooperative strategy. Of course, in so doing, I make myself vulnerable to being let down by him; but in real life few situations are evidently and certainly one-off, and anyone who lets me down on one occasion will forfeit my trust thereafter. In the long run I shall do worse if I let people down in order to maximize my own pay-off on each occasion than if I respond to each person as he did to me the last time we met, and give those I have not met before the benefit of the doubt and trusting them to behave decently. Being reasonable seems reasonable once we conjugate over persons, and proves to be the best policy once we conjugate over time too.

Conclusion A completely static and purely individualist approach is inadequate and demonstrably irrational: if we are to be rational we must take the values of others into consideration as well as our own, and must be prepared to change our priorities in the light of them. We start by assuming, as the classical economists did, that rationality can be determined in terms of maximizing future pay-offs, and then show that even within its own terms, such a definition is self-contradictory. The Rule of the Road shows that it is better to keep to the rules: each of us should recognize that he is not the only pebble on the beach, that it is not for him to choose which course of events shall occur, and that often the best he can do is to fit in with what other people are likely to do. The Battle of the Sexes shows that it is irrational to have regard only to future outcomes; an agent has a past as well as a future, and should make up his mind what he is going to do with regard to what he has decided in the past as well as what will ensue in the future. The Prisoners' Dilemma shows that he should take into account not only the existence but the interests and ideals of other people, and that it is irrational to ignore the collective point of view. The Altruist's Dilemma shows that the problem is not wanting to maximize one's payoff, but in being tied just to one pay-off through a discussion or negotiation between people seeking different pay-offs.

Contrary to the static solipsistic, future-oriented, exclusively individualistic standpoint of the classical economists, we are forced, by thinking about these four cases, to recognize that rationality is dynamic, leading us to take a longer temporal and wider personal view of what is involved in the decisions we are called on to take.

References

Karrass CL. Give and take: the complete guide to negotiating strategies and tactics. New York: HarperCollins; 1993.

Sennett R. Together: the rituals, pleasures and politics of cooperation. London: Penguin; 2012.

Verhoef PC. Understanding the effect of customer relationship management efforts on customer retention and customer share development. J Market. 2003;67(4):30–45.

Von Neumann J, Morgenstern O. Theory of games and economic behavior. Princeton, NJ: Princeton University Press; 2004.

Wicksteed PH. The common sense of political economy. Abingdon, Oxon: Routledge; 2003.
Stefano and Vera Zamagni. Cooperative Enterprise. Edward Elgar Publishing 2011.

Institutions

International Customer Service Institution, "International Standard for Service Excellence" (ICSI 2012).
Society for Customer Service Professionals (SOCAPE).

4

Money as "Encapsulated Choice"

Lack of money is the root of all evil. George Bernard Shaw

Abstract We can look at money as "encapsulated choice" rather than an inert token of value, because it confers freedom of choice. It is inherently both "slippery" and "sticky"—"slippery" because its value is changing all the time as a result of economic conditions and the unpredictability of consumer preferences, and "sticky" because consumers do not always buy in the cheapest, and sell in the dearest market. Economics is concerned with the quantity of money and its supply and demand, where the debate swings between the "aggregate demand" Keynesian or the Friedmanite "monetarist". People are funny about money and regard it with different approbations. Are we to give it three cheers for freedom of choice, two for selfishness versus altruism, or only one or none for its potential for its capacity for greed and self-aggrandizement? We need a new philanthropic principle for money in economics, which takes a more optimistic view on how people like to spend their money, and provides incentive for "giving back" to society the wealth "Economic Man" is creating.

4.1   Chapter Overview

Money is an essential lubricant in economic and social exchange, because it confers choice. It can be described as "encapsulated choice", because it enables people to exercise a freedom of choice as to how and when they use their money. As such, money is not an inert substance but a token of value, something which raises ethical questions about how we value and use money. In the economics of business it is the token we use for making economic transactions and agreeing contracts between the parties involved—whether supplier, customer or employee. But it is also a "slippery" substance influenced by the variable world of consumer preferences, and the value it derives from the economic conditions of inflation, productivity, competition, raw material prices, and the relative "efficiency" between one national economy and another, which give a "currency" value to money. One tricky problem for economics is how to estimate the future currency values of money, which further complicates the task of putting a value on money between one national currency and another.

Another aspect of money concerns the "How much?" question, which takes us into a consideration of the quantity theory of money (QTM), and the need to answer the question "Quantity of what?" Monetary economics has to grapple with the problem of how we determine the amount of money to be released into an economy, and how we fix the amounts in terms of the MO categories of "narrow" and "broad" money (see Appendix at the end of the chapter). The jury is still out in the debate about money supply and demand between the "aggregate demand" Keynesians and the "monetarist" Friedmanites over the exact relationship between money and prices, and how to get the balance right between monetary demand and supply. Prices at times appear to be "sticky" in not responding to the classic theory of the elasticity/non-elasticity of demand in economics, when people do not necessarily buy in the cheapest markets or sell in the dearest. This is a debate which tends to exclude the businessman and be left to the "economic experts", but he needs to be closely involved in the demand/supply debate in finding the right solutions, in light of the specific business experiences and needs of different economic sectors, which have their own particular supply/demand characteristics.

Money can be regarded as being "funny", not only in the way people earn it and spend it (people do not always buy in the cheapest and sell in the dearest market), but also in terms of its different values of "use" and "exchange", as is seen, for example, with regard to water, which is more useful than diamonds, but has a much lower money "exchange" value. This poses some tricky ethical problems, with egalitarians often objecting to the fact that pop stars and footballers are paid much more money for their work than nurses or schoolteachers. So money can receive different votes of approbation, depending on whether we give it three cheers for its conferral of freedom of choice; two cheers for the different potentials it has for selfishness or altruism; or one, or no cheers at all, for its potential for greed and self-aggrandisement.

All this makes it difficult for economists to propose a coherent and rational "theory of money". We need to base any such theory on an analysis of its uses, the information for which can be provided by the cash flows of any "economic operator", where we can match cash inflows (earnings) against outflows (uses) in establishing guidelines for the use of money. This kind of analysis applies not only to business, but also to the State as an economic operator, and to the individual citizen as a taxpayer. As far as individual economic operators are concerned, this takes us into the fiscal, social and philanthropic areas of "giving back", the information for which exists in any individual tax return reporting gross and net income after tax, social charges and philanthropic contributions, which are all forms of "giving back" money earned. The limitations of published income league tables arise from the fact that they concentrate on gross rather than net income, which is the key measure for evaluating the "giving back" principle we need to include in any comprehensive and coherent theory of money. Philanthropy is a necessary subject of study for new economic thinking in looking at theories about the value of money and its uses, and in deciding how many cheers we are prepared to give to money as a token of economic and social exchange in an economy.

4.2   The Concept of Money

Money is an important part of cooperation in economic transactions. It is not the only part (there may well be non-monetary considerations in non-profit economic transactions), but it facilitates cooperation by enabling it to be jointly beneficial to all parties involved in an economic transaction. Money is an oil that lubricates social interchange, and it is valuable because it confers choice and is regarded as a means for establishing the monetary values in an economic transaction. It works because it is what most of us could do with more of, but it is a scarce and limited resource, which determines the choice of how we want to use it.

Economists are right to say that economics is about the allocation of scarce resources, and the management of money as a scarce resource is fundamental to any theory of economics. In order to work, money has to be valuable to me, because it is valuable to you, and it is valuable to you, because it is valuable to others with whom you might want to do business, and it is valuable to each of them for the same reason. If money is to have value for me, for you and for other people, it must also maintain its value over time. The time interval might be short; I might, for example, take what you gave me straight to the pub, and have a drink. But it would greatly diminish the value of money if it had to be spent straight away. We may well want to postpone spending it to a later time of our own choosing. Since the value of money lies in its encapsulating choice, we want to be able to choose not only to whom to give it, but when. There is a past, present and future aspect to money, depending on all the people involved, whether first, second, or third person singular or plural, which makes it susceptible to the different values the parties concerned place on it at any one point in time. For example, in wage negotiations there is a delicate relationship between what I want now and in the future, and what you can give me now and in the future, where money may have different tokens of value for the parties involved. Money becomes an instrument for defining the values involved, and, as such, for example in industrial relations, requires sophisticated procedures for gaining the cooperation of the parties involved in negotiating wage levels and working conditions, and in defining the criteria for agreeing employment contracts in relation to product output or service provision, productivity, skills and training.

The concept of money is inextricably linked to how we wish to satisfy our consumer preferences, whether for daily survival in keeping the fridge full or paying consumer credit obligations, for pleasure, for educating our children, or for security in the future. If you have money you have to decide to spend it now, next week or further into the future. But next week you may choose to defer choice yet again, so as to be able to choose at some later date. And so on. We can always go on deferring when we spend it, but it has to maintain its value. which is a "slippery" characteristic of money, since its value is not maintained and will change according to factors such as the rate of inflation, the productivity of national economies, or fear of default on national debt, which influences the value of its exchange rate vis-à-vis other currencies. The value of money now and its value in the future will influence how much we need to put aside for future survival, for example, in the form of pension contributions (both statutory and voluntary) for retirement.

The pension "money value" debate between "defined contributions" and "defined benefits" in the end came down on the side of defined contributions, since defined benefits, as a result of changing demographics and future inflation, made it impossible for pension schemes to pay for future defined benefits without an unacceptable increase in contributions to finance such benefits in the future. What money we need to spend now as opposed to what we shall need to spend in future is a challenge for economic thinking in getting the balance right between money consumption today and money saving/investment for the future. So the difficulty for economics in setting assumptions for predictive modelling is how to estimate the future value of money and national currencies; such uncertainty introduces the concept of the modal logic of potentiality, by which we mean the possibility of something happening or not in the future. The potentiality of choice that money confers does not have (necessarily) to be exercised in one way or the other way, but can (possibly) be exercised in either way. We need to distinguish between actually exercising the choice now, or possibly in the future.

This has implications for the study of consumer preferences, since as we can use money to defer choice, we are also faced by the question of when that choice will be exercised or realized. That is, not only do we want to choose, but we also want to have a choice whether to choose or not. If I have money in my pocket, I can choose what to spend it on, but I may not want to make a possible choice in that moment; it may be that I simply wish to be able to make choices when I decide to do so at some time in the future. There is an imponderable conundrum in the use of money between the logic of maybe or the maybe not, of which economic predictive modelling has to take account in defining the assumptions it uses for analysing the monetary values of consumer preferences now and in the future.

There needs to be a very close link between the economist and the businessman in analysing the uses of money for consumer preferences, in order that economic forecasting is based on the "business realities" of today, rather than on experiences of the past which may no longer be valid. Money is valuable in terms of consumer preferences, which gives it a duplicate value of being valuable because it enables us to exercise choice, but also because it has value determined by the specific economic conditions at the time, with the risk that a national monetary value may be devalued. In the 1980s the official value of the Cuban peso vis-à-vis the US dollar was one Cuban peso for one US dollar, while the outside market was saying says "No, I'll give you 20 or 25 pesos, not one, for one US dollar." So, who decides what the currency value of money is going to be? In this case, was it the Cuban National Bank, the US Fed, or the consumer in the peso marketplace?

It is easy to think of money as a substance consisting—as it did in the past—of a quantity of precious metals or today of coins and banknotes. As the word "currency" indicates, however, it is really a token of value intended for current use. Modern currencies are not the same as traditional currencies in the past; the assumption that money is something like gold is mistaken. Its value is determined not by gold, but by those slippery factors of economic productivity and "consumer preferences" in a national economy. Monetarists make many trenchant criticisms of Keynesian supply economics as being inflationary in creating more money to finance economic growth, when they stress that the quantity of money available is the key for achieving low or non-inflationary growth. However, they do not advance a coherent view of what "the quantity of money" is a quantity of. In times gone by it was possible to link it to the quantity of gold, but today what does it mean when we talk in terms of "narrow" or "broad" money? (see Appendix). It is no longer sufficient to talk only of MO money, or narrow money; it has to be extended to other "M" categories of broad money, covering such things as demand

and savings deposits whose values are linked to specific time horizons and confidence in the debt structures of national economies.

But they are not substances, and carry no guarantee of being reliably quantifiable over time on account of the peculiar nature of money which, besides notes and coins, includes credit. Economic transactions can take place with IOU notes just as well as with coins, so long as everyone trusts the creditworthiness of the issuer. In England treasury notes are IOUs, signed by the Chief Cashier of the Bank of England, that promise to pay the bearer on demand the sum of five, ten, twenty, or fifty pounds, the nominal value of which is fixed, but not related to the changing values of currencies. In monetary economics, the quantity theory of money proposes that money supply has a direct, proportional relationship with price levels. For example, if there is an increase in the amount of currency in circulation, there will be a proportional change in the price of goods.

This theory was challenged by Keynesian economics, but subsequently reasserted by the "Monetarist" school of economics. While mainstream economists agree that the quantity theory holds true in the long run, there is still disagreement about its applicability in the short run. Critics of the theory argue that money velocity is not stable and, in the short run, prices are sticky, so that the direct relationship between money supply and price level does not hold. The classic concept of QTM proposes that there is a direct relationship between QTM and the level of prices and goods sold. But real interest rates and prices are determined by non-monetary factors, such as the productivity of capital and time factors (time horizons). Keynes believed that price levels are not strictly determined by money supply, that is, prices are "sticky", meaning that QTM fails to explain variations in the value of money. Money today is fiat money, that is, it is not tied to any other commodity, so that notes are just pieces of paper, whose values—although guaranteed by the central issuing bank—are in the end determined by exogenous factors like wage levels, investment and productivity, but also by the endogenous factors of consumer preferences and confidence in the outlook for the value of a particular currency. So, the value of money is inseparably linked to the slippery nature of consumer preferences in determining how much money we need, or want, at any one point in time, and how we get the balance right between its demand and its supply.

It will suffice at this stage to emphasize that there are still divergences of opinions between economists on these questions whether they are "aggregate demand" Keynesians or Friedmanite "control the money supply" monetarists, with a dissenting view being held by those, such as von Mises, who criticized the overemphasis on the supply of money in the absence of any adequate explanation of the demand for money. As he said, QTM fails to explain the mechanisms of variations in the value of money. So, can differences of opinion about QTM be reconciled in a rational theory of money demand and supply which takes account of differences in global, national and economic sector requirements? For example, the economic sectors of energy, heavy industry, health and consumer products have different money demand and supply characteristics, which economic planning has to recognise if it is to avoid the danger of national policies killing the goose that lays the golden egg.

4.3   Funny Money

As a sticky and slippery commodity it should not come as a surprise that people are funny and unpredictable with regard to money. Some people hoard it, some spend it, some give it away, some steal it, some love it, some hate it, or are just cynical about it, as Somerset Maugham once put it: "Money is like a sixth sense, and you can't make sense of the other five without it."

Viewed in these different ways is there any rationality behind the way we think about and use money? But the different rationalities or irrationality of people's behaviour stem from the fact that it is unsubstantial, whose value is not determined by a substance outside itself. It was not always so. In times past it used to be valued in relation to metals, like gold, silver, brass and even iron, even if today gold reserves are held by countries to back the resources they have for supporting the national debts they incur. Modern currencies are a kind of self-sustaining confidence trick. We value them because we think they are valued by others, who equally value them on the same supposition. The value of money depends on accepting the values other people put on it, which makes it a thing each of us could do with more of. So it is easy then to suppose that I should adopt a maximizing policy with regard to my money. But the inference is invalid. Although it needs to be true that money is what one could do with more of "other things being equal", "other things are often not equal".

Economists postulate "Economic Man", who buys in the cheapest, and sells in the dearest, market, but this is a fleshless abstraction, because in reality people do not always buy in the cheapest, and sell in the dearest, market; indeed, in practice it would be irrational for them to do so. It is rational to buy in the village shop rather than the supermarket, for reasons of convenience or the pleasantness of a conversation across the counter. As we have said, money needs to be scarce, for people to be willing to do things in order to get it. But it is a scarcity imposed by the need for money to be limited if it is to work. If money grew on trees, it would not serve as a medium of exchange. Although necessarily scarce, however, it can be increased in the form of credit, which is extensible money, but with a pay-back obligation.

We tend to think of money as privative (what is mine is mine, not yours), so that if I give you a gold sovereign it is my decision to give up my personal possession of having it no longer. But credit is not privative: if I give you money in the form of credit, it does not follow that I no longer have it. I do, but it depends on trust that one day I will get it back. Trust is a matter of psychology and social exchange, where the reverse side of credit is debt. I do not give credit unless there are terms and conditions as to when the debt you incur with me will be paid back. So, extensible money depends not just on simple trust, but also on confidence that a repayment term will be respected, which brings us face to face with the credit–debt interface inherent in money transactions. This holds good not only for lending cash, but for money in general. Bank notes are converted into a financial network of IOUs, which are money-equivalents, the value of which depends on the confidence of others down the line, for example, the depositors, who make it possible for banks to issue credit. People are funny (unpredictable) about money, because money is funny in the sense that it is insubstantial and indeterminate in the way it is used, both of which characteristics make it a slippery commodity since its value is changing continuously according to the time and circumstances in which it finds itself. From whichever direction we approach it money is inseparable from the concept of value. Adam Smith was right to distinguish between the "value in use" and the "value in exchange", taking water as an example of value in use but of little value in exchange, as opposed to a diamond which has little value in use compared with water but a far greater value in terms of its exchange value. But in talking about values people differ in the way they value things as the variability and unpredictability of consumer choice in economic affairs indicate.

The old adage of "There's nowt so queer as folk" can equally well be applied to money.

4.4   Three Cheers for Money as an Instrument for Freedom of Choice

As we have said, money facilitates cooperation where the benefits make it possible for business to be carried out in a large variety of different ways. It is freely transferable and tradable, and as money encapsulates freedom of choice, it also decentralizes choice. The great and irrational defect of the communist regimes after the Second World War was to believe that the State could allocate resources exactly as it thought fit. Money was just a resource, to be doled out according to some socially approved principle, refusing to recognize that money confers choice on the part of those who have it, and if people are free to choose, they may choose differently from the way we think they ought to choose. As mentioned earlier, egalitarians are affronted at the huge incomes enjoyed by pop stars and footballers. But if people have money, they may all choose to buy the same albums, or give it to the same sports hero.

Money entails the possibility of economic inequality. It also militates against a just distribution according to merit or according to need. Other people's choices may direct funds to the undeserving or those who are not in need. Nurses deserve to be paid more than pop singers: football stars may not need all the money they get, which might be better directed to the poor and ill-nourished. But other people have the choice, and they have chosen otherwise. We may regret this restriction on our power to create a just society—which raises the question of how to decide between the private and the public good in the allocation of monetary resources, where the priorities of each may differ in terms of individual freedom and the need for the State to protect and preserve the civil order. In an ideal world we might not need protection, but in our actual world, there are, besides some bad people, many who would have us do something different from what we want to do. Where that power is exercised through the coercive machinery of the State, we have no choice but to do what we are told. But money does give us the power to say No, and gives us some ability to seek alternatives. However, it does not confer complete protection.

We may be wage-slaves, or too poor to pay for the alternatives available, but money not only provides some freedom from the power of others, especially the authorities; it also, as we have seen, enhances our freedom to choose. It protects and promotes each person's individual identity as a free citizen to choose the lifestyle he wants. Of course, in a world in which there are other people we cannot always get our own way. Many questions have to be decided by authority, or by a vote, or by some other public procedure, which may leave the individual feeling impotent and of no account. It is important, therefore, that there should be some questions on which he cannot be outvoted by others. The institutions of personal liberty and private property are essential bolsters of the individual's status as a decision maker. The former gives him at least a veto over the actions he is to undertake, and the movements of his own body. Money confers a positive choice. With money in my pocket, I can choose whether to buy flowers for my girlfriend, beer for myself, or a ride on the merry-go-round for us both. Often, of course, I may not have money in my pocket, but sometimes I do; and such occasions not only enhance my sense of my own individuality, but also develop it, and constitute an education in responsible decision making.

Money is a private possession, but it also gives me the opportunity to cooperate with others. I am naturally choosy about the people with whom I cooperate, and need to be sure that they do respect or empathize with my values. I need to know that a potential partner or colleague is like-minded with myself, if I am to cooperate with him over many years, but I do not know, nor do I need to know, much about my grocer or tailor, except that he provides me with wholesome groceries and well-fitting clothes. Spinoza was a Jew living in a gentile city and much disapproved of by his Jewish co-religionists. But he was able to make a living by grinding lenses, and since the lenses he ground were good, and enabled spectacle-wearers to see better, they were glad to do business with him without enquiring into his religious beliefs; and he similarly was able to buy the things he needed with the money he earned from tradesmen who were equally unconcerned with his metaphysics.

Money thus promotes freedom. By being impersonal it also confers a cloak of privacy about one's personal values and commitments. I can be more myself, if I have the economic sufficiency which money can provide. Many people find themselves at odds with the society in which they live. J.S. Mill, for instance, felt the pressure of public opinion to be a tyranny. Even if I happily endorse the mores of the society in which I live, I may want to have the space (lebensraum) in which to exercise my freedom of choice. Money gives me space for action, which is unavailable to the person stuck in the poverty rut. Economic justice thus has to be intimately concerned with the question of how we achieve the correct balance between our freedom of choice in how we spend our money and the needs of other people, including the State, whose preferences may conflict with or limit our freedom of choice.

Money does have its defects and raises moral issues as to how "private" it should be. We do wrong to worship it, but we are right to value it. We value it, because being universal encapsulated individual choice it confers freedom on the part of its possessor to spend it as he sees fit, either immediately or at some later time, and for this reason it is inherently desirable, and often desired simply for its own sake. But it only encapsulates choice because it is desired by other people. And why should it be desired? Because it is the medium of exchange with which we can buy things. Why are we able to do this? Because other people value money too, and are willing to exchange goods or render services in return for it.

Thus money is useful for society as a whole because it facilitates cooperation. Money may be, as will be argued, a bad master: but it can be a good servant, and we should be lost without it. As encapsulated choice it is an essential instrument for exercising the freedom of individual choice and for that deserves three cheers before we enter the realm of who decides what that choice should be. But freedom to use money as we want immediately raises the question of the rights and wrongs of exercising that freedom of choice, which, besides the law, concern the ethics for business in exercising its freedom of choice, and the principles of responsible business behaviour. But this defence of money as an instrument for freedom of choice is conditioned by the justice of the way in which that freedom of choice is exercised. It is not a licence for the unlimited pursuit of personal gain which many critics of capitalism believe to be the case, but also the means for "giving back" to, as well as "taking out from," the society of which we are a part. Today league tables of how much people earn are one-sided if they talk only about the "taking out" (total compensation), and do not indicate the "giving back" in terms of income tax paid, social contributions and donations to charities, educational and research institutions, international health and poverty programmes. We need to express such league tables not only in terms of gross income, but also in terms of net income after these "giving back" contributions to the State and social institutions, which quantifies how economic freedom has been exercised in terms both of the inflow and the outflow of money at the individual as well as the corporate level.

4.5   Two Cheers for Money as an Instrument for Selfishness or Altruism

Money has many merits as a facilitator of free choice, but many demerits when selfishness enters in as the motivator of the way it is obtained and used. Nevertheless, we should be lost without it. Moralists who denounce it as the root of all evil are partly right, but they are too undiscriminating in their anathemas. Money has its demerits, true: but often they are merely the other side of merits we value, and the fault lies not in money, but instead in our use of it. Because it enables me to do business with you, even if I do not have your priorities it is assumed that if I do business with you, I need not be concerned with your personal opinion and beliefs. In other words, business does not have to be "non-tuistic", that is, it does not take account of the other's individual point of view in a money transaction, which gives rise to a common belief that in business one need have no regard for anything other than one's own interests, reinforcing the view that when we are dealing with money we tend to become selfish, if not mean, in the way we act.

Yet selfishness is not the fault of money in itself, but of our attitudes towards the way we accumulate and use it. (See P.H. Wicksteed, *The Common Sense of Political Economy* and F.A. Hayek, *The Constitution of Liberty*.) Money is divisible into suitably differing amounts and makes it feasible to equalize or reconcile the different pay-offs in a business transaction, something that is seen nowhere more clearly than in the often-conflicting pay-offs that occur in wage negotiations. Because money is divisible it raises the awkward question "How much?" The awkwardness of this situation arises from the fact that the gain to one party is a loss, or reduction, for the other. Although cooperation does indeed yield a "cooperators' surplus", division of the cooperators' surplus is a zero-sum game: the more one party gets, the less is left for the other party. In itself a monetary transaction thus involves an element of confrontation. Although by cooperating both parties can benefit, when it comes to apportioning the cooperators' surplus, they are no longer just cooperating with each other, but are now competing against one another, which means that money can make us mean, if we are trying to do the other party down, and take advantage of what might be a weaker negotiating position. But dealing with confrontation is a necessary part of business negotiations, and requires skills, rules and regulations for gaining the cooperation of all parties in a business transaction, which can lead to arbitration in highly charged and conflictual negotiating situations. Consequently, money becomes the token for determining what is the fair price or wage in establishing an acceptable pay-off for the parties involved in a monetary transaction. This is one of the main reasons for fixing a scale of fees for professional services, but it is also the principle behind the scale of prices shown in a taxi or hotel room. In these cases the prospective purchaser has a choice, whether to buy or not, but no contest as to how much. But in that case how do we know what is a fair wage and a fair price, which would enable people to do business together without either exploiting the other?

The difficulty is to find a way to determine the just wage or the just price. Typically, there are no natural guidelines, and we are forced back onto the notion of the so-called "going rate" or the "going price", to yield a solution with which each can be happy; or, in more difficult cases, we get a professional valuer to estimate a value "as between a willing seller and a willing buyer". We let other people bargain, and let the market find the level at which the marginal producer and marginal consumer are willing to do business, where competition plays an important role in fixing the going rate or going price. Externally determined wage rates and prices not only avoid hassle, but also confer a level of security. I can make plans for the future if I can predict—within limits—what the cost of particular goods and services is going to be. Economists often deplore the "stickiness" (the unpredictability or unreliability) of wages and prices, and postulate the necessity of creating an ideal market, where wages and prices adjust instantly to changes in supply and demand. But that is not realistic, because wages and prices are elastic or inelastic depending on the nature of the supply and demand at the time. The retail price index is not determined by an ideal market, but by an infinite number of variables which establish a going rate mediated through transactions, but ultimately based on actual bargains made in actual markets.

Money is good in so far as it gives us choices, but this is simultaneously a drawback in that it makes us vulnerable to the choices of others. Money energizes agents who are not necessarily going to be altruistic in their demand or decisions. The underlying difficulty is how money influences our motives in obtaining and using it. I may do a highly professional job—and this may be my prime motive for doing it—but it cannot be removed from the financial incentive for doing so which necessitates a balance between the two motivations. Motives do not always reinforce one another; they can also crowd the other one out. When we seek to carry into effect values we espouse, in helping the aged or the sick, for example, we act wholeheartedly, and we do the best we can. When we become involved in the creation of domestic facilities for such people we have to resolve the economic costs of what then becomes a business with the investment risks involved, which the crisis of homes for the aged brought home with the threat of putting those who needed that care out into the street.

This emphasizes the trust implicit in the use of money, and the need to recognise the trust that the other party may be placing in us in making a monetary transaction between the two of us. Trust is thus an inescapable facet of money, the loss of which has implications for the responsibilities involved in monetary transactions, and the way we use money in providing a product or service to the "other". It is one of the merits of money that it enables us to do business with all sorts of people without our having to have many values in common. where the parties are at arm's length from each other having no other than the value and interests the parties have in reaching an acceptable deal or agreement. Modern money is socially useful in allowing individuals to choose between "what I want", and the need to adapt what I want to the wants of the other in agreeing a business transaction. This confirms the generalized heteronomy of choice, where outcomes can be determined by a force outside the individual's determination of what those outcomes should be. This might appear to contradict Kant's moral imperative, but this is not the case if we accept the moral imperative of "alteritas" in recognizing and respecting the needs and interests of the "other" in business transactions. Such an imperative will condition our attitude towards money as a force for facilitation and not exploitation of the "other".

Money may be good, BUT we may want to give it two cheers rather than three because:

1. Being able to divide the cooperators' surplus can make us mean in the way we divide it.
2. Money can contaminate our motives and let financial motives prevail.
3. Money transactions can conflict and diminish the element of trust.
4. Money is incompatible with complete autonomy; we may have to compromise.

However, money still merits two cheers. Although it can make us mean, it makes possible many cooperative activities where the benefits need to be finely evened out, and which would not take place were money unavailable, although it can crowd out better motives. The anonymity of modern life may be disheartening, but it can be overcome by having family, friends and neighbours with whom we can share values.

Money enables us to do business with those with whom we do not have many values in common, but does not preclude our joining in common enterprises with others with whom we have much in common. Although for some the free life on the open road is the one that fulfils their personal aspirations, for many others fulfilment is found in the "give-and-take" of social relationships, where a willingness to serve others is a sign not of servility but of respect for the needs and interests of the other. Money is not ideal, but then neither is the world in which we live: It is very useful in many situations, but it may have bad side effects of encouraging selfishness and a lack of consideration for the other when we have to use it. But with the suitable conventions of business practice of honesty and fairness these can be minimized. Money is a good instrument for our freedom to choose what we want, and so long as we treat it as such, we also have to realize it is subject to the contrasting motivations of selfishness and altruism.

4.6 One Cheer for Money as a Motivator of Greed and Self-Aggrandizement

Money is a bad master. Too often and too easily it achieves mastery, sometimes through psychological flaws, sometimes through force of habit, often through muddled thinking. Some inner compulsion that psychologists sometimes attribute to inherent nature or upbringing. Even if we take psychologists' findings with a pinch of salt, it is evident that people often fail to think rationally when money is an issue. Making money can become a status symbol, a sign of success. The more money I make, the better I have done. It seems to follow from this that other things being equal, one could do with more of it, and its maximization becomes a moral imperative for "Economic Man," where his concentration on money making may make him forget the ceteris paribus (other things being equal) clause, and the danger that personal relationships can suffer as the result of the money-making ethic. Again, in a sceptical age we feel diffident in robustly defending any particular value, since, values are a matter of personal choice, and so, it seems, just a matter of personal choice. But money is an assured public value, with a token value, whatever private values may be held. (See Keynes, *A Treatise on Money*, vol. II, 1930, p. 290n (reprinted in *Collected Works*, vol. VI, 1971, p. 258n), referring to Freud's *Collected Papers*, Clinical Paper No. IV, and to papers by Ferenezi and Ernest Jones. See also a letter to F.A. Hayek, 28 June 1944 (*Collected Works*, vol. xxvii, pp. 385–8); quoted R. Skidelsky, Keynes, vol. 3, p. 285.)

The idea that only impersonal money has objective value undermines our sense of self, if it engenders a feeling of being only a money-transferring unit, whose value is purely pecuniary. We are wrong to allow money to usurp the realm of private values, and to exclude all the other values that confer meaning and significance in our lives. The risk is that "Economic Man," who always buys in the cheapest, and sells in the dearest, market, and always seeks to maximize his wealth, becomes an empty shell, having no other values than money, which is itself intrinsically valueless, unless there are other worthwhile ends to which it can be a useful means. There are other ends. Our lives are in constant flux, and money is valuable because it helps adjust our lives to constantly changing needs and circumstances.

Economists distort their understanding in concentrating solely on money supply and demand, and forgetting the other values which make money valuable too. It is only in order to facilitate cooperation whereby we can achieve the manifold and shifting purposes of ordinary life that money is useful. But we find it hard to believe. In a society where non-monetary values are often held in lower esteem, money may be the only thing generally esteemed, but being the highest common factor of everyone's set of values does not imply its having to be the greatest value for any one. Indeed, to repeat the argument it cannot be. For it only has value for any of us by reason of its being a means whereby we can induce other people to cooperate with us in achieving the ends we want to achieve. If we had no non-monetary wants, we should have no use for money either.

Economists also risk distorting their understanding in concentrating on money, and ignoring the social context in which transactions take place. Their picture of "Economic Man" is not recognisable in the real world. We do not always buy in the cheapest market. Sometimes, indeed, cheapness is no recommendation, but the reverse. Classical economists not only suppose away the facts of ordinary behaviour, but also idealize away also the limitations of ordinary life, assuming perfect information and instantaneous effects. They imagine an unreal world of stable equilibrium, whereas the real world is one of continual instability, and equilibrium is never reached, but always disrupted by changing exogenous or endogenous factors. It is true that, other things being equal, there is a general tendency to buy at lower prices and sell at higher ones, but it does not follow that the market ever reaches perfect equilibrium. There is a tendency, but no reason to conclude that it will work itself out before other factors supervene.

The economists' idealizations are much less unrealistic when we move from microeconomics to macroeconomics. Whereas ordinary people, workers and housewives have many other things to think about, financiers, stockbrokers and bank managers are primarily concerned with money, and think about it all the time. If I am dealing with hundreds or thousands of shares, it is well worth my while to spend time comparing prices, and seeing where the best bargain can be got. The market may not clear completely, and equilibrium is always being disturbed by adventitious factors, but the fact that large sums are in issue overcomes the resistance to market pressures which is characteristic of ordinary life. This makes for greater economic efficiency, but at the price of macroeconomic instability. To repeat Keynes's analogy, monetary values depend on second-hand opinions about third-hand opinions. I value money because you and others value it, who do so because others do also. But if the reality of money's value is simply its being thought to be so, there is an element of spin in financial affairs, which can prove dangerous. Financiers learn to be lemming-like as they concentrate on what others are going to think that others are going to think. Built-in positive feedback means that mistaken estimates are magnified and can easily become bubbles that go on expanding until they burst. Money may be good, BUT it deserves only one cheer or perhaps none at all if:

1. People get obsessed by money making.
2. Money comes to be thought of as the only thing that has real value.
3. It beguiles economists into ignoring the real facts of life, and the unpredictability of consumer preferences.
4. It encourages lemming-like behaviour, particularly in bear and bull markets.

But we do not abandon money. Panic may encourage the herd to career down steep slopes to their destruction, but we mostly manage to remain on the high ground, doing the shopping with the wages we earn, paying off the mortgage and revising our spending priorities in times of economic downturn. It is microeconomics, with its many inputs (both exogenous and endogenous) from society at large that makes economics real. The macroeconomic world of high finance, interest rates, taxation, investment incentives, banking, and government bonds can provide useful facilities, but these are not self-sustaining unless supported by the wage earners who provide the human resources for economic growth. The Stock Exchange can provide funding for new ventures, making them possible on a larger scale than would otherwise be the case, but the ordinary buying and selling of shares is a zero-sum game where some investors gain, but only at the expense of others.

The only unqualified gains occur when firms do well in their own business, a factor which may be extraneous to stock market values. The macroeconomic world, with its instruments for planning, incentivizing and controlling the exogenous factors of economic growth, is necessary and important, but it is the microeconomic world that provides the drive and resources to make the economy work. The charge that economists are beguiled by their theories into producing fallible forecasts based on unreliable figures has some degree of substance: but other disciplines also give rise to misleading models. Provided we treat long-distance economic forecasts with the same degree of scepticism as we do long-distance weather forecasts, we shall not be greatly misled. More serious is the tendency to impute to economic generalizations a necessity that is properly due only to mathematical truths. People talk about the "iron laws of economics", especially when seeking to justify unpopular taxation or government expenditure decisions. But although the conclusions economists draw in their reasoning are sometimes valid deductive consequences of their assumptions, their assumptions are often mistaken, and the conclusions drawn from them are often erroneous too.

To repeat it yet again, economists need to set their studies in their social context, and should not seek to exclude all non-economic considerations from their thought. In our present age we are often too diffident in defending our core values (social, cultural and political), but even if we are hesitant in taking a stand on any one of them, we still should insist that money is not the only objective value, for the reason we have given, namely that economic activity can take place and money have value only when we recognise a background of our having other values that lead us to cooperate with other people in order to achieve those values. It is noteworthy that the great expansion of economic activity took place against a background of strongly held Protestant values of thrift and individual responsibility, and that Adam Smith, who wrote *The Wealth of Nations*, preceded it with *The Theory of Moral Sentiments*.

Money may be that which we each could do with more of, but it is necessarily not the only thing we value, and nor is it something which we should want to have most of all. Money making can become an obsession. But human beings can also be obsessed by sex, by food, by drink, by power, or even by knowledge and the search for understanding. There are also many motivations which are behind the phenomena of economics, and are an area for the study of "behavioural economics" in trying to understand why people behave as they do, and why sometimes they are greedy and sometimes not.

Greed and the Creation of Value

"Greed, for lack of a better word, is good. Greed is right. Greed works. Greed clarifies, cuts through, and captures, the essence of the evolutionary spirit. Greed, in all of its forms; greed for life, for money, for love, knowledge, has marked the upward surge of mankind and greed, you mark my words, will not only save Teldar Paper, but that other malfunctioning corporation called the U.S.A." Gordon Gekko in the film Wall Street, 1987, with Michael Douglas.

The interesting thing is that we could replace "greed" by "creation of value" without contradicting ourselves. Greed if it means the motivation to create value for oneself, one's family, one's business, one's society can be said to be good but not, as we have said, if it means the self-aggrandizement of the solipsist, who believes he alone is the measure of all that counts. Economic man as a money maker has to temper greed with generosity, or magnanimity as Aristotle would have said, reflected in the quality of sympathy, or empathy, with which Adam Smith opens his Theory of Moral Sentiments.

4.7 "Giving Back"

Money is much misunderstood, because, as we have argued earlier, it is a sticky and slippery commodity, but its underlying moral imperative of freedom makes it an instrument for the way in which that freedom will be exercised within the context of the other two moral imperatives of economic freedom, namely, consideration of the other ("alteritas"), and economic justice. In this way, the basic characteristic of money as "encapsulated choice" makes it a fundamental, and hopefully rational, component of economic philosophy, to which we shall return in Chap. 13.

And in looking at money, we should not forget the opportunity for "giving back" which money has in terms of philanthropy and the financing of charitable activities, which have important implications for the "giving back" principle is economies. In addition to our cost of living and expenditure indexes, we need an index of philanthropic and voluntary giving which quantifies the expenditure and investment in these activities, set against a tax index of how much tax we are foregoing in directing resources towards philanthropy. We shall return to the "giving back" principle in Chap. 13, in which we discuss some new concepts for the philosophy of economics in terms of philanthropy, a principle which widens the definition of "Economic Man" as not only a profit maximizer but also as a creator of wealth and contributor to society in terms of fiscal and philanthropic "giving back".

We need a theory of philanthropy in economics which can assist and motivate "Economic Man" in exercising his encapsulated freedom of choice. There are plenty of examples of "giving back" in economics. A significant example is the founding, by Sir Paul Judge, of the Judge Business School at the University of Cambridge. Following his own education at the University of Cambridge and at the Wharton Business School in Philadelphia he spent a dozen years working at Cadbury Schweppes plc. In 1985, he initiated and led a buyout of all of the food interests of Cadbury Schweppes in the UK, France and Ireland. The management team bought them for £97 million and sold them just a few years later to Hillsdown Holdings for £310 million. Paul Judge used part of his gain to donate £8 million to the University of Cambridge to allow the development of the Judge Business School as he believed that the UK had to have strong business schools in its most prestigious universities. The JBS has flourished and is now rated as having the best one-year MBA in the UK and of producing research which has the greatest impact—a good example of "pure" research combining with "applied" research in economics.

Appendix: Types of Money

Type of money	M0	MB	M1	M2	M3	MZM
Notes and coins (currency) in circulation (outside Federal Reserve Banks, and the vaults of depository institutions)	V	V	V	V	V	V
Notes and coins (currency) in bank vaults	V					
Federal Reserve Bank credit (minimum reserves and excess reserves)	V					
Traveler's checks of non-bank issuers			V	V	V	V
Demand deposits			V	V	V	V
Other checkable deposits (OCDs), which consist primarily of negotiable order of withdrawal (NOW) accounts at depository institutions and credit union share draft accounts			V	V	V	V
Savings deposits				V	V	V
Time deposits less than $100,000 and money-market deposit accounts for individuals				V	V	
Large time deposits, institutional money market funds, short-term repurchase and other larger liquid assets					V	
All money market funds						V

- M0: In some countries, such as the United Kingdom, M0 includes bank reserves, so M0 is referred to as the monetary base, or narrow money. MB: is referred to as the monetary base or total currency. This is the base from which other forms of money (like checking deposits, listed below) are created and is traditionally the most liquid measure of the money supply.
- M1: Bank reserves are not included in M1.
- M2: Represents money and "close substitutes" for money. M2 is a broader classification of money than M1. Economists use M2 when looking to quantify the amount of money in circulation and trying to explain different economic monetary conditions. M2 is a key economic indicator used to forecast inflation.

- M3: M2 plus large and long-term deposits. Since 2006, M3 is no longer tracked by the US central bank. However, there are still estimates produced by various private institutions.
- MZM: Money with zero maturity. It measures the supply of financial assets redeemable at par on demand.
Source: Wikipedia.

References

Coggan P. The money machine: how the city works. London: Penguin; 2015.

Hayek FA. Individualism and economic order. Chicago, IL: University of Chicago Press; 1948.

Hayek FA. The constitution of liberty. Abingdon, Oxon: Routledge; 1960 (2006).

Keynes JM. A treatise on money. Eastford, CT: Martino; 1930 (2011).

Poggi G. Money and the modern mind. Berkeley, CA: University of California Press; 1993.

Rothbard MN. Man, economy, and state. 2nd ed. Auburn, AL: Ludwig von Mises Institute; 2001.

Simmel G. The philosophy of money. Abingdon, Oxon: Routledge; 2004.

Von Mises L. The theory of money and credit. New Haven, CT: Yale University Press; 1953.

Wicksteed PH. The common sense of political economy. Abingdon, Oxon: Routledge; 2003.

Zelizer VA. The social meaning of money. Princeton, NJ: Princeton University Press; 1997.

5

The Moneyed Society

When I was young, I thought money was the most important thing
in life; now that I am old, I know that it is.

Oscar Wilde

Abstract This chapter looks at some of the characteristics of the moneyed society, in terms of freedom of choice, justice and economic value in satisfying the needs and wants of consumer preferences, within the social setting of a moneyed society. It looks at the management of money as a token and store of value expressed in the demand for liquidity, and the recent use of "Quantitative Easing." The importance of trust and feedback, or Reflexivity, in responding to economic changes is discussed, as well as the use of predictive modelling techniques for doing this. Finally, it looks at the financial performance measures of a moneyed society, like GDP, but also quality of life measures, like the Human Development Index (HDI) and the Gross National Happiness Index (GNH).

© The Editor(s) (if applicable) and The Author(s) 2016   **81**
M.R. Griffiths, J.R. Lucas, *Value Economics*,
DOI 10.1057/978-1-137-54187-1_5

5.1   Chapter Overview

Money is a predominant force for the way we live and work together in society, and economics is concerned with the ways it is created and used. A moneyed society manages the freedom of consumer choice in light of the needs and wants of its members, who use money as both a token of value and a store of value. Thus the management of the markets, which exist for satisfying consumer preferences, is a prime responsibility of a moneyed society, as is the creation of economic value, the protection of that value in terms of price stability, and the value of its currency in relation to the currencies of other countries. Capitalism needs to get the balance right between freedom and justice, since a capitalist system may give less importance to justice than to economic freedom. In this sense, the creation of value is a prerequisite for the distribution of wealth in society and for economic justice in the distribution of that wealth among its citizens.

In considering the supply and control of money, we discuss the debate between the aggregate demand theory of Keynesians and the monetarist theory of Friedmanites, and the apparent conflict between those who believe that "money does not matter" compared with the need for investment in economic growth, and those who say that "money matters" as the basic principle for controlling inflation, a debate which continues concerning the need for austerity, or not, following the last financial crisis. We look at the trends in economic experiences since Bretton Woods to see who might have been right or wrong. With the move of monetarism towards a new emphasis on the value of consumer preferences, we ask whether in the work of economists, like Paul Krugman, and those he calls the "MIT Gang", we may be moving towards a new economic synthesis between the Keynesian and Friedmanite schools of economic thought. In looking at liquidity and its demand we consider the questions a moneyed society has to face in deciding "how much" liquidity to release into the market and to where it should be directed in getting the balance right between the issue of credit and the ability to repay. We discuss Keynes's three consumer motives for credit—for transactions, for precaution and for speculation—and consider what are the priorities for the supply and demand for money, covering levels of sovereign debt split between industrial investment, consumer expenditure, and social services, and the need for free trade agreements in global markets, and the elusive search for fiscal harmonization in those markets. We also look at the introduction of "Quantitative Easing" and its effect on inflation and growth in countering the risks of stagflation after the last financial crisis. Its possible effect on the returns for consumer savings and pensions makes us ask the question whether it may be a system of robbing Peter to pay Paul?

The moneyed society has to be seen in its social setting composed of families and firms, which consists of a network of interrelated individuals controlled by the law and an increasing number of norms for controlling possible abuses to modern capitalism, such as insider trading and the rigging of interest rates. Trust and feedback (reflexivity) are essential for the functioning of a moneyed society where feedback enables companies to verify, like any organism, their state of health through processes for employee and customer satisfaction feedback.

An important characteristic of the moneyed society is the relation between the private and public sectors. We look at the provision and management of private and public goods, and the risk of "free riding" in the use of public goods. Also discussed are possible ways of redefining the role of the State, not just in "de-risking" the private sector in the form of "bailouts" following market failures, but also as a risk taker in its own right, as suggested by Mariana Mazzucato in her book *The Entrepreneurial State*, which seeks, as she puts it, to debunk Public v Private Sector Myths. We posit, as a basis for further discussion, the possibility of State projects being financed by the private sector, and the issue of project or State bonds underwritten by the private sector or reinsured.

Predictive modelling is an essential planning and control mechanism for the moneyed society, and requires sophisticated skills in setting assumptions and assessing risks. We make a plea to involve businessmen more in the setting of economic assumptions which will utilize the individual microeconomic experiences of business in validating econometric planning assumptions. In response to dissatisfactions, also on the part of some economists with the current state of the art for economic modelling, we suggest the creation of a high-level study group to study the question, possibly sponsored and chaired by the Bank of England, including economists, regulators, financial analysts, businessmen and the business advisory professions.

The chapter concludes with a discussion of the performance measures for a moneyed society like GDP, and the newer quality of life measures, the Human Development Index (HDI) and gross national happiness (GNH).

5.2   Freedom of Choice

As we have said, money is essential for facilitating economic transactions between members of society, and allowing them to exercise their freedom to choose the way in which their money is to be used. As standardized, generally recognized, encapsulated choice, it is the "raw material" for the management of a moneyed society. It is a token which derives its value from the encapsulated choices of consumer preferences, which cannot be determined by some preconceived social agenda which confuses needs with wants, as the communist state regimes found to their cost, when needs failed to take account of what people wanted. People were told their country needed ballbearings rather than consumer products. There is an example of this which illustrates this point clearly: the New Zealand Auckland agent of a well-known firm of men's toiletries was said, when business was bad, to pray that a Russian ship would put into port. He knew that if it did so, the day afterwards he would be sold out of after-shave lotion, which was unobtainable in Russia, where the regime told people they had no need of aftershave lotion, much as they might have wanted it, in an economy where ballbearings where considered to be more important than western consumer products.

Apart from the function of money as a medium of exchange, a unit of account, a standard of deferred payment and a store of value, its function as a provider of choice remains fundamental in ethical terms, because the concept of choice raises questions of the rights and wrongs of those choices, and also how the supply of money is to be managed and controlled in satisfying those choices. If money is a store of value, how do we determine its exchange value in acquiring other stores of value, such as stocks and shares, property, commodities, works of art, gold and reserve currencies? We need a marketplace where these exchanges can take place in order to satisfy consumer preferences. Thus, the management of markets becomes one of the first priorities of a moneyed society in creating and allocating resources between the various stores of value consumer preferences are looking for.

In thinking about the ethics of money and consumer preferences, we need to remember that we are liable to strong but contradictory attitudes towards money stemming from our own nature as autonomous agents in seeking the cooperation of others, but not always being willing to cooperate with them on their own terms. Money comes to dominate our thinking, both individually, as earners and spenders, and corporately, when businesses have to decide on how to price the products or services they offer. We naturally think about money from our own point of view. But in thinking of it in these partial terms, we can lose contact with the context in which money operates, that complex nexus of needs and wants, which give money its value in terms of customer preferences. The moneyed society at its heart is an instrument for the realization of diverse consumer preferences, which motivate the way in which our freedom of choice is exercised. This freedom of choice is a fundamental principle of liberal economic capitalism, but it needs a theory of moral principles, or sentiments, to use Adam Smith's phrase, which can provide the guidelines for economic activity in reconciling the dictates of self-interest and the social needs of society. We cannot say that "society does not exist", as Margaret Thatcher was purported to have said, since self-interests have to adapt themselves to the social context in which they have to operate. The moneyed society is faced daily with the task of managing this potential conflict of interests between the individual and the State, which arises from the fact that individual citizens may have choices which conflict with those of the State, and means that a moneyed society has to get the balance right between the needs and wants of the private and the public sectors of the economy.

5.3   Freedom, Justice and Economic Value

The freedom of choice associated with liberal political systems that afford each individual a large degree of personal freedom can result in freedom rather than justice becoming the dominant ideal. The free market capitalist often makes minimal assumptions about morality, believing that respect for the sanctity of contracts and the norms of law will take care of justice in economic affairs. The precision of this classical analysis depends on achieving economic equilibrium which results from perfect competition (markets unhampered by state intervention or monopolistic price-fixing practices) in conditions of perfect information, where the customer has the necessary information for making an informed decision to buy or not.

The problem is that economic equilibrium and perfect information are conditions which are changing constantly owing to the volatile nature of consumer preferences, with which the moneyed society has to deal in determining the prices for the things consumers want. Prices, like money, are slippery and sticky, and require the moneyed society to have a chameleon-like quality (maximum flexibility) in the way it assists the functioning of a free market. The challenge is how to balance freedom and economic justice in a free market environment. In economies which attempted to impose prices and regulate the exchange of goods between customer and supplier, the result was a gross distortion and falsification of the value of money. At the height of the communist regime in the former Soviet Union, the value of a pair of shoes was one month's wages, and in Cuba the official exchange rate at one time was one Cuban peso for one US dollar, at a time when the unofficial (or market value) of the peso was 20 to 1. A moneyed society has to exist in a variable currency exchange world, where the value of money is related to the comparative levels of market competitiveness, and national debt. The danger of playing with the value of money in political terms was ironically illustrated in Harold Wilson's remark after the devaluation of sterling in 1964: "The pound in your pocket has the same value (purchasing power) as it did before", when it was patently clear that the value of sterling was then less when compared with the US dollar the day before it was devalued. We need to be clear about how money can lose its value through devaluation of the currency, or through inflation, and how its value can be protected.

This raises the question of how much money is to be made available and controlled, taking us into a world of differing economic theories, between supporters of Keynesian "aggregate demand" theory on the one side and Friedmanite "monetarism" on the other. Monetarists propose that the amount of money available in an economy is the determining factor for eliminating the negative effects of recession, excessive inflation, and stag-flation (minimal inflation and no growth), all of which affect the value of money. This contrasts with the aggregate demand theory of the Keynesians which places a greater emphasis on the creation of demand rather than restricting it through limitation of the supply of money. The moneyed society is faced by the problem of getting the balance right between these two economic theories regarding the demand for and supply of money. The balancing of the demand for money with its supply is a dynamic process, and indeterminate in its outcomes, but money remains the key token for deciding whether we are creating or destroying the value of our currency.

We shall return to the question of value creation in Chap. 8 and the need to see the role of business as a creator and protector of economic value, with money as one, but not the only, measure of value. In intro-ducing the concept of economic value, the moneyed society has to have a coherent quantity theory of money, which aims for price stability and non-inflationary growth. But recently we now have a theory which sees some inflation as conducive to economic growth, if we are to avoid the danger of stagflation. We are often irrational in our attitude towards inflation, with property owners happy with increases in the value of their properties that are way above the national inflation targets being set by the financial authorities. Monetary values, which also depend on the "roll-on" effect of inflation, need to be related to the economic value of the underlying assets, where market values may differ from economic value. The question of economic value, and how it can be measured is discussed in Chap. 8, as the basic metric for measuring the reality of financial expectations which may not reflect the true economic value of the assets on which those expectations are based.

5.4   Money Supply and Control

The spectre of inflation and its control focuses the attention of econom-ics on controlling the amount of money in circulation, and the issue of how to target and manage the growth of the money supply. "Inflation is always and everywhere a monetary phenomenon" became the basic tenet of monetarist theory, as argued by Milton Friedman, who proposed that money supply targets should be set by the central bank to keep or decline the supply and demand in line with equilibrium as measured by growth in productivity. Productivity becomes a key measure in determining whether goods can be produced and sold at stable prices, which are the prerequisite for reducing the danger of inflation or deflation arising from the over- or understimulation of demand. Monetarists stress that the monetary authorities should concentrate on maintaining price stability through a rigorous control of the money supply, and let the market decide on its use and distribution. Keynes, on the other hand, argued for a demand-driven model for money, which would create, rather than deflate, value in conditions of market downturn or recession. Monetarists believe that it is excessive money supply generated by the central bank which causes inflation, while on the reverse side the central bank will create deflationary conditions if it does not support money supply when there is a shortage of liquidity. The monetarist theory that "money matters" contrasts with the view, attributed to Keynes, that "money does not matter" in stressing the importance of getting the balance between supply and demand correct in the context of whether the business cycle at any one time or place is in a phase of expansion or contraction. Friedman restated the quantity theory of money, arguing that demand for money should depend on a number of economic variables such as inflation and productivity, and not on a "social" stimulation of demand in times of market recession or inefficiency. According to the monetarists, the capacity to create wealth and pay back debt arising from investment in industrial capacity or public services should be left to the market, not to state regulation of supply and demand.

In effect, the debate between the monetarists and the supply/demand theorists of the Keynesian school is one of emphasis rather than of fundamental doctrinal disagreement, since both schools of economic thought are in agreement when it comes to the prime importance of liquidity management in stimulating and controlling the economy. The rise of monetarism was also the result of trying to explain the contradictory problems of rising unemployment and inflation following the collapse of the Bretton Woods system in 1972 and the high inflationary increases of the oil price hikes in 1973. How was one to resolve the conflict between reflation to reduce unemployment and deflation to combat the problem of price inflation? Monetarists believe that the Great Depression of the 1930's was caused by a massive contraction of the money supply (between 1929 and 1933 the Fed presided over a decline in the quantity of money by one-third), rather than by the lack of investment as Keynes had argued, although there is, of course, a direct correlation between the supply of money and the ability to invest. Some monetarists proposed going back to the pre-Keynesian view that markets are inherently stable, propounding that active demand management of free market economies through increased government spending is not only unnecessary but also likely to be positively harmful.

When Margaret Thatcher won the UK General Election in 1979 in market conditions of high inflation she used monetarism as the instrument to bring down inflation which, by 1983, was reduced to under 5 per cent compared with the 10 per cent when she came to power. But the social cost of this policy resulted in a recession and the doubling of unemployment from 1.5 to over 3 million. Government spending was reduced in the belief that restraint in this area is the most important means for restraining excessive monetary growth and reducing inflation. This contrasted with a growth in US government spending which, in the first years of Reagan's presidency, increased by over 4 per cent per annum compared with increases of 2.5 per cent during the Carter years. In the ensuing years unemployment remained high in both countries while the central banks raised interest rates to restrain credit, which produced a reduction in inflation in the US from 14 per cent in 1980 to 3 per cent in 1983. The ensuing liberalization of credit and the reduction in interest rates then led to the inflationary economic booms of the 1980s. But was the reduction in inflation due to a control of the money supply, as the monetarists would claim, or to unemployment resulting in a reduction in demand, which the demand/supply economists would argue for?

At the end of the 1980s and the beginning of the 1990s western central banks contracted spending and the money supply ending the economic booms of the 1980s which ended with the crash of 1987. The 1980s and 1990s are a good example of the results of changes in monetary policy from the restriction to the expansion of the money supply, and emphasizes the fact that in economics we are not dealing with steady-state conditions, but rather with a dynamic process where new factors such as globalization and changes in consumer demand and preferences, and in the patterns of wealth, call for a continuous review of conventional economic axioms concerning theories of value in terms of utility, and the impact of government on consumer preferences. How is economics to identify and respond to changes in externalities which manifest themselves in the macro- and microeconomic business worlds, and propose solutions to resolving the economic inequalities in a global world market?

Wasn't it Keynes who said that politicians are usually the victims of some defunct economist, or, in other words, outdated economic theories regarding the management of inflation and deflation? Globalization, and the ensuing changes in the levels of sovereign debt, call for new systems for the management of international liquidity by the IMF and the central banks of the different world economies. Since the 1990s the classical form of monetarism and its belief in the supreme importance of the money supply has been questioned because some economic conditions, such as the decoupling in the US of the money supply from inflation in the 1990s, and the failure of monetary policy to stimulate the economy between 2001 and 2003, are not explicable in monetarist terms. Alan Greenspan argued that the situation in the 1990s was explained, as he put it, by a virtuous cycle of productivity and investment on the one hand and a degree of "irrational exuberance" in the investment sector on the other. Economists of the Austrian School, such as von Mises and Hayek, introduced another aspect of the argument between the Keynesians and the Friedmanites by arguing that monetary policy has to be based not solely on the "quantity of money" theory of classical monetarism, but also on the "value of money", which takes account of the subjective aspect of consumer preferences, and not values imposed by the manipulation of the money supply. The economic debate between these differing schools of thought continues today, where attempts to stimulate demand and investment have seen the introduction of new forms of liquidity management in the form of "Quantitative Easing" and a dramatic reduction in interest rates with the intention of stimulating demand without increasing inflation, and without creating deflationary "austerity" conditions of high unemployment, and the consequent reduction in demand. Are we now witnessing the emergence of a new kind of hybrid Keynesian, Friedmanite, Austrian School economist where apparently conflicting theories are moving towards a new paradigm for economic theory which integrates the thought of all three?

For the businessman economics becomes more complicated, if not more confusing, as these schools of thought compete for supremacy. An economist such as Paul Krugman has been contrasting the Chicago School's advocacy of a free market laissez-faire ideology with the approach of what he calls the "MIT Gang", which consists of people like Ben Bernanke, Mario Draghi, Olivier Blanchard and Maurice Obstfeld, whom he describes as advocates of a more open-minded pragmatic approach, which incorporates a more Keynesian view of the imperfections of markets, and the role monetary policy can play in boosting a depressed economy without the austerity and rigour of classical Friedmanite monetarism. The criticism is that it is a mistake to cut spending in a depressed economy and to reduce high levels of debt via austerity—a frontal attack on classical monetarism (*INYT*, 25 July 2015).

It is this kind of debate in which the economic masters of the 1970s and 1980s are being "redimensioned", if not debunked, which can leave businessmen bewildered, and marginalized. The microeconomic experience of the businessman is important, and needs to be incorporated in full into economic theory. For every panel of economic theorists we need a panel of businessmen who have to deal daily with the problems of operating in a moneyed society, where business experience, in managing the demand and supply of money in the reality of individual cash flows, can make an essential and practical contribution to economic theory. How often do economists talk to businessmen about their theories in the light of practical business experience? The moneyed society has to grapple with economic questions of this kind, but also within the context of the economic justice which a moneyed society is achieving or not in terms for example of inequality of incomes, to which we shall return to in Chap. 9. At this stage in looking at the supply of money and its control in a moneyed society, we need to introduce the concept of the economic value it is creating for its members, and the need to define the metrics for measuring that value discussed in Chap. 8.

5.5   The Demand for Liquidity

Liquidity is a key feature of the moneyed society. It represents deferred immediate choice. Although Ricardo was right in seeing consumption as the ultimate rationale for holding money, Keynes was more accurate in seeing it as a shield against uncertainty in protecting ourselves from a reduction in our purchasing power and our ability to meet commitments both to ourselves and to those for whom we are responsible. The rational response to uncertainty is to be ready to meet unforeseen negative circumstances, whatever they turn out to be, and to go liquid if I do not have confidence that all is going to be alright. In this sense confidence and liquidity are inversely related; the more confidence the less need for liquidity and vice versa. Debts and other obligations are a form of negative liquidity which determine how liquid I can be. But liquidity comes at a price since it may defer my choice to spend, which means foregoing economic activity.

Economists are concerned with the nature of economic activity and how to achieve and control economic growth. Important as growth may be in creating wealth to pay back the interest on public debt, it also has to be judged in relation to the level of private savings, where consumers are limiting their willingness to consume things by committing their savings, that is, their liquidity, to investment in public debt instruments. For this reason the management of liquidity cannot ignore consumer preferences in establishing the correct relationship between consumption and saving. One basic problem of liquidity management by the central banks remains how the liquidity released into the local banking systems is to be directed. Is it to be to government bonds, social infrastructures, or industrial investment, including research and new technology?

Targeting the requests for liquidity is a complex task, and at national levels requires a sophisticated analysis of the economic profile and needs of the country concerned, in which different sectors are looking for financial resources. Following the Aberfan disaster in 1966, and the radical restructuring of the Welsh mining and steel industries, the Welsh Development Authority under Peter Walker, the Secretary of State for Wales, supported by government-directed liquidity, was able to transform the Welsh economy through an aggressive inward investment strategy to encourage outside investors—both British and foreign—to establish manufacturing and distribution operations in Wales. This was an interesting example of combining government liquidity management with "let the market decide" when it came to the individual investment decisions of the companies who judged Wales to be a profitable investment opportunity.

In macroeconomic theory liquidity preference refers to the demand for liquid money. Keynes developed the concept to explain how interest rates should be determined by the supply and demand for money. He proposed that money as an asset depended on the interest forgone by not holding bonds. In this sense interest is not a reward for saving, but a reward for parting with liquidity. According to Keynes, demand for liquidity is determined by three motives: the transaction motive, the precautionary motive and the speculative motive. In the case of the first motive, people require liquidity to make basic transactions with the amount being determined by the level of income; the higher the income, the more liquidity available for increased spending. In the case of the precautionary motive, people require liquidity for unexpected problems which need unusual costs, with the amount of money demanded for this purpose increasing with income. Finally, for the speculative motive, people retain liquidity to speculate when bond prices or equity prices fall.

The liquidity preference relationship can be represented graphically as a schedule of money demanded at different interest rates. In the IS/LM model, the supply of money together with the liquidity preference curve in theory interact to determine the interest rate at which the quantity of money demanded equals the quantity of money supplied. This theory was rejected by Murray Rothbard, who argued that interest rates are determined by "time preference" rather than "liquidity preference". This is one example of how the debate between economists, in this case, liquidity management, is still at the stage of open discussion, if not dispute, which, following the recent financial crisis, has led to a call to rethink the liquidity axioms of economics, covering the management of global sovereign debt, income inequality, global trade agreements and the possibility of global fiscal harmonization. We now have the introduction of "Triple Bottom Line Accounting" which takes economics into the area not only of economic "value" accounting, but also of social and environmental "value" accounting, with the liquidity requirements for these three kinds of "value".

This call for a rethink of economic theories has led to the creation of the Institute for New Economic Thinking (INET), strongly supported and financed by George Soros, the motivation for which was well expressed by an economist, Andy Haldane, the Executive Director of Financial Stability at the Bank of England: "I think one of the great errors we as economists made was that we started believing the *assumptions* of economics, and saying things that made no intellectual sense. The hope was that, by basing models on mathematics and particular assumptions about 'optimizing' behaviour, they would become immune to changes in policy. But we forgot the key part, which is that the models are only true if the assumptions that underpin those models are also true. And we started to believe that what were *assumptions* were actually a description of reality, and therefore that the models were a description of reality, and therefore were dependable for policy analysis." What are the assumptions we need for new economic thinking regarding all the mechanisms of the moneyed society for creating economic value and protecting the value of money within the context of managing liquidity preferences?

Liquidity is a key component of money distribution, and is linked to how much money should be released for circulation without increasing inflation, and putting price stability at risk. "Quantitative Easing" has now arrived as a new way of providing liquidity with the objective of increasing the money supply without increasing inflation, but who are the recipients of this "new" money? Will banks hold the money to meet new solvency requirements, or for increasing credit, and, if so, will the credit be for property or industrial investment? And will there be negative effects for saving where negative interest rates reduce the capital of pension funds. Do we run the risk of stealing from Peter to pay Paul?

5.6   Quantitative Easing

"Quantitative Easing" is an unconventional monetary policy used by central banks to stimulate the national economy when conventional monetary policy has become ineffective. A central bank buys financial assets to inject a predetermined *quantity* of money into the economy. This is distinguished from the more usual policy of buying or selling government bonds to keep market interest rates at a specified target value. A central bank implements quantitative easing by purchasing financial assets from banks and other private sector businesses with new electronically created money. This action increases the excess reserves of the banks, and also raises the prices of the financial assets bought, which lowers their yield. Expansionary monetary policy typically involves the central bank buying short-term government bonds in order to lower short-term market interest rates (using a combination of standing lending facilities and open market operations). However, when short-term interest rates are either at, or close to, zero, normal monetary policy can no longer lower interest rates. "Quantitative Easing" may then be used by the monetary authorities to further stimulate the economy by purchasing assets of longer maturity than short-term government bonds, and thereby lowering longer-term interest rates further out on the yield curve. "Quantitative Easing" can be used to help ensure inflation does not fall below target. Risks include the policy being more effective than intended in acting against deflation—leading to higher inflation, or of not being effective enough—if banks do not lend out the additional reserves.

If the man on the Clapham Omnibus finds it hard to understand this bank technospeak in putting the case for quantitative easing, he is at least entitled to an evaluation of how successful quantitative easing has been in reducing the risks of recession and in providing credit for renewed economic growth. How have banks used the liquidity released through quantitative easing, apart from strengthening their reserves, in channelling finance to industrial companies in a recessionary environment which increases the credit risk of their lending? What are the assumptions for establishing the money risk involved in a bank's loan portfolio and its ability to call back loans when default is likely?

If quantitative easing is to become a new economic axiom it needs to be tested by a rigorous process of risk analysis in light of its past experience and define what is its time frame of reference when it is phased out by a period of "tapering".

5.7   The Social Setting of a Moneyed Society

In the moneyed society, with its continuous demand for money for exercising choices in making economic transactions and as a token of value, people are tempted to overlook the social setting within which monetary transactions take place, and to assume that because business is business, ethical considerations and social obligations are secondary to the right to freedom of choice. That is a mistake if it ignores the justice of how that freedom is exercised. Although it is true that ethical considerations in business, for example, fairness, are different from those in private relationships, such as loyalty, some values are implicit in a money transaction. The typical transaction is not, pace Hayek, a South Sea trader exchanging beads for copra, a one-off transaction, but rather a relationship between suppliers (vendors) and buyers (emptors), who may return, thus confirming that relationships are often not one-off transactions. The customer and the shopkeeper each have their own values and each have expectations of the other; the customer wants reliable goods, and expects the shopkeeper to supply him with such; the shopkeeper expects the customer to pay in good currency, and not to shoplift or to tender dud cheques. There is an element of mutual trust limited, indeed, but nonetheless an inherent component of a business transaction.

Thus, every economic transaction takes place against a social background of values, some of which may be shared, others not. Business transactions are primarily privative, that is, each party does not have to have the same values, but at the same time they are non-privative, because, there has to be some recognition, if not acceptance, of the other party's values. This is not an oxymoron or contradiction of terms because some degree of sharing is essential in cooperation, which means that neither party can be exclusively governed by unmodified individual self-interest. Self-interest may motivate me to cooperate, but, as we have said, active cooperation requires me to modify or adapt my self-interest in light of what the other party expects from me when we agree on the specific costs and prices involved in an economic transaction.

The cost/price mechanisms which determine the value of money in any given transaction remain a key study for economics. Predictive modelling techniques are important, but the assumptions on which they are based are even more important since assumptions are not static, and have to be re-examined continuously in the light of experience. Predictive models can never be cast in stone, but need to be flexible in adapting or changing the assumptions when the "initial conditions" on which economic models were based are no longer valid. Economic transactions are subject to changing customer preferences influenced by the social mores of the times in which people live. The fashion business is never static, as we move from the mini-skirt to baggy trousers, and from corduroys to jeans. The complex web of shared values, expectations and degrees of trust varies greatly, depending on the transaction involved, whether it be a new suit, a Ferrari or a contract to purchase a new house. And there are laws spelling out what each side is entitled to expect. The laws against insider trading and on how company takeovers should proceed are complicated in their attempt to articulate best practices in the world of high finance. In each case legislation not only crystallizes but also defines mutual expectations. Legislation would not make sense, however, if there were no antecedent understanding of what the parties to a transaction might reasonably expect of the other, and what ought to be avoided as being unfair to one or the other of them.

In this sense the law used to be unfair to divorced couples and homosexuals until it was changed in response to changes in the social and moral norms regarding such relationships, confirming the legal positivist concept of law as a social construction which reflects the social standards of the time. Some Legal Positivists dislike the idea that laws largely depend on shared social and moral norms, claiming that this undermines the autonomy of law, and that we should regard law simply as the enforceable commands of the sovereign power whether it be the monarch or parliament. But the problem remains of how the law is to keep pace with social changes, as changes in the "unfairness" of insider training practices and price-fixing practices have called for legislative changes. Similarly, the cases of business fraud which emerged in the Enron and World Com scandals produced the Sarbanes Oxley (SOX) legislation in the USA designed to improve the veracity of financial statements, and to regulate and control those responsible for auditing them in a modern example of the old Roman dictum "quis custodiet ipsos custodies" ("Who guards the guards themselves"). However, the law has often been slow to legislate to prevent unethical business behaviour, which in complicated financial situations makes the need for self regulation even more important as the recent spate of regulations by the financial control authorities has indicated.

Compliance has now emerged as a new business function to ensure that companies and financial institutions are conforming to an ever-increasing set of norms for economic behavior, the cost of which is not insignificant. It has been estimated that the cost of compliance for the Fortune top 500 works out on average at $5 million per company. Two facts emerge. First, although the arm's-length nature of monetary transactions makes business ethics and the generality of "fair dealing" different from the ethics of personal moral codes, such as "faithfulness" in private relationships, it is not the case that there are no shared values. In any negotiation an understanding of where the other side is coming from is essential in deciding if there can be any meeting point for negotiation, even if the final result may be "we beg to differ". Second, the widespread belief among economists, that it is up to the legislature to lay down the rules, and that, provided he keeps within the law, the businessman is free to make money in any way he pleases, is unsustainable. Just as the law breaks down if witnesses are not trustworthy, judges are not honest, and jurors do not try to give a true verdict, so commerce breaks down if each party is trying to get as much as he can get away with to the disadvantage of the other party. Economists, too, who have claimed that their discipline is an autonomous one, are similarly mistaken. Although economics is about money, and money is about choice, it is not a matter of choice alone, but of choice allied with trust. The tag "caveat emptor" captures the element of choice, but needs to be complemented by the equally essential element of trust implicit in the tag "caveat vendor". Trust raises the question of obligations inherent in the sell/buy relationship and needs a clear understanding, if not statement, of why two parties in an economic transaction trust each other.

Traditionally, when looking at business we distinguish the professions from business because a lawyer or a doctor has an obligation to seek the client's interests rather than his own. The fiduciary nature of the professions differentiates it from business where the nature of trust between the parties involved is not specified in the same way as it is for the professions, which have clearly laid down "professional standards" of behaviour. However, even in business transactions both parties are under some obligation to each other: the buyer to pay promptly in sound currency, the vendor to sell a product or service which accords with the quality standards of what he sells. Most transactions are not only bilateral, but limited in scope, being taken by different decision makers, each with his own standpoint, and so with his own perspective. I am responsible for my own family, my own firm and, to a lesser extent, my own locality, my own country, church, interest groups, and many other commitments, and these naturally loom larger in my scheme of things than in someone else's. Our lives are constituted by a web of social obligations, leading to specific duties incumbent on different agents in virtue of the place they occupy in society.

A moneyed economy decentralizes decision making, and requires each decision maker to be responsible for what he does not only in respect of the law but in respect of the less codified responsibilities of honesty and fairness. The underlying logic is the necessary conjugation between the first person singular and the first person plural. "What is good for the United States is good for General Motors" is often quoted (and often misquoted). Although often condemned, it is true. We cannot only quote it for the underlying altruism it represents but argue for it on games-theoretical grounds which contest that business is a zero-sum game. Being in business does not cancel obligations to other parties.

What has emerged from our discussion is that to understand the moneyed society we need to think of it from a general, social, as well as a limited individual, point of view. Although the value of money lies in each person being able to spend it as he thinks fit it is not rational to think only of oneself, and each agent in making up his own mind how to exercise his choices has to take account of the society of which he is a part, but also in terms of his actions on other people. A moneyed society consists of a set of interrelated individuals. Margaret Thatcher's claim that "there is no such thing as society" arose from her dislike of the State as "big brother" telling individuals what to do, but she confused State with Society, failing to recognize the individual as a "social animal", which was the original Greek concept of politics as a social activity in which individuals participate willingly without State coercion to do so.

To extol freedom is a basic ethic of business, but such freedom has to be exercised in the social context of how money is spent and of cooperating with all the stakeholders in a business enterprise, which has important implications for the corporate governance and the social responsibilities of sustainable business. Corporate social responsibility (CSR) is now a recognized as a part of economic activity in its wider social setting, which we look at in Chap. 11.

5.8   Families and Firms: The Feedback Principle

Families and firms are entities in a moneyed society that have economic relations with one another. They can be distinguished crudely as those that primarily spend money, families, and those that primarily make money, firms. The distinction is neither rigid nor complete: there are extended families, networks of friends, family businesses, trade associations and global conglomerates; and within the context of firms we should not omit such entities as religious bodies, charities, museums, or universities, all of whom engage in shared activities and work towards shared goals. This sharing provides the basis on which members may also cooperate without money changing hands, for example, the breadwinner does not pay the housewife for carrying out domestic chores. This raises the question of voluntary contributions for economic activities where we do things without being paid for doing so, the value of which is left out of the equation when we calculate the monetary value of gross national product.

Families and firms, both profit and non-profit, are entities that last, sometimes over many generations. Like biological entities they survive because they are homeostatic, that is, they respond and adapt themselves to the outside world in order to secure and protect their internal structures. They adjust their activity in the light of economic conditions where, in the moneyed society, money is an important feedback factor in assessing economic viability, both at the level of the family and the firm, but it is not the only one. Feedback, which can take the form of positive or negative criticism on the part of those who participate in whatever kind of economic entity, has an important qualitative side where, "how good or bad we are we in doing what we do", has to respond to a process of quantitative feedback in deciding "how successful are we in matching our costs to income?".

Biological entities have innate systems for responding to positive and negative feedbacks, or inputs, which they receive from outside, such as diet or disease, and exist in a context of other biological entities. Just as one cell coexists with many others, one organism with some others, one territorial tribe with its neighbours, one species with some others, so economic units operate in a variety of contexts involving feedback both positive and negative from their customers, employees, suppliers, and competitors, and society in general. But cells, organisms, populations, species, and families, although not isolated, are insulated, and have membranes, skins, territorial boundaries, ecological niches, which separate them and protect them from the rest of the world. Similarly families and firms need to have an internal membrane or structure which requires a viable economic structure if they are to survive.

Thus, internal equilibrium is a powerful motivator for both families and firms, but it cannot be achieved by complete isolation from the world outside, and has to be receptive to both positive and negative feedback from the environment or market in which they exist and operate. The Chief Executive of a firm stands by his employees, but may fail to instil in them the importance of ethical behaviour in business dealings. In spite of statements telling people about the mission of a company, firms like families may be impervious to complaints and criticisms. The mark of a good business leader is that he leaves it to others to say how well he has done, but concentrates on responding to negative feedback which can alert him to where his company is falling down. Many complaints, of course, are fractious or fictitious. But they should be listened to, and not automatically rejected. Adequate response to feedback both from within or outside the family or firm is an essential requirement for responding to change, and procedures for doing so will involve challenges for the established hierarchies of how families and firms are organized. Single-parent families are a social reality today which only a few generations did not exist, as is the reality of the "virtual" firm in recent times. A virtual business uses electronic means to transact business as opposed to traditional business relying of face to face contact transactions. Amazon.com is a virtual business as an online bookstore delivering bookstore services without a physical retail store presence.

George Soros uses the word "reflexivity" in relation to the circular feedback relationship between cause and effect where markets tend towards disequilibrium as prices affect the basic fundamentals of supply and demand which determine the nature of economic activity at a given time. He discusses the nature of pro-cyclicality of lending when banks are willing to ease lending standards for real estate when prices are rising, and then raising those standards when prices are falling, thus contributing to the economic phenomenon of boom and bust in economic activity, or the self re-enforcing cycles of bear and bull markets which complete the loop of circular feedback. The cyclicality of business is a phenomenon of economic activity which require systems for managing product/service life cycles, where regular feedback on market performance and trends is an essential part of business management. Who foresaw when the once ubiquitous telefax machine would be replaced by internet connections which have revolutionized communications and access to feedback information systems? The system for obtaining and managing feedback as an essential component of any business is well expressed in Apple's open invitation for feedback on its website saying "we would love to hear your comments of our hardware and software products", where concern for client feedback is characteristic of a company for whom "customer service" is an essential part of its mission for doing business. Ramaprasad in 1983 produced a tortuous but useful definition of feedback as "information about the gap between the actual level and reference level of a system parameter which is used to alter the gap in some way" ("On the definition of feedback", Behavioural Science vol 28, issue 1 January 1983). The definition rightly emphasizes the concept of a "gap" between objective and performance in the management of an economic enterprise, where a system of continuous feedback to answer the question "how well are we doing?" can assist in deciding what we need to do to fill those "gaps" in performance.

5.9 Public and Private

The moneyed society is based on a division between the public and private sectors of an economy, resulting in the concept of private and public goods, which leads to the dichotomy in a capitalist economic system between private and public ownership. This division of ownership results in a ongoing debate as to the economic efficiency of the two sectors, where it is often propounded that the private sector is more efficient in its use of economic resources financed and accounted for by shareholder investors who require a profitable return on those privately owned resources, whereas the public sector without the need to pay a dividend to its owners is less efficient in its use of resources, because devoid of the discipline of the profit motive makes it less susceptible to the requisites of cost control and return on assets measured in terms of dividends to its owners.

The State, it is claimed by its critics, is in this sense impervious to the strict profit disciplines of the private sector. At its most negative the State is seen as a burden on the private sector called on to finance the public sector, even if it is recognized that there is an economic need for the State to provide public services for the private sector in terms of social infrastructures which the private sector is unable to provide by itself. Cooperation between the two sectors has increased through the outsourcing of public services and a move towards the privatization of public services, for example, in the transport sector. The early days of nationalization when the State took command of key industrial sectors, such as coal and steel, have given way to privatizations as the means for financing public services without increasing the level of the public debt. But the image remains of "private efficiency against public inefficiency" where it is said that State bureaucracy lacks the entrepreneurial spirit and profit discipline of the private sector.

Such an attitude belies the reality of the cooperative relationship which exists between the two sectors in terms of how efficient they are in the creation of national wealth and well-being. A recent book by Marianna Mazzucato, *The Entrepreneurial State*, has made a contribution to the dispelling these kinds of false images of the State in proposing that "in seeking to promote innovation-led growth, it is fundamental to understand the important roles that both the public and private sector can play". The book makes a strong plea for seeing the State "as an active, entrepreneurial, risk taking agent".

The challenge is how to strengthen and improve the role of the State in the area of innovation, not leaving it to focus on creating the conditions for innovation to happen in the private sector. This will require a national programme for defining the innovation needs of the national economy which involves both the public and private sectors in which the State is an innovating proposer at the national level. As the State is expected to engage in a world of uncertainty, with inevitable winners and losers, it needs to become a professional risk taker, which can partake in the profits as well as the losses of risk-taking projects. This could call for specific project bonds which will repay loans and possibly participate in the profits of these projects. This will require new thinking on how to manage the ROI of these projects in a way which might involve private as well as State investors in such projects.

Such a new approach to what Mazzucato calls the "ecosystem" of innovation will require the State to be involved not just in the "de-risking" of the private sector and correcting "market failures", but in the market financing of projects at the drawing board stage. This will place a new emphasis on the importance of defining the economic value of State projects and their intrinsic value in terms of national well-being. In this way we need to devise new measures for valuing the outcomes of State innovation projects, whose investments would be monitored and controlled in light of those outcomes. This approach would extend the metric of economic value to State investment projects, which might include the provision of private capital for such projects. Is it beyond the imagination that private equity could also be used for finding capital for specific State investment projects in new initiatives between the public and private? We now take of "social impact bonds" which include private capital in their issue.[1]

Public goods, as opposed to private goods, are an important part of the moneyed society. Public goods are classified as being both non-excludable and non-rivalrous in that individuals cannot be effectively excluded from use and where use by one individual does not reduce availability to others. Examples of public goods include fresh air, knowledge, lighthouses,

---

[1] See center for Global Development Report Oct 2013 on development impact bonds (DIB).

national defence, flood control systems and street lighting. Public goods that are available everywhere are sometimes referred to as global public goods. Many public goods may at times be subject to excessive use resulting in negative externalities affecting all users; for example, air pollution and traffic congestion. Public goods problems are often closely related to the "free rider" problem or the so-called "tragedy of the commons", in which people not paying for the good may continue to access it. Thus, the good may be under-produced, over-used or degraded. Public goods may also become subject to restrictions on access and may then be considered to be club goods or private goods, restricted for public use in term of exclusion mechanisms such as copyright, patents, congestion pricing and pay television. Private goods, unlike public goods, are rival and excludable. What is mine, is mine, and what is yours, yours. There are important philosophical issues here for economics in deciding whether business is a privative, or non-privative, or a combination of both, activity, which is discussed in Chap. 13.

5.10 Predictive Modelling

In trying to estimate the likelihood of what income, expenditure and investment levels in the moneyed society will be in the future we enter the world of economic modelling where the predominant empirical tool is that of linear regression, used for measuring consumer spending, fixed investment spending, inventory levels, the demand for liquid assets, exports, imports, and employment. In doing this we move into a world of uncertainty, which in the main is indeterminate, where we seek to understand the variables involved and their volatility. The problem is that all these economic factors are not unchanging scientific facts but change according to time and circumstances; they are dynamic and never static. They are heavily dependent on human behavior and preferences which make the accuracy of the assumptions we make difficult to verify and define. The key question for economic modelling, and econometrics in general, concerns the validity of those assumptions and how quantifiable they are in terms of their nature (inner construct) and duration. In this respect economics has to be concerned with the behavioural sciences which looks at how and why people act and behave as they do.

Why was it that the predictive modelling processes of economics was unable to predict the last financial crisis? As a leading industrialist and banker put it in a private and off-the-record conversation:

"If I could offer a partial view of why things have gone as badly as they have, it would be along the following lines. First, models banks used made assumptions about the liquidity of markets which turned out to be unfounded in very stressful conditions. There have been times when there has been no market in many instruments, making risk mitigation strategies inoperative. Second, and partly as a result, a lot of hedging strategies were based on assumptions about the possible range of price movements which turned out to be unfounded. In other words people were hedged down against a certain size of price fall, but thereafter were not effectively hedged. Risk management models tended to focus on net exposures, assuming that hedges were effective, when in the circumstances gross exposures were more relevant.

More fundamentally, perhaps, in the mortgage market at least assumptions were made about the credit worthiness of borrowers which were unrealistic. Subprime mortgages were only about six per cent of the total mortgage pool in the US in 2001, while by 2006 they were 23 per cent of the total. It is quite clear that the average quality of those mortgages was therefore significantly lower than in 2006, yet the pricing did not reflect that change. The rating agencies did not respond to this change in quality by adapting their ratings. At an even more fundamental level one can point to the very significant macro imbalances, especially China and the US, and the rapid increases in consumer indebtedness in the US and the UK (and elsewhere) which in retrospect do not look to have been sustainable. I believe these underlying issues are much more important than the technical flaws in risk management.

And I am not quite sure what short selling really has to do with the story. I think that where investors believe that assets are overvalued, they will sell them short, and that was certainly the case with many banks over the last year. You ask why 'predictive models' like Black–Scholes failed to predict the problems we have seen. My understanding of Black–Scholes is that it is essentially a pricing model which prices options based on observed volatility in the underlying asset. So if there is a very sharp and significant change in volatility, Black–Scholes will not be a good basis for pricing. But I would not see it really as a predictive model, it is simply a way of expressing value of a contract based on past experience."

This well-expressed opinion indicates the complexity and unreliability (if the assumptions are incorrect) of economic modelling. This does not mean that we dispense with economic predictive modelling, but it does mean asking economists to come out of their empirical tower, to take better account of those subjective and often indeterminate preferences and motivations which influence human behaviour when making their assumptions, and to indicate the extent plus or minus that the conclusions of those predictions may be wrong. In the aftermath of the 2007–2009 global economic meltdown, the profession's attachment to unrealistic models is increasingly being questioned and criticized. After a week-long workshop, one group of economists released a paper critical of their own profession's unethical use of unrealistic models. Their *Abstract* offers a criticism of fundamental practices:

> The economics profession appears to have been unaware of the long build-up to the current worldwide financial crisis and to have significantly underestimated its dimensions once it started to unfold. In our view, this lack of understanding is due to a misallocation of research efforts in economics. We trace the deeper roots of this failure to the profession's focus on models that, by design, disregard key elements driving outcomes in real-world markets. The economics profession has failed in communicating the imitations, weaknesses, and even dangers of its preferred models to the public. This state of affairs makes clear the need for a major reorientation of focus in the research economists undertake, as well as for the establishment of an ethical code that would ask economists to understand and communicate the limitations and potential misuses of their models.[2]

We need a radical rethink of economic and financial modelling which should involve all the professions, accountants, lawyers and actuaries, economists, financial analysts, government regulators, and, last but not least, representatives from the Fortune Top 500. The sponsors need to be drawn from authorities including the IMF, the World Bank, the ECB, the BIS, and the stock exchanges, with a brief to examine the present state of the art in assumption setting for predictive and risk management modelling, analysis of current strengths and weaknesses, and recommendations

---

[2] See also "why economists failed to predict the financial crisis" Wharton university.

for the future. Predictive modelling is of such importance for new economic thinking that it requires a high level study group composed of economists, regulators, financial analysts, businessmen and professional advisors, perhaps with a pilot "kick start" project sponsored and chaired by the Bank of England, and other authorities like the Fed and ECB.

5.11 GDP and Welfare

The regulation and control requirements of a moneyed society are discussed in Chap. 10. In the rest of this chapter we look at systems for measuring the performance and results of a moneyed society, including quality of life measures like the Human Development Index. GDP per capita (per person) is often used as a measure of a person's welfare. Countries with higher GDP may be more likely to also score highly on other measures of welfare, such as life expectancy. However, there are serious limitations to the usefulness of employing GDP as a measure of welfare:

- Measures of GDP typically exclude unpaid economic activity, most importantly domestic work such as childcare. This leads to distortions; for example, a paid nanny's income contributes to GDP, but an unpaid parent's time spent caring for children will not, even though they are both carrying out the same economic activity.
- GDP takes no account of the inputs used to produce the output. For example, if everyone worked for twice the number of hours, then GDP might roughly double, but this does not necessarily mean that workers are better off as they would have less leisure time. Similarly, the impact of economic activity on the environment is not measured in calculating GDP.
- Comparison of GDP from one country to another may be distorted by movements in exchange rates. Measuring national income at purchasing power parity may overcome this problem, but GDP does not directly take account of changes in currency values which will affect the national GDP value of an economy vis-à-vis another economy against whom its currency has been revalued or devalued.

Devaluation may give an economy competitive advantage in terms of export pricing, but a "devalued GDP" may divert attention from the need for productivity improvements on which competitiveness depends.

- GDP does not measure factors that affect the quality of life, such as the quality of the environment and security from crime. This leads to distortions—for example, spending on cleaning up an oilspill is included in GDP, but the negative impact of the spill on well-being (through, for example, the loss of clean beaches) is not measured.
- GDP is the mean (average) wealth rather than median (middle-point) wealth. Countries with a skewed income distribution may have a relatively high per capita GDP while the majority of its citizens have a relatively low level of income, due to concentration of wealth in the hands of a small fraction of the population. See the Gini coefficient for assessing the distribution of income in an economy.

Because of these limitations, other measures of welfare, such as the Human Development Index (HDI), the Index of Sustainable Economic Welfare (ISEW), the Genuine Progress Indicator (GPI), gross national happiness/wellness (GNH) / wellness (GNW), and sustainable national income (SNI) are now being used to measure the economic health, or value, of an economy beyond the purely monetary value of GDP measures.

5.12 The Human Development Index

The HDI's definition of economic freedom is "The highest form of economic freedom prides an absolute right of property ownership, fully realized freedoms of movement for labor, capital, and goods, and an absolute absence of coercion or constraint of economic liberty beyond the extent necessary for citizens to protect and maintain liberty itself." The index scores nations on 10 broad factors of economic freedom using statistics from organizations like the World Bank, the International Monetary Fund and the Economist Intelligence Unit:

- Business Freedom: Business freedom is a quantitative measure of the ability to start, operate, and close a business that represents the overall burden of regulation as well as the efficiency of government in the regulatory process.
- Trade Freedom: Trade freedom is a composite measure of the absence of tariff and non-tariff barriers that affect imports and exports of goods and services. Different imports entering a country can, and often do, face different tariffs.
- Monetary Freedom: Monetary freedom combines a measure of price stability with an assessment of price controls. Both inflation and price controls distort market activity. Price stability without microeconomic intervention is the ideal state for the free market.
- Government Size/Spending: This component considers the level of government expenditures as a percentage of GDP. Government expenditures, including consumption and transfers, account for the entire score.
- Fiscal Freedom: Fiscal freedom is a measure of the tax burden imposed by government.
- Property Rights: The property rights component is an assessment of the ability of individuals to accumulate private property, secured by clear laws that are fully enforced by the state.
- Investment Freedom: In an economically free country, there would be no constraints on the flow of investment capital. Individuals and firms would be allowed to move their resources into and out of specific activities internally and across the country's borders without restriction.
- Financial Freedom: Financial freedom is a measure of banking efficiency as well as a measure of independence from government control and interference in the financial sector.
- Freedom from Corruption: Corruption erodes economic freedom by introducing insecurity and uncertainty into economic relationships. The higher the level of corruption, the lower the level of overall economic freedom and the lower a country's score.
- Labour Freedom: The labour freedom component is a quantitative measure that looks into aspects of the legal and regulatory framework of a country's labour market.

The 10 factors are averaged equally into a total score. Each one of the 10 freedoms is graded using a scale from 0 to 100, where 100 represents the maximum freedom. A score of 100 signifies an economic environment or set of policies that is most conducive to economic freedom. The methodology has shifted and changed as new data and measurements have become available, especially in the area of Labour freedom, which was given its own indicator in 2007. The origins of the HDI are found in the annual *Human Development Reports* of the United Nations Development Programme (UNDP). These were devised and launched by the Pakistani economist Mahbub ul Haq in 1990 and had the explicit purpose "to shift the focus of development economics from national income accounting to people centered policies". To produce the *Human Development Reports*, Mahbub ul Haq brought together a group of development economists, but it was Amartya Sen's work on capabilities and functionings of economics that provided the underlying conceptual framework.

5.13 Gross National Happiness

The measures of GDP and HDI are now being supplemented by work and research in the area of "happiness economics". The assessment of gross national happiness (GNH) seeks to define an indicator that measures quality of life or social progress in more holistic and psychological terms than just the economic indicator of gross domestic product (GDP). The term "gross national happiness" was coined in 1972 by Bhutan's fourth Dragon King, Jigme Singye Wangchuck, who has opened Bhutan to economic modernization, which aims to build an economy that will serve Bhutan's culture, which is founded on Buddhist spiritual values. The concept was developed by the Centre for Bhutan Studies to survey the population's general level of well-being. Two Canadians, Michael and Martha Pennock, assisted in developing the Bhutanese survey, and developed a shorter international version of the survey which has been used in their home region of Victoria, BC as well as in Brazil. Like many psychological and social indicators, GNH is easier to state than to define with mathematical precision. The four components of the Bhutanese index are the promotion of sustainable development, the preservation and promotion of cultural values, the conservation of the natural environment, and the establishment of good governance. These components are then specified into eight general contributors to happiness: physical, mental and spiritual health; time-balance; social and community vitality; cultural vitality; education; living standards; good governance; and ecological vitality.

There is no exact quantitative definition of GNH; however, elements that contribute to GNH are subject to quantitative measurement By contrast, the Genuine Progress Indicator (GPI) has been developed to find quantitative measures of well-being and happiness. With 26 indicators divided into three categories of indicators—economic, environmental and social—which attempt to define economic success not only in terms of the money spent and goods consumed, but also by the quality of life in society, and in the moneyed society in particular. A second-generation GNH concept, treating happiness as a socioeconomic development metric, was proposed in 2006 by Med Jones, the President of International Institute of Management. The metric measures socioeconomic development by tracking seven development areas including the nation's mental and emotional health. GNH value is proposed to be an index function of the total average per capita of the following measures:

1. Economic Wellness: Indicated via direct survey and statistical measurement of economic metrics such as consumer debt, average income to consumer price index ratio and income distribution.
2. Environmental Wellness: Indicated via direct survey and statistical measurement of environmental metrics such as pollution, noise and traffic.
3. Physical Wellness: Indicated via statistical measurement of physical health metrics such as severe illnesses.
4. Mental Wellness: Indicated via direct survey and statistical measurement of mental health metrics such as usage of antidepressants and rise or decline of psychotherapy patients.
5. Workplace Wellness: Indicated via direct survey and statistical measurement of labour metrics such as jobless claims, job change, workplace complaints and lawsuits.

6. Social Wellness: Indicated via direct survey and the statistical measurement of social metrics such as discrimination, safety, divorce rates, complaints of domestic conflicts and family lawsuits, public lawsuits, crime rates.

7. Political Wellness: Indicated via direct survey and statistical measurement of political metrics such as the quality of local democracy, individual freedom, and foreign conflicts.

The above seven metrics were incorporated into the first Global GNH Survey. We are still in the early days of using these new performance measures and they need to be related to the existing systems for measuring business and consumer confidence which are already in use, and also the individual employee and customer satisfaction information companies are already reporting on in social balance sheets and sustainability reports (see Chap. 11) as part of their corporate social responsibilities. However, the ten economic freedom measures of the HDI are a useful checklist for reporting in the social balance sheet or sustainability report.

We return to the basic concept of economics as being the science for determining the amount of scarce resources available, and how to allocate them between consumer preferences. Because of the inherent scarcity of economic resources we enter a world of continuous trade-offs between different priorities, interests and beliefs, which lie behind those preferences. Since the economic reality of poverty (one of the social indicators impacting on human happiness) is a basic fact of the world we inhabit, "happiness economics" has now arrived as the study of how it can contribute to resolving the inequalities of income, poverty; access to health and education services, which remain key priorities for human well-being.

In this chapter we have tried to examine the challenges which the moneyed society has to face in managing the interface between the amount of money available and the demands for investment and consumption. The fundamental question remains: "Can a nation's GDP be consumed without undermining its ability to produce and consume the same GDP in the future?" In essence, HDI and GPI are metrics for measuring what needs to be done to ensure sustainable economic development in future, balancing the opportunities for monetary profit with the potential degradation and depletion of the resources on which GDP depends.

References

Coyle D. GDP: a brief but affectionate history. Princeton, NJ: Princeton University Press; 2014.

Finlay S. Predictive analytics: data mining and big data: myths, misconceptions and methods. Basingstoke: Palgrave Macmillan; 2014.

Frees E, Predictive Modelling of Insurance company operations, University of Wisconsin, 2013.

Kearns J. The Fed eases off. Bloomberg QuickTake, 16 Sept 2015. http://www.bloombergview.com/quicktake/federal-reserve-quantitative-easing-tape.

Lerner AP. The economics and politics of consumer sovereignty. Am Econ Rev. 1972;62(2):267–78.

Mazzucato M. The entrepreneurial state: debunking public vs. private sector myths. London: Anthem; 2013.

Mueller J. Understanding financial liquidity. Investopedia, October 2015. http://www.investopedia.com/articles/basics/07/liquidity.asp?view=print.

Predictive Modelling for life Insurance, *Society of Actuaries.*

Ramaprasad, On the definition of feedback, Behavioural Science, vol 28, issue 7, January 1983.

Rawls J. A theory of justice. Cambridge, MA: Harvard University Press; 1999.

Rothbard MN. Man, economy, and state. 2nd ed. Auburn, AL: Ludwig von Mises Institute; 2001.

Ryback TW. The U.N. Happiness Project. New York Times, 28 Mar 2012. http://www.nytimes.com/2012/03/29/opinion/the-un-happiness-project.

Samuelson P. Foundations of economic analysis. Cambridge, MA: Harvard University Press; 1947.

United Nations Development Programme, "What is human development?" Human Development Index (HDI), April 2012.

"Why economists failed to predict the financial crisis" The Dahlen Report, Wharton university of Peninsylavia.

Wolf M. Keynes v Friedman: both can claim victory. Financial Times, 21 Nov 2006. http://www.ft.com/cms/s/48d6ff46-7994-11db-90a6-0000779e2340, N6cp.

6

Boom or Bust

Abstract This chapter looks at the boom and bust conditions which occur during business cycles. Before the economic crisis of 2008 some experts were claiming that the boom–bust syndrome had been resolved, only to be proved wrong by a crisis which has resulted in a legacy of high unemployment, low economic growth and high levels of sovereign debt. We try to look at boom and bust through the eyes of the businessman, call for an analysis of the bubbles that have occurred over the past twenty years, and propose four key questions for new economic thinking, which would also look at how a sample of individual companies from 16 economic sectors have responded to these crises.

6.1 Chapter Overview

In business the inherent life forces of growth and decay manifest themselves periodically in business cycles, which are characterized from time to time by economic boom–bust conditions, and which can cause havoc to economic prosperity and asset values. Until the most recent financial

© The Editor(s) (if applicable) and The Author(s) 2016   **115**
M.R. Griffiths, J.R. Lucas, *Value Economics*,
DOI 10.1057/978-1-137-54187-1_6

crisis of 2008 certain experts were starting to claim that the boom–bust problem had been resolved, only to be proved wrong by a crisis which left a legacy of unemployment, low economic growth and high levels of sovereign debt. Reflecting on the hubris of such commentators, the US Nobel Prize-winning economist Joseph Stiglitz made the following observation: "The only surprise about the economic crisis of 2008 was that it came as a surprise to so many". The causes of the last financial crisis are now well researched, and actions have been taken to prevent or manage such bubbles occurring again, including better financial regulation, new systems of liquidity management, and the control of sovereign debt. Whether these actions will suffice still remains to be seen. This debate is taking place within a lively exchange between those who are proposing more austerity and those who favour more investment, since the impact of such policies on future economic growth, prosperity and the creation of economic value is often unclear or hazy at best.

How will it ever be possible to agree national policies for the management of business cycles to reduce or alleviate possible boom or bust conditions, until we have clear and agreed criteria for measuring the long-term economic value of businesses and national economies? In this chapter we discuss these issues, and their possible implications for new economic thinking on the management of business cycles, in linking economic value to the levels of public and private debt being incurred. The market will continue to be an important mechanism for pricing the value of assets, but it will always be subject to market sentiment, and to the irrationalities of the "greater fool" theory, which lie behind boom and bust conditions. We need to understand the reasons for the various bubbles that have occurred over the past two decades, from the Black Wednesday of 1992 through to the financial crisis of 2008 and the problems of European sovereign debt in 2010.

We call for an analysis of nine specific financial crises, which occurred over these two decades, and the lessons learned—or not—for economic planning in the future. We propose four key questions for future economic thinking based on the experience of these bubbles which we hope can contribute to a better understanding of what is involved on the part of economists, regulators and businessmen. However, we believe that answers to these questions must consider the experience of specific economic sectors (both private and public) over the past twenty years, and should focus on the experience of a representative sample of individual enterprises operating in those sectors. Economic theory needs to distinguish between those economic enterprises, which are creating, or destroying, economic value over the long term, and the reasons for these changes in economic value.

This will take us into the area of how to estimate the economic value of government enterprises, which we shall return to in Chap. 8. For the purposes of a "bubble analysis project" of this kind, however, we believe it would also be useful to analyse the experience of public enterprises during times of boom and bust, to see the effects they have had on the investment profiles and cost–benefit performances of State enterprises during these periods. One of the causes of the 2008 "bubble" cycle was the imbalance between the level of national public debts, and the ability to repay that debt in terms of interest and the time horizons for repayment of the loan capital granted by its creditors. In managing the globalization risks inherent in boom and bust cycles, we need ways of establishing what levels of sovereign debt should be in relation to the capacity of national economies to support and repay that debt. Why was it impossible, for instance, for the regulatory authorities to intervene before allowing Greek public debt to reach nearly 200 percent of GNP?

6.2   Business Cycles

Business cycles in OECD countries after the Second World War were less prone to the dramatic boom and bust phenomena of earlier cycles like the Great Depression of 1929. In the period from 1945 to 1973 the OECD world was not subject to heavy recession, and it was not until 2008 that these economies suffered the effects of a global economic downturn and a financial crisis which defied previous predictions. Until then it was felt that fiscal and monetary policies had solved the worst negative effects of a series of financial crises which we highlight in Sect. 6.4 of this chapter. During this period, it had been claimed on several occasions that the problems of business cycles—or at least the problem of depressions—had been solved.

The first claim in the late 1960s was attributed to the Phillips curve (the correlation between increasing employment and higher rates of inflation) as the way for managing the economy, but the stagflation (high levels of inflation with low economic growth and high unemployment) of the 1970s showed that economic theory had still not found the key to maximizing employment. The second claim was made in the early 2000s, following the stability and growth in the 1980s and 1990s in what came to be known as the Great Moderation (a period which had seen a reduction in the volatility of business fluctuations). In 2003, Robert Lucas, in his presidential address to the American Economic Association, declared that the "central problem of depression-prevention [has] been solved, for all practical purposes". Unfortunately, he was to be proved wrong by the 2008 global crisis still ongoing.

So, we appear to be back to square one with regard to finding a viable theory for managing business cycles in the future. There are an abundance of explanations for the development of this last crisis, including a failure to manage sovereign debt levels adequately in a global environment, the lack of an effective system for managing currency exchange rates, changing competitiveness between one OECD economy and another, restrictive work practices, and liquidity restrictions imposed for austerity requirements, all of which impacted negatively on the economic growth required to provide resources for public debt reduction and future investment. There is plenty of material here for new economic thinking in tackling the perennial problem of getting the balance right in economics between growth, debt and investment in managing "business cycles", where globalization and the sophistication of new financial debt instruments have complicated life for economists, and the recommendations they make to governments and businesses for the management of "moneyed" societies.

6.3   Economic Bubbles

Why is that economies suffer from the hiccups of boom and bust cycles? One reason is that asset values become subject to irrational market pricing, which, for one reason or another, become removed from the intrinsic (or long-term) value of those assets. Bubbles occur when market values move ahead of intrinsic values until, in times of economic downturn and declining profitability, those "over-optimistic" market values begin to decline. At this point investor confidence starts to fall, resulting in people "playing safe", selling their investments, and going liquid, moves which prick the bubble of "over-inflated" assets concentrating attention on the value of those assets, and whether in fact they exist at all, as were the false assets of the Koretz "Ponzi" investment schemes offering fake mortgages or worthless stocks.

We enter the world of the "greater fool" theory, where over-optimistic investors (the fools) buy overvalued assets hoping to sell them to other optimistic investors (the greater fools) at a higher price. It is a situation similar in some ways to the "self-fulfilling prophecy" of the herding instinct where investors tend to buy or sell according to the market trends prevailing at the time. Another cause of bubbles is excessive monetary liquidity, which, when coupled with inadequate lending standards by banks, can make markets vulnerable to volatile asset price inflation caused by short-term speculation. In the words of Axel Weber, a former president of the Deutsche Bank: "The past has shown that an overly generous provision of liquidity in global financial markets in connection with a low level of interest rates promotes the formation of asset-price bubbles." When interest rates are low, investors tend to avoid putting their capital into savings accounts, taking advantage of cheap money to leverage their "borrowed" capital by investing in alternatives such as property for rent or in the stock market. Consequently, with too much liquidity chasing a limited number of assets, the prices of those assets inflate until such time as any loans have to be repaid, and the funds are no longer available to meet those debt obligations. "Elementary, my dear Watson", we might say, but at that point when banks start to take liquidity out of the system by calling in loans or raising interest rates, thus instigating a "contractionary" monetary policy, the bubble of inflated prices bursts, and there is no one left to buy the assets the borrower requires to sell to pay back his leveraged debt.

Another factor is that of "moral hazard", where people take on more risks than they can afford, because they believe someone else will take on the burden of that risk. This phenomenon was observed during the last crisis when the government offered bailouts to prevent bank failures, being caught on the petard, as some might say, of the "too big to fail" doctrine of those years. In the USA the Troubled Asset Relief Program

(TARP) in 2008 was introduced to bail out financial institutions who had speculated in high-risk financial instruments during the housing boom, which the *Economist* described in 2005 as follows: "The worldwide rise in house prices is the biggest bubble in history". Ben Bernanke was also honest enough to admit his error when he stated that "I and others were mistaken early on in saying that the subprime crisis could be contained." Bubbles are also influenced by price inflation, which was one of the causes of the property boom, during which prices increased at a much higher rate than national inflation. Where was the economic rationality for these increases in property prices, which syphoned off liquidity from industrial investment when the stock markets did not keep pace with the increase in property prices?

Bubbles have also been studied through experimental and mathematical economics. For example, the mathematical modelling of Gundaz Caginalp and others. Using assumptions that the supply and demand of an asset depends not only on valuation, but also on the trend in prices, and that both cash and assets are finite, it was found that the bubble would be larger if there was initial undervaluation, and that when the initial ratio of cash to asset value was increased the bubble would be larger. This confirmed what was already recognized by those who believe that excess cash and market trends are key factors in creating bubbles, and that "cheap money fuels markets". If that is the case, it strengthens the case of the Austrian School in proposing that monetary policy is the key for non-inflationary economic planning, in countering the Keynesian tenet that "money does not matter", when it comes to the priority of eliminating recession through increasing rather decreasing demand. If too much money results in the creation of boom conditions, or too little leads to bust conditions, what are the economic policies we need to put in place to control the risk of economic bubbles?

6.4   Questions for New Economic Thinking

In looking at business cycles and financial crises resulting in the bursting of bubbles, which are caused by an unrealistic valuation of assets and a falsification of fundamental, or intrinsic, values, one might expect to find agreement about the causes of these events, and adequate reporting systems for preventing them in the future, but we do not find that the experts (both economists and financial) are in agreement. Is austerity the answer, or is it more investment in productive resources to stimulate demand, encourage innovation and improve competitiveness? It is unsurprising that the businessman and the man in the street on the famous Clapham Omnibus are confused and—in the light of past experience—distrustful that the experts will get it right in the future. We might use Bertrand Russell's adage that the important thing for philosophical enquiry is to ask the right questions, and then consider how the great minds of the past have tried to answer them. In economics who have been and are today the great minds to whom we might turn for answers in defining rational and successful policies for managing the economies of the world? We could start by considering the crises which have plagued economics over the past twenty years in analyzing why they occurred and the lessons which they taught, or did not, teach us.

1. Black Wednesday of 1992.
2. The default of Mexican debt in 1994.
3. Asian devaluation and banking crises in 1997.
4. Russian financial crisis in 1998, repeated in 2014.
5. Argentine economic crisis 1999–2002.
6. Iceland financial crisis 2008.
7. The dot-com bubble of 2001.
8. Global financial crisis 2007–2008.
9. European sovereign debt crisis of 2010.

Economists need to explain why these crises occurred, and why the predictive techniques of econometrics were unable to forecast them. There is a crisis of confidence here with regard to the competency of the experts on the part of the businessman and the man in the street. As Matthew Parris, the *Spectator* journalist and former Conservative MP, put it, "The collapse of confidence is not irrational; it's the correction to a long run of irrational confidence", on the part we might add not only of the man in the street, but also of his financial advisors. There is a clear need for explanation and basic economic education, if confidence is to be restored fully in the economic and financial "experts" who are responsible for defining economic policy, and advising economic operators on what to do. We might leave aside for the moment general post-event analysis, and consider the experience of how businesses survived during these economic crises, and take soundings from a sample composed of leading companies drawn from key economic sectors, as to the effects of the last financial crisis on their fundamental economic values, as opposed to the monetary, or paper, value of their stock prices. (See Sect. 6.5 for the possible components of such a sample.) An "experience research" project of this kind could help to identify the "success" stories of individual business enterprises during boom and bust market conditions, which could provide a realistic basis for setting sectoral economic assumptions for the future, and designing appropriate financial and fiscal incentives.

Let us concentrate more on the economic values of individual companies, based on their underlying intrinsic values, as a metric for comparison against market stock price values. Such information could also provide important inputs for evaluating the sovereign debt of individual economies based on their industrial and tertiary capacity to support the public sector in terms of fiscal income for the national exchequer. So far, we have been talking about the private sector, but this research could be extended to the public sector in analysing how government departments as economic enterprises have been affected by the last economic crisis. (See Sect. 6.5 of this chapter for a discussion of how this might be done.) With the "hard fact" findings arising from the experience of successful and unsuccessful economic enterprises, we could then formulate the kind of questions new economic thinking needs to address in analyzing the bubbles which arise from boom–bust market conditions.

1. What is the correlation between the creation of economic value and the key performance indicator (KPI) of growth, inflation, investment, debt, currencies and economic value, and how do these factors change during conditions of boom and bust? It would be useful to have a six-point matrix composed of these factors to highlight how each impacts on the others in light of the "business experiences" described above.

2. How do we measure competiveness in the global marketplace and how it varies between the economic sectors of individual economies during boom and bust conditions?

3. How are capital and liquidity to be provided for economic enterprises, both private and public, particularly during boom–bust conditions, and in what form, covering credit, variable interest rates, debt instruments, including securitization, project bonds and equity financing?
4. What are the standards and procedures required for managing and controlling sovereign debt levels during business cycles, using the economic criteria identified by answers to the three questions posed above, and how should sovereign debt be categorized between private and public debt, and quantified in terms of "Triple Bottom Line Accounting", covering economic, social and environmental performance?

None of the answers to the four questions posed above can avoid taking a position on what we mean by economic value and how it can be created. In other words, "value" needs to be a basic criterion for planning and measuring economic activity, particularly during boom and bust conditions, which affect the economic value of business enterprises (see Chap. 8). The final question at the end of the day for any businessman, and the same applies to the economist, banker or government policy maker, has to be: "What contribution are my actions, advice or decisions making to the creation of economic value?" Whether it's boom or bust, "economic value" has to be the measure of how successful we are in managing business cycles and in understanding how much value is being created or destroyed at each and every stage of those business cycles.

6.5 Private and Public Business Cycle Management

In analysing the experience of managing business cycles in conditions of boom or bust, we believe it would be useful, in addition to analysing the nine bubble crises described in Sect. 6.4, to analyse the experience of different economic sectors and a sample of companies operating in those sectors. We propose that such an analysis could include, for example, the following economic sectors and companies.

1. *Retailing*: Wal-Mart and Tesco.
2. *Oil*: Exxon and Royal Dutch Shell, with possibly an invite to China National Petroleum.
3. *Computing*: Apple and Microsoft.
4. *Motor*: General Motors and Volkswagen.
5. *Airspace*: Boeing and Airbus.
6. *Chemical*: DuPont and ICI.
7. *Pharmaceuticals*: Pfizer and Astra Zeneca, and possibly Sinopec for the Chinese experience.
8. *Engineering*: GE and Siemens.
9. *Food*: Kraft and Nestlé.
10. *Metal*: Arcelor Mittal and Nippon Steel, and possibly TATA for the Indian experience.
11. *Electrical*: Sony and Philips.
12. *Banking*: JP Morgan Chase and Société Générale.
13. *Insurance*: AXA and Allianz.
14. *Diversified*: Berkshire Hathaway and Black Rock.
15. *Beverages*: Coca Cola and Heineken.
16. *Trading*: Glencore and Mitsubishi Corporation.

The objective would be to analyse the experience of business leaders during the period of the last global financial crisis. The list above is not intended to be exhaustive, and is provided to stimulate discussion, both as to how such a research project could be conducted, and by whom it should be sponsored. In defining the objectives and contents of the research a wide range of people should be consulted: all influential business decision makers and their industrial associations; economic and research institutes; government agencies and departments; business schools and opinion leaders.

And who should be the sponsors? Possible candidates might be one, or a combination of, the following: the IMF, the OECD, the WTA, the NYSE, the SEC, the Fed, the Bank of England, the ECB, or perhaps the Institute for New Economic Thinking founded by George Soros. The important principle is that this is not an academic project, but would instead be a "businessman-oriented" opinion project, which would draw on the experience and opinions of businessmen which are being sought in contributing to new economic thinking, and as a platform for establishing the criteria for measuring economic value.

The findings of such a project would have implications for the methodology of predictive econometric modelling, and for "Triple Bottom Line Accounting" in times of economic crisis. All of the above concerns the activities of the private sector, and makes no mention of the public sector, which leaves a serious gap if such research does not analyse the experience of the public sector in times of economic boom or bust conditions. We should like to see public services, as economic enterprises in their own right, included in this research, if only as an experiment in analysing the experiences of the State as an economic operator subject, like any private business, to investment constraints and the return on any investment, as well as the need to determine income and expense budgets, measured in terms of cost–benefit efficiency. We could perhaps start with health and education as two State service enterprises. If it is accepted that economic value should become a criterion for measuring economic value, then the public sector should be held as accountable as the private sector for the economic, as well as the social, value it is creating for society (see Chap. 8).

References

Caginalp G, Porter D, Smith V. Financial bubbles: excess cash, momentum, and incomplete information. J Psychol Financ Market. 2001;2(2):80–99.

Gale T. Business cycles, theories. International Encyclopedia of the Social Sciences; 2008. http://www.encyclopedia.com/doc/1G2-3045300261.html.

Greenspan A. The age of turbulence: adventures in a new world. New York: Penguin; 2007.

Krugman P. Too big to fail fail? New York Times, 11 Jan 2010. http://krugman.blogs.nytimes.com/2010/01/11/too-big-to-fail-fail-2/.

Krugman P. Bernanke, blower of bubbles? New York Times, 9 May 2013. http://www.nytimes.com/2013/05/10/opinion/krugman-bernanke-blower-of-bubbles.html?_r=0.

Krugman P. A moveable glut. New York Times, 24 Aug 2015. http://www.nytimes.com/2015/08/24/opinion/a-moveable-glut.html.

Lucas Jr RE. Models of business cycles. Cambridge, MA: Basil Blackwell; 1990.

Mazzucato M. The entrepreneurial state: debunking public vs. private sector myths. London: Anthem; 2013.

Solomon D. Light at the end of the bailout tunnel. The Wall Street Journal, 12 Apr 2010. http://www.wsj.com/articles/SB10001424052702304846504575177950029886696.

7

Work and Employment

Abstract In this chapter we look at some of the key issues facing work and employment today, with particular emphasis on unemployment, and the paradox of why there has been an increasing inequality between the rich and poor in terms of the distribution of employment income. We look at the demand of employees for greater participation in decision making and in the profitability arising from increased productivity, and at how the "future of work", as depicted in the "Shamrock" and "Hollywood" models, may change the ways in which people will be employed in future, and how we should define full employment. The important principle for industrial relations is to see employees and employers as stakeholders in the economic value of the companies for which they work, and in the negotiations for new work models of employment.

7.1   Chapter Overview

In the face of growing economic inequalities and high levels of youth unemployment, do we need a new paradigm for work and employment which achieves the correct balance between the capital investment in

© The Editor(s) (if applicable) and The Author(s) 2016   **127**
M.R. Griffiths, J.R. Lucas, *Value Economics*,
DOI 10.1057/978-1-137-54187-1_7

innovation and technology, and the benefits for employment in terms of jobs and remuneration? Is the decline of union membership an indicator that the traditional representatives of labour are losing the support of their members in terms of job creation and pay as they respond to the challenges of technological change and restructuring? What are the challenges of the "future of work" in a global environment where both the nature of work and the way in which it is organized are changing? These are all questions with implications for new economic thinking about how work and employment need to be organized in the future, and how employees can participate and share in the economic value of the companies for which they work. There are implications here for the philosophy of economics which we discuss more fully in Chap. 12.

This chapter looks at the paradox of increasing inequalities between capital and labour where, in the words of the economist Paul Krugman, "the old-fashioned, almost Marxist discussion, about capital versus labour seems to be reviving", or, as the *Economist* put it, "Labour Pains: All Round the World Labour is Losing Out to capital", *The Economist*, 2 November 2013.

We look at some of the recent research, such as the 2012 IMF report *Rise of Inequality at Center of Economic Crisis*, and call for unions, in the face of declining membership, as is occurring in the USA, to broaden and raise the level of debate, by taking it beyond the fundamental tasks of wage negotiation, into considering issues such as the greater participation of employees in decision making and profit sharing. In terms of employee representation and participation we propose that "efficiency, equity and voice", discussed in John Budd's book, *Employment with a Human Face*, should become the keywords in industrial relations. In looking at the future of work and the implications for employment, we consider the changes which were envisaged by Keynes in his paper "Economic Possibilities for our Grandchildren", and the present-day changes that are outlined in the Russell Sage Foundation research project "Low Wages in a Wealthy World", and Dooley and Prause's book *The Social Costs of Underemployment*. We look at current trends in unemployment, identifying the significant differences between one economy and another, and the implications for full employment, and what might be an acceptable "natural" rate of unemployment, taking into account new forms of work organization, such as the "Shamrock Organization" and the "Hollywood Model".

The current changing environment for work and employment calls for the development of a new paradigm for industrial relations, based on increased participation and sharing on the part of employees in their companies, covering consultation in decision making, and new ways of participating in the profitability, and possibly the ownership, of those companies. In this way the basis of the employer/employee relationship becomes one of cooperation between the two parties, who are both stakeholders in the economic value of the business enterprises in which they work.

7.2   Capital Versus Labour

In recent years the age-old struggle between capital and labour has resurfaced again. In an article by Leo Panitch and Sam Gindin published in the *Guardian* (January 2013) entitled "The New American Paradox: Capital v Labour" it was argued that corporations and banks are sitting on their cash while workers suffer. This theme was also taken up by the economist and Nobel Prize winner, Paul Krugman, when, in commenting about low levels of investment in the USA, he raised the question of why it is that high unemployment lingers even though corporate profits are improving. Is it because corporations with more cash are investing in new technology rather than people? As he put it, "The old-fashioned, almost Marxist discussion about capital versus labour seems to be reviving." According to the argument advanced by Panitch and Gindin in their article, the roots of all this in the USA date back to the political response to the labour militancy and profit squeeze of the 1970s, and the Federal Reserve's determination, under the leadership of the chairman Paul Volcker, to break wage-push inflation, which was achieved by setting high interest rates and the ensuing unemployment, the opposite of what the Fed's subsequent commitment to low interest rates was intended to achieve. So we must ask: Where does this leave labour in the debate about the desirability of high or low interest rates? The antagonistic nature of the contest between capital and labour was confirmed by Volcker's recognition that what did "even more to break the morale of labour" was Reagan's dismissal of the air traffic controllers and the decertification of their union in 1981. Subsequent policies to liberalize trade, deregulate financial services, and capital flows, and the economic restructuring which followed weakened the trade unions, whose membership in US manufacturing declined from 7.5 million in 1983 to 1.5 million in 2007. Many welcomed the breaking of what some had labelled union monopoly power, but it has done nothing to resolve the problem of increasing inequality in incomes.

The IMF survey *Rise of Inequality at Center of Economic Crisis*, published in June 2012, demonstrated that this inequality had gone so far as to undermine demand (further exacerbated by austerity policies), which is why corporations are currently unwilling to invest. These considerations require new economic thinking in finding ways in which the conflicts regarding employment and wage levels between capital and labour can be reduced. The anti-union animus, which perhaps reached one of its most acrimonious points during the UK miners' strike in 1984/1985, still exists, and was given fresh expression in an article by Leo McKinstry (*The Spectator*, July 2015), which asserted that trade unions have ceased to serve working people, and that it was time to act against them, and, to borrow from Thatcherite terminology, to put the unions "in their place". How does one draw a line under this rant and rave debate? The end of the miners' strike in the UK was seen as a victory for Thatcherism (characterized by policies of monetary discipline and low inflation) in restructuring the coal mining industry, which declined from a figure of 174 mines in 1983 to just six in 2009, although it should be noted that the demand for coal in 2013 was 60 million tons, 50 million of which were imported. Such figures show the complexity of industrial restructuring and productive competitiveness in a traditional industry, and the challenge for unions to become a proactive force, rather than an obstacle, for economic change.

We also need a new initiative on the part of the unions themselves to raise the quality of the debate. This could start by taking this debate beyond the job/pay objectives of union representation (which will always remain the bedrock of the unions' mission), into advocating greater worker participation in joint consultation decision making, covering economic education, investment and participation in profits and ownership on the part of employees. This is a plea not for state ownership, but rather for a greater participation on the part of the workforce in sharing the economic value of an enterprise through profit sharing and share ownership, using possibly non-tradeable or deferred shares to increase the participation of employees in the equity of the business enterprises for whom they work. Such developments could open up a new role for unions in contributing to the organizational procedures for employee cooperation, and the sharing of information. They will still have their role of ensuring that the externality of the employment relationship is protected by agreements which protect both the short- and the long-term interests of their members, but these interests today involve deciding how jobs and skills are going to change as a result of technological innovation and new scenarios for the "Future of Work". Such an enhanced role for unions could help them to overcome the "luddite" mentality of the past, which has at times characterized union behavior, as, for example, in the famous Fleet Street printers' union dispute in the UK regarding the move towards the adoption of digital methods such as desktop publishing.

And last, but not least a more proactive role for union representation could involve unions in the fundamental question not only of how to increase productivity, but also how employees could participate financially in the increased profitability which arises from improvements in productivity. This is a highly topical subject for industrial relations as recent research has shown in the USA that worker compensation is lagging behind productivity improvements. See "The Compensation Productivity Gap" by Fleck, Glaser and Sprague (*Monthly Labour Review*, June 2011) and "Why the gap between workers' pay and productivity is so problematic" by Gillian White (*Atlantic Business*, February 2015).

7.3 Employee Representation and Participation

Trade unionism has been the traditional mechanism for representing the interests of employees, but in recent decades declining membership indicates that unions are losing the confidence of their members in protecting existing jobs, or assisting in the creation of new or alternative jobs arising from technological change. The result of advancing technology had been highlighted by the economist Robert Solow as long ago as 1956 when he stated that "Economists have lots of different theories about how long-term growth and prosperity come about, but nearly all of them agree that technological progress plays a significant role." Union concentration has always focused primarily on the creation and protection of jobs, and on the securing of fair relative wage levels through collective bargaining. But if jobs and pay will always remain key priorities for employees, there are also other interests which need to be taken into account in achieving the full representation of their interests, including benefits, the changing nature of work, training, economic education, consultation and partici-pation in decision making, and in the profits (the cooperators' surplus), and, possibly, in ownership.

In his *Employment with a Human Face: Balancing Efficiency, Equity and Voice*, John Budd argues that the employment relationship is not purely economic, with business wanting increased efficiency and work-ers higher incomes, and that notions of equity and voice should be seen as equally important. He defines equity as the entitlement to fair treatment, but the term could also be extended to participation in the equity of a firm. "Voice" is related to inputs into decisions, which is the same as the idea of consultation mentioned above. Efficiency, equity and voice could become the keywords for a wider concept of indus-trial relations. So, when talking about the issues of representation and participation for employees we need to consider them in the light of the principles of efficiency, equity and voice, each of which have ethi-cal implications for fairness, honesty and transparency in the systems for representing the interests of employees, which will enable them to participate actively—rather than passively—in a business enterprise. All of this calls for new economic thinking regarding employee representa-tion and participation in business enterprises which respond fully to the interests and needs of employees as stakeholders in those enterprises. The concept of employees as stakeholders in an enterprise is essential for emphasizing the participative nature of the employee/employer rela-tionship, and the need for union representation to become a proactive mechanism for facilitating cooperation and innovation, for the creation of new job opportunities in the workplace, and how employees are to share in the economic value resulting from the work they do.

7.4   The Future of Work

What is the future of work going to look like in terms of the jobs available and the skills required to perform them? In his book the *Future of Work*, discussing work and life in a post-industrial society, Domenico de Masi refers to a paper written in 1930 by Keynes entitled "Economic Possibilities for Our Grandchildren" which has some observations that are particularly apposite today.

> At this time, we are affected by a serious attack of economic pessimism which I believe is seriously erroneous in the face of what is actually happening. What we are suffering from are not the pains of old age, but from the disturbances of a growth consisting of changes too rapid to avoid the adjustment pains arising from passing from one economic era to another. Technical efficiency is intensifying at a pace too rapid for us to solve the problem of how to absorb the existing work force. In the space of very few years, I mean our lifetime, we shall be able to perform all the operations of agriculture, mining and manufacturing with a quarter of the human energy we have been used to so far. The pace of change is faster than that which we require for finding new ways of re-employing an existing workforce. But this is only a transitory phase of disequilibrium. Seen in the right context this means that humanity is proceeding to identify solutions for its economic problems. Will this be a good thing? If we only believe a little in the values of life, it will open up possibilities that it will become a 'good thing.' In a period of organizational change, during which work will diminish drastically without completely disappearing, we shall need to redistribute what work remains, so that everyone can be employed for a minimum amount of time.

As Keynes goes on to say, "We need to operate in a way which distributes what remains among as many people as possible. Three hour shifts for a total of fifteen hours a week could tackle the problem for a good period of time. Three work hours a day are more than sufficient to satisfy the old Adam which exists in all of us." The idea of a three-hour working day flies in the face of traditional employment wisdom, of course, but the very "shocking" nature of such a proposal might help us to take a new look at employment outside the straitjacket of the eight-hour day.

In the USA since its inception in 1994 the Russell Sage Foundation (RSF) has been looking at the future of work through various programmes that have examined the causes and consequences of the long-term deterioration in the availability and quality of jobs in the lower tiers of the US labour market. The RSF conducted studies to assess the evidence that a number of factors had put downward pressure on the wages of poorly educated workers, including foreign outsourcing, immigration, the decline of unions, deregulation and technological change. Other research looked at the skills required in the modern economy, and at how the increasing computerization of the economy might change these skills in future. In 2003 the RSF published *Low-Wage America: How Employers are Reshaping Opportunity in the Workplace*. Case studies revealed that in responding to economic pressures firms had sought to hold the line by freezing wages, cutting benefits, and reorganizing production. Where unions were weak, minimum wages were low, there were large numbers of workers with limited education, and low-wage work was widespread; where unions were stronger it made it more difficult for firms to compete by reducing wages and job quality. Among the other ways identified for responding to negative economic conditions were investment in training and capital to increase productivity. Further studies included an analysis of five low-wage jobs in five European countries, as in the USA, covering call centre operators, food processing workers, nursing assistants, retail clerks and hotel housekeepers.

Further study of the future of work was collected together in the book *Low-Wage Work in a Wealthy World*, which showed that the incidence of low wages ranges widely between countries—from a low of 8 percent in Denmark to around 25 percent in the USA—and that these differences are influenced by the "inclusiveness" of each country's industrial relations system, including collective bargaining agreements and minimum wage laws, and the level of social benefits, such as health insurance, pensions, family leave, and paid holidays. In terms of looking at the future of work, RSF has also looked at a growing segment of the low-wage sector, covering activities such as care of children, the elderly and the disabled, and also home-based health care. Care work is moving increasingly from the family to the market, entailing a mix between family, public provision and private, including voluntary assistance. Care in this sense represents another opportunity for new jobs in the future, which involve other tertiary sectors such as culture and the growing demand for tourism covering museums, art galleries, theatres, concert halls, festivals, exhibitions and guided tours, many of which fall into the category of low-wage jobs, which are still not regarded as being "productive" in the same way as it is attributed to the factory shopfloor. New economic thinking needs to study how the future tertiary "service" sector will be structured, and its cost/investment profile in providing services to its customers, which at the same time, like culture, produce induced economic benefits for firms which supply this tertiary sector with products, transport and accommodation facilities.

7.5   The Chimera of Full Employment

It is not our intention here to enter into all the details of full employment theory; rather, we shall restrict ourselves to considering some of the issues with which businessmen have to grapple in providing employment in an environment which is seeing changes in the nature of jobs and work, and where the levels of unemployment vary significantly from one economy to another. Neither do we enter into a full discussion about the trade-off between employment and inflation with which the theory of NAIRU (the Non-accelerating inflation rate of unemployment) is involved, but any such study needs also to examine the Friedmanite concept of "natural" employment, and the Keynesian concept that raising aggregate product demand will increase the aggregate demand for workers. Full discussion of these issues can be found in Wikipedia's entry on "Full Employment".

It is the nature of employment to go hand in hand with unemployment, produced by structural unemployment, arising from technological and globalization changes, and frictional unemployment, arising from individual decisions moving from one job to another in search of better employment. The result is that 100 percent full employment is unachievable, which poses the problem of how to define what are acceptable levels of unemployment or not.

An ILO report estimated that worldwide 200 million people are unemployed, representing about 6 percent of the total workforce. So, is 6 percent an acceptable metric for measuring the level of unemployment? Probably not, because there are wide discrepancies between economies, and also between categories of employee, particularly in terms of age. Eurostat estimates that in March 2015 nearly 24 million men and women were unemployed in the 28 European countries, of whom just over 18 million were in the euro area. The *seasonally adjusted* unemployment rate for the euro area was 11.3 percent in March 2015, stable compared with February 2015, but down from 11.7 percent in March 2014. Among the Member States, the lowest unemployment rates in March 2015 were recorded in Germany (4.7 percent), and the highest in Greece (25.7 percent in January 2015) and Spain (23.0 percent). This compares with an unemployment rate in the United States of 5.5 percent, the same as in February 2015 and down from 6.6 percent in March 2014. In March 2015, nearly five million young people (under 25) were unemployed in the European Union, of whom 3.2 million were in the euro area, with percentage rates varying from 7.2 percent in Germany, 10.5 percent in Austria, and 10.8 percent in Denmark and the Netherlands, to 50 percent in Greece and Spain, 45 percent in Croatia, and 43 percent in Italy. These widely varying rates emphasize the extent of unemployment in the European Union and the difficulty in reducing unacceptable levels of unemployment.

What should the target unemployment rate? After the Second World War, Beveridge proposed that the rate should be 3 percent, but the OECD talks in terms of a range of 4–6 percent. A 6 percent rate as a measure of unemployment may be an acceptable measure for Germany or the United States, but how is one to achieve this target in a country such as Italy, where the figure for total unemployment—at nearly 12 percent—is twice the 6 percent metric (and the figure for young people (43 percent) is around seven times this rate). What are the reasons for this in a country where per capita income has declined since the 1990s, and industrial production by nearly 25 percent over the past ten years?

The main reason has been a decline in productivity following the introduction of the euro which has removed the option of currency devaluation as a means for regaining competitiveness. There are, however, wide differences between economic sectors which calls for the promotion of microeconomic policies which will support those sectors which are creating economic value, or which have the potential to do so. Such policies must also control the level of national debt within acceptable levels of the cost of public debt, which needs to be structured in a way which differentiates between debt for economic investment, and debt for the financing of public services and administration. It is a complex task to achieve acceptable levels of "full" employment when taking into account the factors of frictional and structural unemployment.

Solutions are closely linked to price competitiveness which is linked inseparably to labour costs, including social security costs, which in Italy, for example, amount to about 55 percent of gross salary, compared with an average of 27 percent in the European Union. The UHY International, a network of independent accountants and consultants, produce statistics on this relationship, which demonstrate the substantial difference in social security costs between one country and another. Another factor which influences the creation of employment is how companies finance themselves, particularly the small business sector, which in Italy is heavily dependent on bank as opposed to equity finance, where it is estimated that 52 percent of small businesses resort to bank finance compared to about 5 percent in the USA.

How can access to cheaper finance be created? New ways are starting to emerge, for example the creation of investment funds for small businesses businesses, and project bonds for specific investment and development projects where bond holders might also be employees. Employment costs are part of a company's investment in its future, and we need to move towards the concept of seeing employment as investment, and not simply as a cost. This means taking a new look at linking pay to increases in productivity and the investment in technological innovation and research. In this sense productivity needs to become a key national and sectoral measure of economic efficiency, which requires the accurate reporting of how much an economy is investing in productivity, which distinguishes productivity by economic sector, and compares it with other countries.

In looking at ways to reduce unemployment, we also need to consider the question of disguised unemployment which arises as a result of a number of factors, including both overqualification (that is, people doing jobs for which they are overqualified, such as a taxi driver possessing a university degree) and outsourcing (taking work away from an established labour force); and of overstaffing (labour hoarding of more people than is strictly necessary). (See Dooley and Prause, *The Social Costs of Underemployment: Inadequate Employment Disguised as Unemployment* (2004).)

This situation has an interface with the ways in which traditional jobs are changing, which has been labelled the "Shamrock Organization", where a workforce is reduced to a number of core workers feeding the outsourcing of work, and the employment of temporary workers for meeting seasonal production requirements. These changes also reflect the move towards the greater flexibility of work, where work sharing can increase levels of employment, albeit resulting in a reduction in the income per employee. The "precariousness" factor, whereby workers are subject to the lack of guaranteed employment provided by full-time contracts without a specified time horizon, has been tackled in Italy by the passage of the recent Jobs Act, which sets a time for converting short-term "precarious" work into full-time contracts, but also makes it simpler for employers to shed labour in times of economic downturn, bringing Italian labour practices more into line with practices in more efficient economies such as Germany. Unemployment guarantees remain a contentious industrial relations issue, but the damage to the employee in the event of job losses is now covered by statutory unemployment benefits, which can also be supplemented by specific unemployment insurance. This requires some new thinking on the part of both employers and unions on how to manage this kind of risk within the context of greater employee participation in a business enterprise argued for in this chapter.

Finally, it can be helpful to consider work and employment in the way we manage employment and job creation as suggested by the OECD guidelines for jobs covering national macroeconomic policies (public investment, inflation and aggregate demand management); the diffusion of technological know-how; work flexibility; entrepreneurial capacity; wage and labour cost structure; unemployment benefits; technical training; the identification of skills and competencies; and pension provision. Such an approach covers all aspects of employment management, which, in times of economic crisis, requires the management of unemployment in the form of temporary or permanent "laying off" of personnel. The direct costs of unemployment are covered by state social security systems, which need to be managed and controlled as part of total social security costs financed by the State, including contributory pensions. The Economic and Social Research Council in the UK has calculated that total annual benefits for unemployed people amount to about £5 billion, about 2.5 percent of total social security. Public awareness of these "social costs" of doing business needs to become part of social accounting and reporting in the Social Balance Sheet where all employees can understand the composition of all employment benefits, both direct and indirect, including unemployment benefits when applicable, provided by the company and the State through the company's social contributions, which contribute to the creation of economic value (EVA), and how much of it can be distributed to employees as stakeholders in their enterprise.

7.6   Changing Work Models

If the future of work and its related employment opportunities are likely to be determined by changes in the organization of work, in consumer preferences, and the globalization of markets, we are going to require some radical rethinking about the future nature of work and employment.

More than two decades ago Charles Handy, in his book *The Empty Raincoat*, alerted us to likely changes in the future shape of work organization and employment. More and more we shall see organizations divide their work into project teams, task-forces, small business units, clusters and work groups. These groups will change shape and membership as the needs of the organization change. Individuals may well work for more than one group at the same time, with one group having an operational responsibility, another an advisory role, a third having a temporary project assignment. Organizations are no longer guaranteeing to provide planned careers but are offering "career opportunities." And, more recently, we have been introduced to the "Hollywood Model", in which a project is identified; a team is assembled; it works together precisely as long as needed to complete the task; then the team disbands. This short-term, project-based business structure is an alternative to the corporate model, in which capital is spent up front to build up a business, which then hires workers for long-term, open-ended jobs that can last for years, even a lifetime. It is also distinct from the Uber-style "gig economy", which is designed to take account of extremely short-term tasks, manageable by one person in less than one day".

The results of these changes mean that work is probably going to be increasingly structured around short-term project-based teams, rather than the long-term, open-ended jobs that characterized the past. This new economic reality raises important issues regarding fixed-term employment, and short-term, part-time employment. How are the two to be reconciled? The solutions will require new economic thinking regarding not only the time span of jobs, but also the way they are compensated, including a new look at fixed and variable pay systems. Employees are understandably concerned about the "precariousness" of employment, and look for some degree of long-term security. We might look at the introduction of employment credits for employees who have part-time, or limited-time jobs to protect their pension rights when they are experiencing "out of work", so that they do not lose the time necessary to acquire pension rights. We need to find incentives for the flexibility inherent in shorter- or fixed-term employment which are acceptable to both employee and employer. It will require management and unions to break out of the straitjacket of permanent employment as the sole criterion for jobs, in order to investigate ways of reducing unemployment through greater flexibility and work sharing for young employees. We have already discussed the possibility of employees participating in profits, and the role of unions in taking a wider view of compensation, which goes beyond fixed rates for the job and in to the area of variable rates of pay linked to productivity and profitability.

We need a new paradigm for work and employment that can incorporate management, employees, and unions, where the keywords for these stakeholders are cooperation, participation and sharing, in the creation of economic value for the companies in which they work, and in deciding how the "cooperators' surplus" can be distributed equitably between them. An essential starting point for putting these things into practical effect will be a programme of economic education to improve the economic literacy and the informed decision-making capacity of management, employees and their representatives.

References

Appelbaum E, Bernhardt A, Murname R, editors. Low wage America: how employers are reshaping opportunity in the work place. New York: Russell Sage; 2003.

Adam Davidson, "Hollywood as Model for Economy", INYT, 9 May 2015.

Budd J. Employment with a human face. Hum Resource Manag. 2005;44(1):109–11. ILR Press, Ithaca, NY.

Dooley D, Prause J. The social costs of underemployment. Inadequate Employment Disguised as Unemployed. Cambridge: Cambridge University Press; 2004.

Dufty NF. Organizational growth and goal structure: the case of the ILO. Int Org. 1972;26(3):479–98.

Fleck S, Glaser J, Sprague S. The compensation-productivity gap: a visual essay. Mon Labor Rev. 2011;January:57–69.

Gillian While, Why the gap between worker's pay and productivity is so problematic, Atlantic Business, February 2015.

Handy C. The age of unreason. Boston, MA: Harvard Business School Press; 1990.

Healy S. Cooperation, surplus appropriate, and the law's enjoyment. Rethinking Marxism J Econ Cult Soc. 2011;23(3):364–73.

IMF Survey Online. Rise of inequality at Center of Global Economic Crisis. International Monetary Fund, 14 June 2012. http://www.imf.org/external/pubs/ft/survey/so/2012/int061412a.htm.

Keynes JM. Economic possibilities for our grandchildren. In: Pecchi L, Piga G, editors. Revisiting keynes: economic possibilities for our grandchildren. Cambridge, MA: Massachusetts Institute of Technology; 1930 (2008).

Kowalski R. Free agents and the Hollywood model. Center for the Study of the Workplace, 22 Feb 2012. http://www.studyofwork.com/2012/02/free-agents-and-the-hollywood-model/.

Mazzucato M. The entrepreneurial state: debunking public vs. private sector myths. London: Anthem; 2013.

Panitch L, Gindin S. The new American paradox: capital v labour. The Guardian, 4 Jan 2013. http://www.theguardian.com/commentisfree/2013/jan/04/us-balance-labour-capital.

The Economist. Labour pains: all around the world, labour is losing out to capital, 2 Nov 2013. http://www.economist.com/news/finance-and-economics/21588900-all-around-world-labour-losing-out-capital-labour-pains.

Tortora J. Are unions useful anymore? AFL-CIO, 22 Oct 2015. http://www.
aflcio.org/Blog/Organizing-Bargaining/Are-Unions-Useful-Anymore2.

Trumka R. Future of unions: new models of worker representation. AFL-CIO,
3 July 2013. http://www.aflcio.org/Blog/Organizing-Bargaining/Future-
of-Unions-New-Models-of-Worker-Representation.

8

Economic Value and Intrinsic Value

Abstract We need to differentiate between monetary wealth and the value it is creating, which takes account of the way we establish value not only for shareholders but for all stakeholders in an economic enterprise. Economic value, which is a component of the intrinsic value of a business, is one of the first metrics for value investing and value-based management, and for validating the target share prices which investment analysts recommend. The chapter looks at the various dimensions of value, and poses some questions which businesses, professional advisors, and regulators need to answer and agree, if economic value reporting is to become a basic metric for measuring the creation of corporate value, the future sustainability of a business, and how people are paid for creating economic value.

8.1 Chapter Overview

What do we mean by "value" in economic affairs, and what distinguishes it from the creation of "monetary wealth"? How should we distinguish between the various dimensions of value, that is, economic value, market

© The Editor(s) (if applicable) and The Author(s) 2016   **143**
M.R. Griffiths, J.R. Lucas, *Value Economics*,
DOI 10.1057/978-1-137-54187-1_8

value, shareholder value, net asset value, intangible assets value, embedded value, intrinsic value, and social (human welfare) value, and report on and monitor these values? We define economic value as NOPAT less cost of capital, and propose that it becomes the first metric for valuing a company, and the starting point for calculating intrinsic value in terms of the other dimensions of value (defined in Sect. 8.5), which are used by investment analysts to set target market share prices. Defined in this way, economic value links with the simpler measures of value, such as net asset value, and free cash flow, which, alongside profitability, are practical measures used in the day-to-day management of a business, and for setting key performance indicators (KPI).

Economic value provides the basis for calculating intrinsic value, which is a more complex and less definitive measure of value, but which remains an essential measure for the investment analyst, as Warren Buffett describes its importance: "Intrinsic value is an all-important concept that offers the only logical approach to evaluating the relative attractiveness of investments and businesses. Intrinsic value can be defined simply: It is the discounted value of the cash that can be taken out of a business during its remaining life" (Warren Buffett Annual Report, 2014. pp. 107–108). The goal is to identify a stock with intrinsic value that exceeds its current market value.

We need to consider value in terms of the time horizons involved in economic activity and to distinguish between the short term and the long term, and how we price financial products in terms of present and future earnings. The concept of "value investing" needs to take account not only of the price/earnings (P/E) ratio, but also of the intrinsic value of the company in which an investment is being made. If we agree how to define the various components of value, we can start to design systems for "value-based management", and the related compensation systems for rewarding the creation of short- and long-term value. These systems have implications for the way in which we report on and control economic value, and raise a number of questions that are discussed at the end of the chapter, the answers to which will require inputs from business, and the "Accountability" professions of chartered accounting, actuaries, lawyers, and chartered analysts, in proposing standards on which the regulatory control of economic value can be based. There are also implications for new economic thinking on the part of economic, university and business institutions and the way that thinking relates to economic justice and to the creation of economic value in terms of "Triple Bottom Line Accounting."

The chapter also includes the perspective of an investment analyst on the question of intrinsic value and its use for market stock pricing.

8.2   Components of Economic Value

This chapter looks at the creation of wealth and the economic value that monetary wealth is creating. The problem in talking about economic value is to distinguish between the different ways in which we can put a value on the worth of economic activities. It can be misleading to talk of value solely in terms of monetary wealth, and we need to relate economic value not only to shareholder value, but also to stakeholder value in general.

How are we to define "monetary value"? What is the monetary "value" of a business or a non-profit enterprise? What is the monetary "value" of a stock or a share, and other financial products, such as derivatives? What is the monetary "value" of a research and development department? What is the monetary "value" of a hospital or educational institution? And so on. To answer these questions we need to put a value on the "worth" of what we are doing economically (whether the enterprise is for profit or non-profit, private or public), in terms of the various dimensions of value we discuss in Sect. 8.5. We start first by looking at how we put a worth on something, and how this is related to the creation of wealth.

8.3   Concept of Worth

How do we put a worth on what we do? A comprehensive discussion will take us into the philosophical study of value, or axiology (deriving from the Greek word "axia", meaning both value and worth), which is related to the values people have and the worth they put on things. In Greek philosophy these values covered both ethics (right or good conduct), and aesthetics (beauty and harmony), and the principles on which they are based, for example, justice, which Plato discussed in the *Republic* in examining what we mean by justice both in the individual and in the State. Although economics is not always directly concerned with these philosophical concepts, there are cogent normative reasons why economists need to take account of them when analysing how markets work in terms of consumer preferences, and the underlying human behaviour. Markets are shaped by the way people value economic things, which raises the questions of why, how, and to what degree people put a worth on things, whether it be a new suit, a financial investment, a sporting event, family health and education, a work of art, or the performance of a Shakespeare play.

Adam Smith, in his book *Of the Origin and Use of Money*, introduced the concept of distinguishing between the value of use, and the value of exchange, which takes us into the paradox of value, and questions such as why, for example, water, which is much more useful than diamonds, has much less value in terms of exchange value than diamonds. This poses a basic problem for economics when it seeks to answer the question "What is the price someone is willing and able to pay for a specific good or service?" We shall return to this question later in this chapter in considering how markets price things, whether they be stocks and shares, property or a Van Gogh painting of sunflowers. How much something is worth is a daily concern for economics, whether it be an insurance underwriter putting a value on a human life, a property developer in Hong Kong, a Christie's art auctioneer, or a housewife deciding between different cuts of meat at the butcher's.

8.4   Creation of Wealth

In any discussion about wealth and how it is created, we talk about it primarily in terms of its monetary value. We talk often about wealth in monetary terms, but less about the way we put a value on that wealth. A first question is to look at how wealth is created. In *The Origin of Wealth*, Eric Beinhocker proposes new ways of looking at how wealth is created, and how it may be created in future. He advances the notion of what he calls Complexity Economics in terms of the basic tenet that economics is a dynamic evolutionary process, which highlights the fact that economics is also an indeterminate process, where the key to success in creating wealth is to manage flexible systems, which are in a state of continuous evolution where business has to decide how to realize (or actualize) its potential for creating wealth.

Drawing on the theory of thermodynamics Beinhocker sees business organizations as carrying out irreversible transformations of matter (production), energy (the power to produce) and information (the feed-in and feed-back mechanisms we need to operate a business). This transformation process, implicit in the creation of wealth, requires us to convert high entropy inputs (the inherent nature of systems and organisms to decline unless renewed) into lower entropy inputs (systems which manage the risk of decay and decline in business organizations), where innovation and productivity are key inputs for growth and the creation of wealth. In other words, we reaffirm the essential homeostatic nature of business, which, like any human organism, has to be self-adapting, if it is to realize its potential to grow and to survive. Without wishing to over-complicate business organizational theory, we need to see the creation of wealth as an indeterminate and evolutionary process of growth and decay (the entropy principle), where renewal is the key to future sustainability.

In his chapter on the implication of Complexity Economics for finance, and the ways we price assets (monetary wealth) and the cost of capital, Beinhocker makes the important point that "price does not equal value", although he does believe that the market is the most efficient way to price assets. However, his innovative analysis of the way we create wealth and value needs to be completed by distinguishing between wealth and value to avoid confusing the two different things. Wealth is a concrete measurable thing relative to a unit of currency (money). Value, by contrast, is the worth we put on the use to which that money is put in allocating economic resources. We need to avoid the danger of defining wealth solely in monetary terms and to extend its definition also to the value which it is creating. This requires an analysis of how we measure value, and distinguish between the different dimensions of that value discussed in the next section.

8.5   Defining Value

The vocabulary of economic value has become increasingly diverse as we have moved into the world of embedded value, intrinsic value, fair value, and market-consistent embedded value (MCEV), all of which build on the simpler definitions of value in terms of profitability, earnings and cash flow. All of these concepts of value derive from the starting point of "economic value" which we define as NOPAT less cost of capital, as a basic measure of value deriving from an economic enterprise (whether for profit or non-profit). In considering the multivarious nature of value it can be helpful to start from the cash value of any business measured in terms of its cash flow, which provides a bird's-eye view of how its financial resources are being generated and spent, and then to move on to the other dimensions of value described below. Economic Value, as defined above, can then be "filled out",[1] as it relates to other dimensions of value, whether economic, social or environmental. As a starting point, economic value—defined as NOPAT less cost of capital (which Apple calls "Economic Profit")—is a measure which adjusts operating profits to take account of the cost of capital. However, it is a statement of value at one point in time, without taking into account the discounted value of future profits (DCF). Therefore, in this sense economic value is an incomplete statement of value, which needs to be "filled out" in consideration of other value measures, such as intrinsic value. But it has the advantage of being a simpler and more immediate measure than other more complex measures of value like MCEV, even if the cost of capital is not necessarily a simple calculation.

Dimensions of Value

– *Cash flow value*: generation and use of funds, which can be extended to free cash flow to identify resources available for distribution after cash needs for running the business.
– *Accounting or economic profit*: profitability gross and net.
– *Net asset value (NAV)*: the remaining surplus after accounting for all liabilities (*Book Value*). Return on net assets (RONA) divides net operating profit after tax (NOPAT) by the fixed assets plus working capital.
– *Economic value added (EVA)*: value created in excess of the return required by the investors is a measure of a company's performance based on the residual wealth after deducting the cost of capital from net profit after taxes, which is also referred to as economic profit.

---

[1] As we move into further refinements for defining value, such as Return on Risk Adjusted Capital (RORAC) and its variation Risk Adjusted Return on Capital (RAROC), and then Risk Adjusted Return on Risk Adjusted Capital (RARORAC), it becomes more important to have a common starting point which NOPAT less COC can provide as the basic metric of economic value (EV).

– *Value at risk (VAR)*: threshold value of how much a mark to market loss in the portfolio might impinge on this value (assuming normal market conditions and no trading in the portfolio).

– *Distributable earnings value*: funds available for the remuneration of capital. Earnings per share (EPS) is a basic measure for establishing shareholder value but, as Terry Smith says in an *Financial Times* article, "Shareholder value is an outcome not an objective", EPS takes no account of the capital required to generate shareholder value, or the required return on that capital.

– *EBITAD value*: earnings before interest, taxes, amortization and depreciation, variations of which can be EBIT or EBT, a measure of operating efficiency and productivity.

– *Share price value*: mark to market value based on the P/E ratio. Used as the basis for defining stock option compensation systems and when those options can be realized. As a metric for measuring management performance, it may not reflect the intrinsic value of the enterprise.

– *Shareholder value (SV)*: the measure of the return on the equity invested (ROE), which also takes account of dividends and capital appreciation of the share price, at the same as measuring the net cash flow profits as a percent of capital employed (ROCE) in terms of equity and net debt (see Terry Smith, what exactly do we mean by shareholder value? Ficbm 2015).

We need to decide how we relate shareholder value to stakeholder value (enterprise value), in general, and the more recent concepts of sustainability value (see below).

The cost of capital (COC) requires the calculation of a company's funds, both debt and equity, which reflects the minimum rate of return required above the risk-free rate, required by the providers of debt and equity capital, to calculate the company's weighted average cost of capital (WACC), covering the costs of debt, preference and equity capital. In determining the cost of capital required for creating shareholder value, the cost of debt is relatively simple to calculate as it consists of the interest paid. The cost of equity is more complex as it is broadly defined as the risk-weighted projected return required by investors, where the actual rate of return is an unknown. It is commonly calculated using the capital asset pricing model (CAPM), but in a globalized market environment CAPM needs to be international rather than local—a factor which increases the difficulty of calculating the cost of capital necessary for defining share-holder value.

- *Market capitalization*: the total value of the issued shares of a publicly traded company calculated by multiplying the share price by the number of shares outstanding.
- *Sustainability value*: a comparatively recent addition to the vocabulary of value which measures "sustainability" performance in terms of the value created by the use of the three "triple bottom line" (TBL) resources (economic, environmental and social) on which the future sustainability of a business depends. See, among other examples, the example of BP's calculation of sustainable value; DuPont's "clean technology" strategy to improve industrial efficiency and cost effectiveness; and the Dow Jones Sustainability Index (DJSI) for measuring the performance of leading companies in terms of economic, environmental and social resources.
- *Enterprise value*: equity value plus creditors and preferred stock. More comprehensive than market capitalization, which only includes common equity.
- *Embedded value*: the discounted value of future profits from existing business.
- *Intrinsic value*: NAV plus embedded value (value of existing business), plus the value of new business production or services, and new ventures, including acquisitions.

There is debate on how intrinsic value should be defined and used compared to simpler measures of value such as cash flow and NAV, but as a value "investor", like Warren Buffett says, "intrinsic value is an all-important concept that offers the only logical approach to evaluating the relative attractiveness of investments and businesses. Intrinsic value can be defined: simply: it is the discounted value of the cash that can be taken out of a business during its remaining life" (Buffett Annual Report, 2014). But he sees it as "an estimate rather than a precise figure to be changed if interest rates move or forecasts of future cash flows are revised. "That is one reason we never give you our estimates of intrinsic value. But we supply the facts we use to calculate this value, regularly reporting our per-share book value, an easily calculable number though one of limited use" (Berkshire Hathaway 2014 Annual Report).

Investment analysts are concerned with setting share target prices, and in this sense are dealing with the "intrinsic value" of a stock, when using the various methodologies for calculating value, covering the Dividend Discount Model (DDM), the Residual Income Model and Discounted Cash Flow (DCF). These methodologies enable the calculation of a target share price (its intrinsic value) allowing the share to be categorized as being over- or undervalued. The "target value" approach can also assist the process of linking market share prices to economic value targets for value-based management, and setting management performance objectives.[2]

- *Fair value*: value which takes into account factors which mark to market value may not have fully recognized, that is, embedded and intrinsic value. The IFRS standard defines fair value on the basis of an "exit price" notion which results in a market-based, rather than a business-specific, measurement of value, which may be different from net asset value (NAV) and market price value of an economic enterprise
- *Intangible assets value*: this dimension of value covers an enterprise's reputation and its investment in know-how, branding, patents, innovation, research and development, economic education and employee professional development. This value, in the absence of projected profit flows deriving from these assets, can be related to the investment in these activities the benefits of which will be demonstrated in the long term, and monitored as a percentage of total assets (tangible and intangible).

---

[2] Concept of intrinsic value: In finance intrinsic value refers to the value of a company, stock, currency or product determined through fundamental analysis without reference to its market value. It is also frequently called fundamental value. It is ordinarily calculated by summing the discounted future income generated by the asset to obtain the present value. It is important to note that intrinsic value has different meanings for different assets—that is, economic, environmental and social. It is contrasted with instrumental value (or extrinsic value), the value of which depends on how much it generates intrinsic value. Human welfare has intrinsic value, while a business may not have intrinsic value as an end in itself, but does have an instrumental value, since it contributes to human welfare.

The term intrinsic value was first used by John Ruskin in his book *The Maintenance of Life* (1860) where he defines it as "the absolute power to support life. A sheaf of wheat of given quality and weight has in it a measurable power of sustaining the substance of the body; a cubic foot of pure air, a fixed power of sustaining its warmth; and a cluster of flowers of given beauty, a fixed power of enlivening or animating the senses and heart. It does not in the least affect the intrinsic value of the wheat, the air, or the flowers, that men refuse or despise them. Used or not, their own power is in them, and that particular power is in nothing else."

– *Social value*: the least quantified value in terms of economic analysis and business thinking. For business the starting point can be the fiscal contribution an enterprise makes to society. Tax value is an essential part of economic value often just regarded as "burden based", but, nevertheless, an essential part of social economic value, which makes the case for economic value to be clearly expressed both before and after taxation. The other aspects of social value, apart from the essential "social values" of employment and customer demand satisfaction, regard a business's contribution to environmental protection and conservation, which focuses on the cost structure and environmental performance of a company in relation to the possible liabilities arising from pollution and operational risks.

These value-related considerations have led to the publication of sustainability reports (see examples from Shell, British Petroleum, Vodafone, and Weyerhaeuser, among others) arising from the UN Division for Sustainable Development, and the guidelines contained in the Global Reporting Initiative (GRI) aspects such as ecological footprint reporting, and "Triple Bottom Line Accounting" (TBL)[3].

---

[3] Calculation of social value (human welfare): But there is another aspect of economic value which concerns the value of non-profit enterprises operating in the area of public social services for health, education, law and order, and the infrastructure of logistics and transportation. Apart from the investment in providing these services, it is more difficult to put an economic "value" on these services which are vital for the efficiency of the private sector of an economy. The original ancient Greek word for economy was "oikonomia", meaning management of a household, seen as the basic unit of economic activity which remains so today, even if we need to recognize the diverse nature of economic units, which cover individuals, families, firms, associations and communities. A move towards defining social value in terms of these economic units, which include both profit and non-profit enterprises, has been made by the development of the Human Development Index, which seeks to define how successful economies are in satisfying the welfare needs and aspirations of their citizens. Attempts are also being made to measure human happiness in terms of "eudaimonia" (happiness) originally discussed in Aristotle's *Nicomachean Ethics* where the word also has the connotation of "human welfare".

How do we put a monetary "value" on human welfare (well-being)? We return to the concept of economic value as a contribution for doing this. We have proposed the idea of calculating the economic value of State public service enterprises, such as health and education, which could provide a monetary measure as to how much is being invested in these enterprises, and their cost and capital efficiency in providing these services. This raises the question of how we calculate the income side of the cost–benefit equation, which could be provided by identifying the standard unit costs of these services and relating them to the number of users using the services. One might call this "consumer income", but there can also be other sources of income arising from services provided to other institutions or foreign countries. An indirect value of such an approach would be to focus attention on the innovation and productivity performance of State enterprises.

In conclusion, the calculation of the economic value profile of a business, which takes account of all the dimensions of economic value described in this section, will contribute to quantifying the value which business, both private and public, is contributing to society, and provide a quantified data base for a rational debate of what we mean by economic justice, and how economic value is being distributed and "shared" between members of society.

8.6   The Time Dimension of Value

There is a time dimension to value in the sense of how present value will be sustained in the future. Intrinsic value seeks to define future value, in terms of the ability, or sustainability, of an enterprise to create value in the future. In other words, economic value cannot be judged solely at only one point in time, measured by the annual balance sheet, but also needs to be judged continuously in terms of its future sustainability. The risk of future decline in, or destruction of, value (the entropy principle) has to take into account the pro-cyclical nature of economic activity and the nature of business cycles, which remain key areas of study for economics. At which stage of those cycles is a business at any one point of time, in terms of growth, maturity or decline? This takes us into the world of potentiality and actuality, which Aristotle first investigated in terms of realizing potential ("becoming") in light of a final end (teleology), whether it be an individual human life, a business enterprise or a social institution.

The annual profit and loss account (which one might call the neurological structure of an economic enterprise) and balance sheet, with its structure of assets and liabilities (which one might call the physiology of an enterprise) are the starting points for reporting on the value of an enterprise at any one time in its business cycle, but this reporting of value needs to be complemented—or supplemented—by a definition of future value, which requires an assessment of those intangible assets on which future sustainability depends. Statutory reporting needs to place more emphasis on the future viability of a business, and quantifying present and future value on which business objectives can be based.

This has important implications for the way in which we can reward the creation of value in getting the balance right between the short and the long term. In talking about the time dimension of value, we need "feedback" systems which provide information on "how well we are doing". The profit and loss structure of a business is similar to the neurological system of an organism which determines the way in which it responds to the positive and negative forces which impact on its being. The balance sheet is similar to the physiological structure of an organism with its interacting structures and systems which provide the physical components for its being. Both provide the feedback mechanisms for monitoring the health (economic viability) of a business and its ability to survive in the future. In the same way as physical bodies are homeostatic in the sense of adapting themselves to changing circumstances through their inbuilt "immune systems", so businesses can be seen as organisms which require efficient "immune" systems to monitor the value they are creating over the time horizon of the business cycle in which they operate. "Feedback" mechanisms on value creation over a period of time and how they should be organized need to be part of new economic thinking.

8.7   Shareholder Value

The creation of value for the shareholders of a business enterprise has always been, and will remain, a cardinal principle of a capitalist economic system, which evaluates value in relation to the market share price, determined by "market sentiment" which may or may not take account of the P/E ratio, and the dividends received. The market is the reference point for the investor in evaluating the acceptability of the return on his investment, but how the market decides what the price of a share should be is not always rational and may be based more on short-term considerations than on the longer-term value considerations discussed in Sect. 8.5 above. The debate on what shareholder value is, or should be, is a complex one and there is no agreed definition of what it is and how it should be measured. As one insurance analyst put it when asked for his definition:

You are asking me a question which has many answers. If you take Damodaran or other text books which assess shareholder equity value, you can see there are different answers for different business models. For instance, if you have a capital-intensive business model you will apply P/BV, while if you have a capital light model, you will apply a discount cash flow model. Hence, it is not easy to give you a clear and short answer to what we mean by shareholder value as it will depend on the measure we use in assessing equity value in a particular situation.

A key question for debate and agreement in the context of new economic thinking is whether the maximization of shareholder value should be the primary, if not the sole, objective of a business enterprise. One of the more recent contributions to this debate has been the book *The Shareholder Value Myth* by Lynn Stout, which takes as its theme the observation attributed to Jack Welch, former CEO of GE, in a *Financial Times* interview about the 2008 crisis that "strictly speaking, shareholder value is the dumbest idea in the world". Criticizing the concept that corporations are required to "maximize shareholder value", the book highlights the dangers of "short termism", criticizing its excessive focus on short-term results at the expense of long-term sustainability. Since the accounting metric of earnings per share (EPS) is the main criterion for judging investment performance, the danger is that managers may take decisions to cut expenditure on research and development, and maintenance (as was revealed by the DeepWater Horizon disaster at BP's oilrig in the Gulf of Mexico) or investment in people, in order to hit quarterly earnings targets. So, if short-term "profit maximization" becomes the determining factor in creating shareholder value, it may jeopardize the creation of value for the other stakeholders in a business enterprise.

Achieving this balance between the short- and the long-term creation of value is a critical and difficult task, and means that the investment analyst's definition of the "target share price" needs to show that it takes into account all of the dimensions of value described in Sect. 8.5 above. Changes in these dimensions of value will lead to changes in the "target share price", which requires analysis to be based on a "real-time" approach to managing the macro- and micro-economic changes which affect the economic value of an enterprise. In this way the market share price can be compared with the other dimensions of value, as, for example, Berkshire Hathaway does when it compares the book value and market value of its shares against changes in the S&P index (including dividends). As Lynn Stout says in the Preface to her book; "Put bluntly, conventional shareholder thinking causes corporate managers to focus on short-term earnings reports at the expense of long-term performance." Howard Schulz, the CEO of Starbucks, makes a similar point when he says "companies need to have a larger purpose than merely raising the stock price" (see J. Nocera, INYT 2012).

And in a recent *Harvard Business Review* article, "What Good Are Shareholders?", Justin Fox and Jay Lorsch argue that shareholders are not well suited to become "corporate bosses", as they are too diffuse and too short-term-oriented, now that high-frequency trading dominate the markets. Also, the theory which regards shareholders as "principals", and managers as their "agents", as Fox puts it, means that "managers get away from seeing themselves as stewards of an organization with lasting value". So, that takes us back to what is the "value metric" a business uses when talking about its economic value. As Fox and Lorsch put it: "the function of business is not just a return to investors, but to provide goods and services, to provide employment, to pay taxes, and so on". As discussed above, how are we to put a value on these things, which contribute directly to the earnings of an enterprise, and to the willingness of investors to invest or not? The shareholder will always be looking to maximize the return on his investment, but that return needs to recognize all the elements which contribute to the economic value of an enterprise.

This means that P/E ratios need to be based on an analysis of economic value, when setting the assumptions on which they are calculated. In this way, we can redefine the concept of "shareholder" value and its maximization in terms of all the dimensions of value which make up the totality of what we mean by economic and intrinsic value. Return on capital employed and the dividends paid on the shareholders' capital will always remain fundamental shareholder value objectives, but this value needs to be set in the context of maximizing the return for the other stakeholders measured in terms of the value metrics discussed in Sect. 8.5, where the short and long term come together in the relationship between annual cash flow and profitability, and the intrinsic value of NAV (book value) measured in terms of discounted future profits.

Such a wider approach to defining shareholder value requires new ways of reporting and rewarding economic value, which analyses the "value profile" of the business (see Appendix 1) in setting objectives for maximizing value for all the stakeholders as partners in the enterprise. This has implications for the way statutory accounts report on "value" in terms not only of annual profit and loss, and balance sheet "robustness", but also of intrinsic value. New economic thinking needs to address the whole question of "value reporting", for all stakeholders, shareholders included, and to look at the way in which "Triple Bottom Line Accounting" (TBL), which combines economic, environmental and social accountabilities, can contribute to a wider concept of shareholder value.

8.8   The Pricing of Shares and Economic Value

The way we price the value of shares has become increasingly complex not only for the investment analysts, but even more so for the man on the Clapham Omnibus as he grapples with the decision of how to invest his hard-earned savings. There have been many examples of incorrect or even fraudulent pricing of shares and financial products, ranging from the pricing of Enron shares before the company collapsed to the pricing of Bernie Madoff's financial products. In each of these cases a more accurate calculation of value at risk could have warned investors of the risks involved in making the investment decisions which they did. The risks involved in being seduced by the attraction of high returns inadequately risk evaluated have caused many casualties, from holders of Argentinian government bonds to Lloyds names in the aftermath of underpriced asbestos insurance products.

In illustrating the complexity of how these kinds of value pricing decisions we take an example, reported by Martin Vander Weyer in an article published in the *Spectator* on 15 June 2013, which discussed some of the valuation issues involved in the possible public offering of Lloyds Banking Group shares that could raise up to £17 billion, where UK Financial Investments, which manages the Treasury's shareholdings in Lloyds, RBS and the rump of Northern Rock, had been advising against a quick sale of the Lloyds stake, fearing that, if the share price soared afterwards, the

UKFI could be accused of failing to maximize the taxpayers' interest. So, what is the "right" price? That raises the question of what was the underlying intrinsic value of Lloyds shares at that time and how it was calculated. Does the mark to market pricing mechanism take sufficient account of long-term value? Were P/E ratios at that time an adequate measure of the intrinsic value of Lloyds? Public offerings underwritten by the banks hired to place shares rely on estimates of value which are based on earnings projections over a limited period of time, but not on a full evaluation of all the dimensions of value at risk described in Sect. 8.5 of this chapter. Share offerings require underwriters willing to guarantee the offer price, but the assumptions made in determining that price need to be stated clearly in the Prospectus, which in order to be complete needs an evaluation of all the dimensions of value discussed in Sect. 8.5, and also the various risks involved. Valid assumptions then become an essential input when analyzing future performance, and the benchmarks for variance reporting.

The same article also commented on the way Project Verde, the proposed selling off of 632 Lloyds branches to the Co-operative Bank, was being handled. The bigger the black hole revealed in the Co-op Bank's balance sheet, the more it appeared that Project Verde had been a politically motivated scheme in defiance of evidence that the Co-op was never strong enough to go through with the purchase. Furthermore, who was to agree a price for the Lloyds branches, and on the basis of what valuation? The sale in fact never took place, but at the time the need was to decide how the Coop stock was to be priced, and a black hole in its financing to be filled. The solution could have been bad news for the small Co-op Bank bonds and preference shareholders should they have been forced to take a 30 per cent 'haircut' as part of a capital reconstruction to fill the black hole—having been encouraged to hold them not only on the strength of the parent Co-op group but also on the understanding that the bank would be supported by the government. Might have this been another example similar to the fate of the pensioners who lost £100 million of savings on Barings' "perpetual subordinated notes" in 1995, having bought them in the belief that the Bank of England would always stand behind a historic member of the financial establishment. These examples illustrate the uncertainties of pricing shares or assets, which requires at all times an assessment of the underlying "values" involved, which a "Value Profile" analysis can provide, to assist the methodology used by the CAPM in pricing assets. Although these examples highlight the importance of "caveat emptor" in investment pricing decisions, they also highlight the importance of "caveat vendor" in the pricing of investment products, shares or otherwise. But, most importantly, they raise the question of how we "value" financial products, whether they be Lloyds' Bank shares, the price the Coop Bank should pay for the 632 Lloyds branches, or Barings' subordinated notes. What are the principles, procedures and systems that are required for valuing financial products? And what is our value dimension or criterion to be? Is to be net asset value, or market pricing value with its bias towards the short term in times of financial crisis, or the intrinsic value of a business long term? We need a unified analysis of all the "value criteria" described in Sect. 8.5. As we have said, such an approach has implications for the way statutory accounts report on economic value in the annual accounts.

In conclusion, new economic thinking needs to take a fresh look at the adequacy of current statutory reporting in terms of "value reporting", not only in terms of the annual balance sheet, but also in terms of present and future economic value.

8.9 Mark to Market Pricing

There is considerable debate surrounding the completeness and validity of "marking to market" as a measure of value since market prices may not take sufficient account of intrinsic value. In the absence of value metrics for measuring economic, as discussed in Sect. 8.5, the "market" will be the only way to "price" assets, as the "auction" markets demonstrate all the time. For example, a sale of contemporary art at Christie's in July 2013 saw the painting of Michel Basquiat "Untitled", painted in 1982 when the artist was 21, set a world auction record for the artist at £18.76 million.

So, who could claim that this was the intrinsic value of the painting where the price was determined by an auction process where individual buyers with different risk appetites seek to outbid each other with the asset going to the highest "bidder"? The market will always remain an important means for pricing assets at any one moment in time, but it will not necessarily reflect intrinsic value. We need a system for comparing market prices and intrinsic value as part of the value reporting system so that the veracity of both values over time can be measured to highlight the disparities which can occur between the two. In determining the value of a Lloyds Bank share or the modern equivalent of a Baring's subordinated note, we are not operating in the auction world of the art market, but the principle of market pricing remains the same. However, we need reporting systems which distinguish between "price" and "value" when an economic transaction takes place, even if the price exceeds or falls beneath the intrinsic value. New economic thinking needs to find effective ways of financial value reporting, which combines mark to market "pricing" and economic value.

8.10 The Variability and Uncertainty of Future Economic Value

Value is a dynamic and evolutionary concept, which means that balance sheet management cannot be a static process to be undertaken only at specific moments in time, but needs to be a day-to-day, if not a second-to-second, real-time process set up to manage change and uncertainty. We enter a world based on the Heisenberg and Gödel principles of uncertainty and incompleteness, which emphasize the stochastic, or random, nature of analyzing future economic value. This analytical process requires continuous attention on managing the unpredictability of risk-taking where the value at risk (VAR) will change according to the external (exogenous) conditions, such as new competitive structures, changes in technology, and the globalization of markets, and according to internal (endogenous) conditions arising from changes in human behaviour and consumer preferences at work within the markets in which "we have chosen to operate". Such changes will have profound implications for business models, and the definition of the "value propositions" on which product and service offerings are based.

The starting point has to be a clear statement of the economic value objectives of the business at any one point of time during the investment cycle of that business, and a definition of the variance analysis process for measuring economic value "performance" in the future. An "Economic Value Profile" (see Appendix 1) arising from an analysis of the information provided by the statutory and intrinsic value reports could become a key analytical tool for measuring success or failure in achieving the creation of economic value.[4,5]

The measurement of the volatility of values has become an analytical science in itself. Most option traders are familiar with the Black–Scholes model of option pricing in their quest for a methodology to measure the rate and magnitude of changes in market prices where fair market value can be out of line with actual market values—something which can result in option mispricing. The variables will be influenced by the time and expiration of the stocks involved, the historical patterns of volatility, and strike price experience. We enter the esoteric world of Beta finance, derivative pricing, financial economics, implied volatility and standard deviations. The trouble is, as Nassim Taleb put it in a paper in the *Journal of Portfolio Management*, "We don't quite know what we are talking about

---

[4] Heisenberg's uncertainty principle and Goedel's incompleteness theorem: Heisenberg's Uncertainty Principle purports that in quantum mechanics we can never know simultaneously the exact position or speed of an object. This has implications for economics in terms of analysing the uncertainty (probability) of realizing economic value objectives in light of the value metrics chosen to measure those objectives.

[5] Heisenberg's uncertainty principle and Goedel's incompleteness theorem: There are deep mathematical reasons why rationality can never be captured completely in any tight definition, and whatever tight definition we give, we can find some action or inference which is not covered by that definition but is evidently rational nonetheless. The implication for economics is that economic theories will always be subject to change many of which are unpredictable e.g. the evolution of the Chinese Communist State-controlled economic system into a system of free market capitalism. This requires a continuous real time risk management process which reviews the assumptions on which economic theories are based, and uses an appropriate and predefined system of "feedback".

K. Gödel, "Some Basic Theorems on the Foundation of Mathematics and their Implications", in *Collected Works*, vol. III, ed. S. Feferman, Oxford, 1995, p. 308; J.R. Lucas, "The Philosophy of the Reasonable Man", *Philosophical Quarterly*, vol. 13, 1965, pp. 98–106; J.R. Lucas, *The Freedom of the Will*, Oxford, 1970, esp. p. 171; R. Penrose, *The Emperor's New Mind*, Oxford, 1989, pp. 64ff; R. Penrose, *Shadows of the Mind*, Oxford, 1994, chs 1–3; J. Myhill, "Some Remarks on the Notion of Proof", *Journal of Philosophy*, vol. LVII, 1960, p. 462, expresses it well: " Gödel's argument establishes that there exist, for any correct formal system containing the arithmetic of natural numbers, correct inferences which cannot be carried out in that system."

when we talk about volatility", as the failure of models to predict prices in the last financial crisis indicated.

The insurance industry has always tackled the risks inherent in short and long tail business, and has developed methodologies for reserving during insurance cycles, including reinsurance. In times of extreme uncertainty and extraordinary risk we need to apply the principle of reinsurance to complex financial products, such as CDS, where portfolio managers could well have benefited from people ready to reinsure, that is, to accept the risks inherent in their portfolios. An "Economic Value Profile" (see Appendix 1) needs a section on the volatility of future economic value and the hidden costs implicit in covering the risks for example of high return government bonds, or Ponzi schemes, where we may be robbing Peter to pay Paul, or derivative instruments the risks of which were not properly understood as happened in the Leeson Barings debacle. The uncertainty of future economic value requires a clear statement at least annually, or at the moment of the introduction of a new product, whether it be a bar of soap, or a derivative product, an indication of the future profit assumptions on which the launch of that product is based. However, one of the greatest problems regarding the variability and uncertainty of economic value concerns the inherent volatility implicit in that "irrational exuberance" to which market sentiment can be subject, which we addressed in Chap. 6, where speculation can take over from rational thinking about the underlying economic value of share prices. Are they over- or undervalued? As we have said, this requires a reporting system for monitoring the volatility of share prices against economic value.

8.11 Value Investing

In any discussion about economic value, we cannot ignore the experience and opinions of value investors, such as Warren Buffett, where the creation of value through maximizing the investment return for themselves and their clients is the first and main objective. Although value investors accept the concept of intrinsic value, they prefer to estimate that value by looking first at data which is verifiable now, such as net asset value, which is the monetary value of what is being bought or sold. Warren

Buffett recognizes that future profits are an important part of goodwill, but future earnings are notoriously subject to unpredictable levels of uncertainty. For this reason, he places great emphasis on understanding the nature of the business and the capacity of managers to deliver earnings growth in the future. The nature of a business and the competence of management are intangible components of net asset value, but they also impact on intrinsic value, which will determine the confidence the investor has in the future "profit" sustainability of an enterprise. The resulting P/E ratio becomes the value metric for the investor, but as prices are determined by market sentiment, where excessive market exuberance or depression may result in the over or underpricing of asset values, there needs to be a way for indicating any misfit between share prices and the underlying intrinsic value of those assets.

The challenge for the value investor is how to turn this potential misfit between market sentiment and economic value to his profit. Bruce Greenwald's book *Value Investing from Graham to Buffett and Beyond* looks at the experience of eight successful value investors which confirms that the overriding priority of value investing is the maximization of value for the investors. But it also confirms the importance of intrinsic value in making the decision either to invest or disinvest, although the index makes does not mention the word "value", whereas "earnings power" and "valuation" get frequent mentions. Value is seen in terms of how much "Mr Investor wants his money to become". The prime motivation is the creation of monetary wealth, which, although it is an essential contributor to the social and human welfare dimensions of economic value, cannot be divorced from the value that wealth is creating, whether it be economic, social or environmental. A potential conflict of interest for the "value investor" lies in the question as to whether in investing he is making a commitment to the long-term development of the business, or whether this remains secondary to the need to maximize his return when he decides to sell irrespective if that decision impacts negatively on the longer term value of the enterprise, or not.

As Warren Buffett put it: "Our long-term economic goal is to maximize Berkshire's average annual rate of return in intrinsic value on a per share basis (Annual Report 2014)." He defines intrinsic value as the "discounted value of the cash that can be taken out of a business during its remaining life. But it is an estimate rather than a precise figure which must be changed if interest rates move and forecasted cash flow change. "Two people looking at the same set of facts inevitably come up with different intrinsic value figures. This is one reason why we never give you our estimates of intrinsic value (Annual Report 2014)." Is this a cop out? Not to declare intrinsic value assumptions means that we can never have the information to show over a period of time the differences between price earnings P/E value (market sentiment) and intrinsic value, which we need for judging "value performance" and the investment analyst's capacity for estimating correctly the value of a business over the long term.

This is a "value reporting" need, which, if it is considered to be too complex and uncertain when compared to the quantifiable data provided by statutory reporting, there is no reason why intrinsic value information cannot be provided as a supplementary note to the statutory accounts. Such information will enable both the company and the market to see how reliable future earnings and the related P/E ratios have been over a period of time compared with intrinsic value. Value investing remains an important part of economic value reporting in establishing how we should allocate capital for investment in the stock market, but its procedures and results need to be reported in a way which can supplement the statutory procedures for establishing the solvency and intrinsic value of an economic enterprise. By its nature "value investing" is not a purely financial process; it is a process which evaluates the management capacity and strength of a company to achieve positive future earnings, expressed in Warren Buffett's principle of investing in businesses "we understand" and whose management "we trust".

But at the end of the day the basic value metric for the value investor remains "earnings power" (the ability to generate positive cash flows in the future). The challenge for the value investor is how to put a value on the intangible assets of a business enterprise (know-how, image and reputation, research and development, and managerial competence) in addition to the value of the tangible assets of people, products and profits, when defining the assumptions on which his "target price" recommendations are made. Another area for new economic thinking regards the way in which we need to measure the value of those intangible assets which, although they may not be specifically accounted for in the statutory accounts, make a vital contribution to the future sustainability of a business.

8.12 Implications for Value Based Management

Value Based Management has sometimes suffered from a failure or imprecision in defining what we mean by the creation of value. If the value of a company is determined by its discounted future cash flows, the creation of that value, needs to be set in the context of a wider analysis of economic value as discussed in Sect. 8.5. This requires us to move on from the traditional NAV approach, and even beyond FNAV (future net asset value), to include the value of intangible assets and the sustainability values discussed in Sect. 8.3, so that corporate social responsibility (CSR) becomes not just a fashionable "catchphrase", but a contributor to the creation of value in the sense of Triple Bottom Line accounting (economic, environmental and social).

As a leading banker put it, *"Opponents of Value Based Management (VBM) used to say that because it appears to be about maximizing shareholder value it must also by definition imply that other stakeholders—customers, employees, the general public, etc—get ignored or worse, exploited. In other words, this is a zero-sum game in which more value for shareholders comes at the expense of less value for other stakeholders. My view is that any company which ignores these other stakeholders cannot maximize shareholder value—because it won't have a sustainable business model and shareholders will eventually suffer as customers and key employees leave and/or society legislates against the firm. Value creation is a positive-sum game. Apple is a great example of a company which is delivering massive value for its shareholders by delivering superior customer value, although they have had their own issues with employee exploitation (at a supplier in China), and more recently in resisting the investigation by the United States Justice Department into whether the company was complying with antitrust laws concerning the fixing of prices for e-books. The financial crisis has demonstrated the importance of business ethics vividly. The shareholders of banks which lost sight of customer value, or otherwise abused their position, in the name of short-term profits have lost huge amounts of wealth. So for me there is no contradiction between shareholder value maximization and good business ethics—the former requires the latter.*

The contradiction is between short-term profit maximization and good ethics. But, of course, there is almost always a conflict between short-term profit maximization and shareholder value." (Sir Winfried Bischoff, Chairman Financial Reporting Council, former Chairman Lloyds Bank Group PLC.)

This is a good example of the challenge in managing different or conflicting investment interests and objectives, and the need for value-based management to start from a clear definition of what any business means by economic value. The "Economic Value Profile" (see Appendix 1) of a business seeks to encompass the value criteria illustrated in Sect. 8.5, and could become a tool for reporting value in terms of its different dimensions, and for setting the assumptions on which value based management can be based.

8.13 Implications for Economic Value Reporting

If we accept the different ways in which we can define and measure economic value, there is a strong case for revisiting the way in which statutory reporting measures and reports on value. If the "Economic Value Profile" approach (Appendix 1) proposed in Sect. 8.5 is considered to be a valid and useful tool for the way we report on value, we need an opinion from the professions, accounting, actuarial, legal, and investment analysts, that this is indeed the case, and that this kind of value reporting could become a useful adjunct to traditional statutory reporting. It also requires an input from the financial regulatory control authorities regarding the way in which economic value reporting could assist them in their basic task of evaluating the financial solidity and capital adequacy of financial institutions. First of all, however, we need to answer and agree a number of questions which can establish the criteria on which a new approach to the calculation and control of economic value reporting could be based, all of which have implications for new economic thinking:

1. Do we agree that we should distinguish between the creation of wealth and value in economics?
2. Is it useful to accept the different dimensions of economic value, and to report on them individually?
3. Do we agree that intrinsic value reporting should become an integral part of economic value reporting?
4. Should intangible asset reporting become a part of statutory reporting?
5. Is it time to report on "social" value as a part of statutory reporting, and how should it be done?
6. Are we in agreement about what we mean by shareholder value?
7. How should P/E ratios and market pricing take account of intrinsic value?
8. How should we relate market volatility to economic value?
9. How should we compensate the creation of economic value in reconciling short- and long-term value objectives?

Answers to these questions will have implications for business efficiency and accountability, and also for business ethics and legitimacy, since each question has an ethical dimension in terms of the way business is conducted and managed. In any discussion of economic justice, the value of what we are doing is paramount and needs to be the raison d'être for the way in which businesses can rationally and convincingly demonstrate that they are creating the long-term economic value on which future sustainability depends. This will require some new thinking on the part of business, including merchant banks and investment analysts, and the "Accountability" professions (chartered accounting, actuarial and legal), regarding the measurement and reporting of economic value and whether changes in the way we do these things are appropriate.

In an attempt to answer these questions, we interviewed a leading investment analyst whose replies are contained in Appendix 2 at the end of this chapter. The important thing to emerge is that intrinsic value is included in investment analysts' calculations of target prices, which has implications for how market prices are compared against these target prices. If that is the case, statutory reporting needs to include, at least in the form of a supplementary note, information on economic value performance, which can relate market share prices to economic value. How this could be done could be the subject of a special study conducted by the CFA Institute in collaboration with the accounting and actuarial professions, and the regulatory authorities. It might also be useful for companies to include a report on how investment analysts are fixing target prices for companies' share prices to indicate how these are under- or overvaluing companies' economic values.

Appendix 1: Criteria for an Economic Value Profile

METRIC	|–5	|–4	|–3	|–2	|–1	Current year	|+1	|+2	|+3	|+4	|+5
Income											
Costs											
Net Profit											
Free Cash Flow											
Net Asset Value											
Distributable Earnings											
NOPAT (less COC)											
Value at Risk (VAR)											
EBITAD											
P/E Ratio											
Share Price											
Volatility Measures											
Market Capitalization											
Enterprise Value											
Embedded Value											
Intrinsic Value											
Fair Value											
Intangible Assets											
Sustainability Value											
ALM Measures											

5 year past experience and future 5 year projections

Source: Author's check-list proposal.

Appendix 2: Intrinsic Value and Economic Value Reporting: An Investment Manager's View

(Massimo Figna, Managing Director of Tenax Capital and manager of Tenax Global Financial Fund (Long/Short) hedge fund. Previously Responsible for UBS insurance investment research)

1. Intrinsic Value Considerations

Question. What is your opinion about calculating intrinsic value?

Answer. The Gordon Growth Model is talking about intrinsic value where Price over Book Value equals ROE (minus growth) over COE (minus growth), the Damodaran thesis, which is the same as saying that DDM (the Dividend Discount Model) equals the value resulting from the Gordon Growth Model. Damodaran's book explains how to move from Discounted Cash Flow to the formula P/BV = ROE/COE. They are equivalent and they are the most used worldwide recognised methods to value equity. P/BV is used for capital-intensive balance sheets like bank and insurers, and historically has been preferred to DCF (discounted cash flow). When you have to value a telecom company, a utility or a cyclical company you need to use the DCF method which is a better measure of value than P/BV. A worked example may help to understand the concept.

Example: Banca Intesa target price

$$P / BV = ROE / COC$$

$$Cost\,of\,capital\,(COC) = Risk\,free\,(10\,years\,government\,bond\,yield) + Beta\,(1) \times Equity\,risk\,premium\,(from\,4\,to\,8\%)$$

Intesa 2016 ROE estimated is 8 %

$$COC = 2\% + 5\% = 7\%$$

Target price of Banca Intesa is determined by multiplying the target P/BV by the BV of Banca Intesa

Target P / BV = 8 / 7 = 1.14

BV per share 2.86 € (Bloomberg estimate, May 2016)

Target price per ordinary share = 1.14 € × 2.86 = 3.27 €

Current price per ordinary share 2.10 € (May 2016)

The example is based on data at one point in time, and is subject to changes in Bloomberg data and assumptions on EPS.

2. Increasing Complexity

Question. What is your opinion about Solvency 2?

Answer. The increase in complexity in calculating value in relation to capital adequacy derives from new accounting and regulation requirements. Moving from a parametric approach (Solvency 1) to a stochastic approach (Solvency 2) makes it difficult to make comparisons and analyse outcomes. It was possible to recreate a Solvency 1 parametric model for an insurance company using the statutory balance sheet. When you know some of the key parameters of the balance sheet, such as P&C, life reserves, etc., you can model the impact of changes, for example, higher growth, M&A activity. With Solvency 2, it is not possible to determine the outcome for the solvency ratio, since you can't recreate the model because there is not enough information in the statutory balance sheet, and the model is too complicated to be replicated, and it is difficult to determine the impact of some of the assumptions. It will be important to ensure that Solvency 2 provides a workable tool for calculating solvency and the amount of capital required to support the business risks without reducing the capital available for developing the business.[6]

---

[6] "In my view, the "black-box" involved in Solvency 2 is far too complex and some of the calibrations leave much to be desired. Deep in the workings are assumptions and variables, in some cases based on very little data, which can have significant impacts on the results. A complex computer simulation gives an impression of accuracy but, because of its nature, judgment is required to interpret it appropriately, yet external users of the information are left very much in the dark. Solvency

3. Statutory Accounts and Intrinsic Value

Question. Would it be feasible and useful for statutory accounts, in addition to reporting on NAV, to include an estimate of intrinsic value based on clearly defined and verifiable assumptions, which can be monitored through variance analysis over time?

Answer. In principle I agree but I think the complexity of Solvency 2 will not allow companies to do this, a view also expressed by a number of insurance company CFOs.

4. Some Economic Value Reporting Questions

Premise. Every businessman should be able to answer the question: "What is the economic value (not just the market value) of your business?" If this is the case, the need for defining what we mean by economic value, and how we measure it, becomes paramount. Within this context how would you answer the following questions relating to economic value?

1. Do you agree that we should distinguish between the creation of wealth and value in economics?

   Answer: Yes

2. Is it useful to accept the different dimensions of value, and to report on them individually?

   Answer: I don't think the market will look at it, but will continue to look at value in terms first and foremost of share price value

3. Do we agree that intrinsic value reporting should become an integral part of economic reporting?

   Answer: Yes, but only if it is also used as a remuneration target for the management.

4. Should intangible asset reporting become a part of statutory reporting?

   Answer: No, too difficult to value.

---

2 has without doubt much value in forcing companies to articulate their risk appetite and therefore think harder about what sort of company they wish to be, and what their risk profile ought to be as a consequence, but if financial analysts are unable to validate the results and do their own scenario testing when assessing corporate economic value, Solvency 2 will end up being a missed opportunity for the industry." Andrew Milton, FIA-former principal of Tillinghast Towers Perrin and Independent Non-Executive Director of Generali Paneurope.

5. Is it time to report on "social" value as a part of statutory reporting, and how should it be done?
   Answer: Yes, but I don't know how.
6. How would you define shareholder value?
   Answer: Shareholder value is always going to be related to the "price on the screen" with the big "caveat" that the assumptions behind the price on the screen are clear and understood. As Warren Buffett has said, price may not be a reliable measure of shareholder value, and needs to take account of the fundamental, or intrinsic, value behind the price on the screen.
7. How should P/E ratios and market pricing take account of intrinsic value?
   Answer: With a premium or discount on the multiple versus its peers
8. How should we relate market volatility to economic value?
   Answer: I don't know, but we could monitor economic value over time compared with the volatility of the market share price.
9. How should we compensate the creation of value in reconciling short- and long-term value objectives?
   Answer: Some banks have been using EVA (economic value added), but probably it is not the best measure, because of its complexity in calculating the cost of capital. NAV, FCF, share price and economic value are simpler metrics for evaluating management performance and relating it to compensation.

References

Beinhocker E. The origin of wealth. London: Random House; 2007.

Bristow R. Online discussion: sustainability reporting. The Guardian, 18 Apr 2011. http://www.theguardian.com/sustainable-business/online-panel-discussion-sustainability-reporting.

Damodaran, Aswath. Damodaran on Valuation: Security Analysis for investment and Corporate Finance. 22 Aug 2006 Amazon.

eFinanceManagement. Economic value added (EVA)—the measure of real wealth creation, 25 Apr 2012. http://www.efinancemanagement.com/

investment-decisions/economic-value-added-eva-the-measure-of-real-wealth-creation.

Fox J, Lorsch JW. What good are shareholders? Harvard Business Review, July–August 2012 Issue. https://hbr.org/2012/07/what-good-are-shareholders.

Greenwald BCN, Kahn J, Sonkin PD, van Biema M. Value investing: from Graham to Buffett and beyond. Hoboken, NJ: Wiley; 2001.

Greenwalk B, Kahn J. Competition demystified: a radically simplified approach to business strategy. London: Penguin; 2005.

Guerrera F. Welch condemns share price focus. Financial Times, 2009. http://www.ft.com/cms/s/0/294ff1f2-0f27-11de-ba10-0000779fd2ac.html#axzz3mfnmBKoH.

Holton GA. Value at risk: theory and practice. San Diego, CA: Academic Press, Elsevier; 2003.

Investopedia. Weighted average cost of capital—WACC, October 2015. http://www.investopedia.com/terms/w/wacc.asp.

Koller T. What is value-based management? McKinsey Quarterly, August 1994. http://www.mckinsey.com/insights/corporate_finance/what_is_value-based_management.

Lev B, Daum JH. The dominance of intangible assets: consequences for enterprise management and corporate reporting. Meas Bus Excel. 2004;8(1): 6–17.

Martin Vander Weyer. George Osborne's Lloyds sale will be all about votes just as Mervyn King warned. Spectator 15 June 2013.

Mocciaro Li Destri A, Picone PM, Mina A. Bringing strategy back into financial systems of performance management: integrating EVA and PCV. Bus Syst Rev. 2012;1(1):85–102.

Smith T. Shareholder value is an outcome not an objective. Financial Times 11 March 2015. http://www.ft.com/intl/cms/s/0/pees758e-abb8-11e4-b05a-00144feab7de.html.

Joe Nocera. Shareholders first? INYT 13 Aug 2012.

Scerri A, James P. Accounting for sustainability: combining qualitative and quantitative research in developing "indicators" of sustainability. Int J Soc Res Methodol. 2010;1(13):41–53.

Stout L. The shareholder myth. Oakland, CA: Berrett-Koehler; 2012.

Smith T. What exactly do we mean by 'shareholder value'? Financial Times, 9 Jan 2015. http://www.ft.com/cms/s/0/463abec2-9721-11e4-845a-00144feabdc0.html#axzz3rw6pN6cp.

Taleb NN. The Black Swan: the impact of the highly improbable. London: Penguin; 2008.

The Economist. Triple bottom line. 17 November 2009. http://www.economist.com/node/14301663.

9

Relating Economic Value to Executive Compensation

*You are correct in thinking that both the amount of compensation—
by which I mean the proportion of income paid to employees rather
than shareholders—and the nature—short term rather than long
term vesting with clawback—have contributed.*

Sir Winfried Bischoff
Chairman Financial Reporting Council,
former Chairman, Lloyds Bank Group PLC,
commenting on reasons for the 2008 financial crisis

Abstract The last financial crisis revealed a mismatch between performance compensation and the creation of short- as opposed to long-term economic value, with no well-defined criteria for the connection between the two. The chapter looks at the current state of the art with particular reference to total shareholder value (TSV), and systems for employee participation in the ownership of companies. Are stock options the best way for doing this or not? Also discussed are the measures for relating compensation to value, such as the Chartered Financial Analysts' Institute (CFA) call for simpler cash measures, like free cash flow. Finally, the ethical implications for compensation related

© The Editor(s) (if applicable) and The Author(s) 2016
M.R. Griffiths, J.R. Lucas, *Value Economics*,
DOI 10.1057/978-1-137-54187-1_9

to economic value are discussed, and the need for better annual reporting of value related compensation.

9.1   Chapter Overview

Whatever the role of pay in investment banking for frontline deal makers, and for their corporate leaders, has been, the last financial crisis has led to a welter of proposals for regulating the pay for both of these categories of employees, and for justifying the levels of executive compensation paid out to them. Much has already been implemented, including issued share capital dilution limits. But the need remains to explain the rationale and criteria for the levels of compensation for chief executives in general. What, for example, was the justification for paying Helge Lund, when he moved to run British Gas (BG) from Statoil (the Norwegian oil company), around ten times his previous salary, followed shortly afterwards by a pay-off of £20 million when he left following the takeover of BG by Royal Dutch Shell?

When one looks at executive compensation systems, and those prevailing in the financial sector in particular, we find that there is no well-defined connection between economic value (as discussed in Sect. 8.5 in Chap. 8), and the compensation paid to executives. Although it may be argued that shareholder return (TSR) as measured by the share price and dividends is a sufficient measure of the relation between economic value and compensation, in statutory reporting there is often no clear definition and quantification of what this return on shareholder value is, and its relation to the amount paid out in performance-related compensation and to economic value.

We need to take another look at how we should reward people for the creation of economic value, rather than just monetary wealth. We might begin by asking boards to state the rationale of their executive compensation systems, and to demonstrate how these systems reward the creation of economic value, which is a basic component of value for the shareholder, and how much the company is paying out in performance compensation in relation to that value. This requires a new look at the possible compensation systems, not only for executives but for all employees, covering profit sharing and the allocation of shares, including stock options, deferred shares, restricted shares and/or performance shares, with restrictions about when they can be traded. We believe that statutory accounts should contain a section on how the company defines and measures economic value and how it intends to reward the creation of that value. Companies could then report annually on the relation between the economic value achieved and the compensation paid to answer the question: "What value are we getting from our performance-related compensation systems?" This could contribute to strengthening the legitimacy in the eyes of the general public regarding the reasonableness and fairness of the levels of executive compensation.

Remuneration needs to be aligned with "value creation", which means that boards need to define a policy for performance-related compensation, specifying the "key performance measured indicators" (KPI); the economic value created for setting management objectives, and paying out compensation on the basis of the results achieved. This policy should be approved in a binding note by the shareholders, as is now current practice in the UK, and other countries like Australia and the Netherlands. Such a policy needs to cover not only TSR, but also the economic value which a company is aiming to create for all its stakeholders. This requires a continuous monitoring of TSR, against the economic value of the enterprise.

The chapter also discusses the question of employee participation in ownership, and different ways for doing this covering stock options, deferred stock, restricted shares, or the allocation of shares not linked to stock options, and the wider problems of income inequality raised in Thomas Piketty's recent best-seller *Capitalism in the Twenty First Century*.

9.2   State of the Art

What is today's "state of the art" regarding the link between performance compensation and the creation of economic value? As Katharine Turner (a partner at FIT Remuneration Consultants, and previously with Willis Towers Watson) put it: "My view is that this is the holygrail for which the relentless search continues". The UK Greenbury Report on corporate governance, which was published in 1995, made a number of recommendations concerning executive compensation, but did not make any connection between compensation and value other than to say that it should be linked to performance in achieving total shareholder objectives. It made proposals for reporting on executive compensation in the statutory accounts, but left the definition of the appropriate compensation system to the discretion of individual companies. The Greenbury proposals, and those of subsequent reports and reviews, such as Hampel and Walker have now been incorporated in the UK Corporate Governance Code (2012), which confirms that directors should have long-term performance-related compensation linked to corporate and individual performance. Companies now report on executive compensation, but there is often no clear statement or quantification of the value of that performance in terms of TSR or other metrics of value, such as net asset value (NAV), free cash flow (FCF), or economic value.

The most common performance measure for long-term plans remains TSR, which explains why compensation is related mainly to share price, rather than to other metrics such as economic value, intrinsic value or sustainable value. Post-crisis measures have started to put an increased emphasis on non-financial measures in fixing short- and long-term pay with the objective of combining risk management and prudence to bring compensation more closely in line with directors' duties as specified in the Companies Act 2006. But there is still no consensus on what the ideal compensation system should be—as can be seen from the differences between the John Lewis company-wide profit-sharing plan, and Tesco's highly leveraged approach. It can be helpful to look at various examples and experiences to get the balance right between TSR and other value measures.

The key question is how to link "performance" to the creation of value. Research on the relationship between performance and executive compensation does not identify consistent and significant relationships between executive and company performance. Even a world-leading company like Exxon has been criticized by the voting guidance body Institutional Shareholder Services (ISS) for having an inadequate link between pay and share allocations and performance. What are the best "State of the art" solutions? Is highly leveraged pay for performance, or profit sharing the right answer? Whatever the nature of the adopted compensation system, however, the important thing is to base compensation on clearly defined performance objectives, and quantification of the economic value which has been created. A discussion of what measures might be adopted is given in the following section of the chapter.

There is an important ethical implication regarding difference in levels of compensation. Over the past thirty years shareholders have argued for pay for performance, and tolerated annual bonuses and long-term plans, which has resulted in a much higher share of the value created going to executives in public companies. The difference between executive pay and the average worker in 2014 was estimated to be 277 times, compared with just twenty times in 1965 (see Economic Policy Unit statistics). This is an inequality issue for business and society which still needs to be addressed and answered. Clearer reporting of economic value could be a first step towards showing that there is a justifiable link between executive pay and economic value, and also a justifiable difference between the executive and the shopfloor.

9.3   What Measures?

The CFA Institute of the UK (Chartered Financial Analysts) published a report in 2014 which examines the link between pay and performance for CEOs in large UK companies (see "Measuring and Rewarding Performance—Theory and Evidence in Relation to Executive Compensation"). Two concerns lay behind this research. The first was that current executive compensation emphasizes the interests of equity holders more than bond holders. The second that performance metrics for directors do not ensure that a company earns a sufficient return in light of the cost of capital. In a recent analysis of this research Willis Towers Watson (See "The CFA Executive Compensation Report and Calibrating Directors' Pay with GR:IN Analysis", 2015) proposes that executive compensation needs to take account not only of current profitability but also of a company's growth prospects. To do this they propose taking income-oriented metrics such as free cash flow with more growth-oriented measures which they label GR:IN analysis. These measures could complement the traditional measures of Total Shareholder Return (TSR), Return on Assets (ROA), Return on Equity (ROE), Return on Capital Employed (ROCE), Earnings per share (EPS), and also the alternative measures, which the CFA is proposing, of Free Cash Flow (FCF), Residual Income (RI), and Cash Flow Return on Investment (CFROI). These conclusions are important, and, in particular, the CFA finding that the EPS metric has the potential to encourage "dysfunctional" decision making, as is the finding that there is a "material disconnect" between the key performance indicators (KPIs) companies state to be targets for strategy and those used for determining the incentives used for executive compensation.

These findings—and in particular the CFA focus on free cash flow, and the Willis Towers Watson metric of GR:IN, which would vary incentive compensation according to the projected growth of a company at any one point of its development—support the view that benefits could be gained from increasing the number of performance metrics (selected in accordance with the nature of the company) to be used in determining executive compensation, in order to give a wider dimension to the metric of TSR based on share price. The first requirement, however, is to define what a company means by the term "economic value" and how it intends to use this when deciding the "value" metrics which it intends to use in measuring performance (see Sect. 8.5 in Chap. 8) With no clear definition of all of the dimensions of value there is a risk that compensation systems will not achieve the correct balance between the short and the long term. The key question for companies is: "How do you define economic value and relate this value to your performance compensation system?", an answer to which could help solve the problem of that "material disconnect" and "dysfunctional decision making" identified by the CFA research.

9.4   Partnership in Ownership

Stock Options
One of the most popular ways of compensating management for the creation of value has been through the granting of stock options. These reward managers for delivering share price gains, which, although an important part of shareholder value, are not the only part of it, and with the emphasis on the share price at the moment of granting the option, do not necessarily create an incentive to achieve specific share price values in the future, or to concentrate on the quality of the company's performance over the long term. Are stock options the best way to compensate management for the creation of economic value? When asked if it might be better to allocate shares over a period of time measured against performance to

prevent the manipulation of the share price in exercising stock options, a leading investment analyst agreed that this is a better system.

So, in giving people the incentive to participate in stock ownership do we need to consider alternatives to stock options, which might take the form of the allocation of stock (both equity and preference), deferred shares, and restricted shares with conditions as to when they can be traded, for example, only at the time the manager or employee leaves his employment? Many countries in Europe have already introduced such a system, but it has not been adopted in the USA. The system of stock options has been criticized and there has been argument concerning the interaction of executive options with corporate stock repurchase programmes. In the USA authorities have argued that it may be possible for options to be employed in concert with stock buy-backs in a manner contrary to the interests of shareholders. Share buy-backs might be seen as a way to boost the share price, and hence the value of the options rather than allowing the market to decide it could be seen as a manipulation of the share price not motivated to be the advantage of the shareholder, but to the advantage of executives by increasing the value. It has been estimated that corporate stock buy-backs for the US S&P 500 companies surged to a $500 billion annual rate in 2006 because of the perverse incentive impact of options. This has prompted an examination of alternative implementations of buy-backs to challenge the dominance of "open market" cash buy-backs as the means of implementing a share repurchase plan (see "Scandal" by M. A. Gumport 2006).

Institutional shareholders in the UK have not been in favour of share options for many years; by contrast, in the USA, where such schemes have not encountered this kind of opposition, share options remain common—as do both restricted shares and performance shares. Could we move towards rewarding the creation of economic value through profit sharing, leaving it to the manager to decide whether to purchase shares, or through the allocation of shares related to the creation of that value, similar to cooperatives and partnerships, who provide alternative performance-related compensation systems to stock options? In this sense the CFA is right to call people back to the concept of free cash flow, where we are talking about hard cash, rather than the paper money of stocks which we may or may not want to turn into cash at the time they are allocated to us or when we have the right to exercise a stock option.

Deferred Shares

The banking crisis, and the subsequent decline in the stock markets, also focused attention on whether executive compensation should be more long term in nature, that is, only realizable beyond annual or triennial cycles, and what should be the alignment between compensation in shares and in cash. Deferral of variable pay is now mandatory for identified staff in the financial services sector. A recent Willis Towers Watson report on deferred shares (see Perspectives: Deferred Shares—a partial solution to executive remuneration alignment?) concluded that "the proposal to defer two-thirds of annual cash bonuses into shares could have a significant impact in aligning the remuneration and interests of executives and longer-term shareholders. Differences are likely to be compounded as longer-serving executives would have deferrals from three separate bonuses exposed to the company's share price at any one time." The advantage of this system is that it would automatically include a "claw-back" if future performance failed to reflect the performance at the time the deferred shares were granted as a bonus for performance. It would also link TSR in the future to the bonuses declared at any one point in time also allowing for the clawing back of pay after it has been delivered to and received by the executive.

Restricted Shares

In the UK we are familiar with the Coop model, which has no shareholders, and divides profits among its members. It is perfectly feasible to envisage companies that exist to serve the interests of employees and customers, and which enable them to participate in the profits of the business. The John Lewis Partnership, for example, makes it possible for all employees to participate in profit sharing, but the law allows all sorts of association; it does not have to be for profit, nor need the members of a company be shareholders with tradable shares. Shares can be non-tradable and non-transferable. An agreed solution to offering shares of this kind has not yet been found, but if one were to be developed it could lead to the establishment of another legal definition of the firm.

However, in the meantime the possibility of using restricted shares which are not tradable or transferable, say, until retirement or the termination of a period of employment, could be tried. Employees could be offered the opportunity to take part of profit-sharing bonuses, or even future salary increases, in the form of restricted shares that would only be tradable when the employee leaves the firm. Value in this sense would be deferred but subject to changes in share price values at the time of termination of employment. In some ways this is similar to the statutory deferral of compensation in Italy where every year one month's salary is deferred into a final termination amount, although it is also possible to draw on this amount prior to termination for specific purposes. The deferral amount is based purely on the amount of annual salary, and as such is not based on economic value. The attraction of restricted shares is that they would give employees the opportunity to participate in the share capital of the company during employment, although there would be the downside risk that the price on retirement might be less than the prices of the restricted shares at the time of allocation. That risk could perhaps be reduced if the employee might be given the option to sell at a time of his choice after retirement, or for the company to insure a minimum price on retirement.

9.5   Ethical Implications

As Martin Vander Weyer put it in an article in the *Spectator*, 3 May 2014: "A growing body of opinion regards the bankers' going rate not only grotesquely out of kilter with shareholder returns, but also inherently dangerous in the risky behaviour it continues to provoke despite the lessons of the recent crisis." Such a comment places compensation at the centre of the debate about how value should be rewarded, how compensation packages should be structured, and also whether there should be an ethics of rewards, an issue that had been raised as early as 1975 by Arthur Okun in his book *Equality and Efficiency: The Big Tradeoff*, published by the Brookings Institution. An examination of incentive compensation systems, apart from the principles for deciding what "the rate for the job" should be, will take us into the philosophical area of equality not only between the "employee stakeholders" in an enterprise, but also throughout society, a discussion which has recently been opened up again by Thomas Piketty's book *Capital in the Twenty-First Century*, which challenges the capacity of capitalism to resolve the increasing inequality of wealth in industrialized countries with negative implications for economic justice in terms of a fair distribution of wealth at the macro- (global) and microeconomic (individual) levels. One key finding of his analysis is that the rate of growth of income from capital is several times greater than the rate of economic growth, which results in a declining share going to income earned from wages. Returns on capital of between 4 and 5 percent compare with rates of economic growth of about 1.5 percent a year, which has contradicted the "trickledown effect" predicted during the Reagan and Thatcher years. As we have said, executive pay is now more than 277 times an average workers' pay, compared with twenty times in 1965, according to the Economic Policy Institute.

In 2012 the top 1 percent of US households collected 22.5 percent of the nation's income, the highest figure since 1928, according to Piketty's research. "The idea that you need people making 10 million in compensation to work is pure ideology", he says—although he remarks elsewhere that he has no problem with inequality as long as it is in the common interest. In terms of solutions, he proposes a progressive global tax on real wealth (minus debt) with the proceeds being redistributed to those with less capital: "We just want a way to share the tax burden that is fair and practical." In measuring inequality net wealth is proposed as a better indicator than income. "All I'm proposing is to reduce the property tax on half or three quarters of the population who have very little wealth." He does not propose how such a property tax could be implemented, which would exclude those who have no property to tax. However, the book is an important contribution as to how capitalism needs to tackle the problem of economic inequality.

The subject of the distribution of income has also been taken up by the IMF in addition to its prime indicators for economic success of sustained growth, low inflation and a balanced budget, to establish if there is a connection between inequality and the efficiency on which sustained growth depends. This is a live issue for new economic thinking, which also involves a consideration of the increasing inequalities in income distribution and what the differentials should be. This could emphasise the need to link compensation to economic value, and the need to achieve the correct balance between compensation in the form of stock and in a wider profit sharing for all employees, not just limited to executives.

A number of key issues for study emerge from the considerations discussed in the previous paragraphs. If a large part of executive remuneration is share-based and performance-based, what effect does this have on base salaries and other elements of pay, such as pensions? If participation in the profits for all employees is to become an important part of compensation, how do we determine the amount of the profits to be distributed? What is the link between economic value and the amount of payout which can be afforded for distribution from the "profit pool"? Should schemes to share a percentage of the economic value generated by the management team be extended to all employees? New economic thinking needs to study these compensation issues to see what modifications to existing practices are required (see Willis Towers Watson Executive Compensation Bulletin, "Enduring High-Performance Companies Take the Road Less Travelled in Executive Compensation Design").

All this brings us back to a consideration of the measures we use for defining performance-related compensation and how to quantify them. Compensation has to be linked to the creation of value, and we propose that economic value should be the metric for combining the short- and long-term objectives of a company. Ultimately economic value should be an integral part of shareholder value, which, because it is traditionally linked to the market share price, does not necessarily reflect economic value. We need a system in which shareholder value equates with economic value, and not solely the market share price. In terms of new economic thinking a number of steps would need to be taken to see how shareholder value can be expressed in terms of economic value:

1. Establish clear and understandable criteria for defining economic value in the specific reality of the company or institution concerned.
2. Decide how that economic value will be measured and rewarded over both the short and the long term.
3. Give an annual statement recording the economic value which has been created, and the cost of performance-related compensation, so that all stakeholders (including investors) understand the financial results of performance in terms of the value created and the compensa-

tion costs involved. A value/compensation matrix could be used for reporting results and for establishing budgetary objectives for monitoring management performance year by year.

Compensation needs to be built into the creation of value, and into codes for corporate governance. The five OECD categories of principles of corporate governance, monitored by ISAR (the UN Intergovernmental Working Group of Experts on International Standards of Accounting and Reporting), make no specific mention of value creation or compensation. Sarbanes Oxley in the USA is weighted heavily towards the regulation of the accounting profession with again no specific mention of value and compensation. The UK Corporate Governance Code, by contrast, does include remuneration as one of its five categories: leadership, effectiveness, accountability, remuneration, and relations with shareholders. Remuneration covers the two broad headings of linking rewards to corporate and individual performance, and procedures for developing executive compensation. There is a schedule regarding the design of performance-related remuneration for executive directors, but no specific mention of value creation, and also no guidance for determining what levels of compensation should be in relation to that value creation. It could be useful for control authorities such as the FRC in the UK, to study guidelines for the ways in which economic value and compensation can be defined and reported as part of corporate governance, whose basic purpose is to ensure business sustainability in terms of value creation and accountability to all of the stakeholders in a business enterprise.

References

Belfield R, Little A. The CFA executive compensation report. *Willis Towers Watson*, 27 Jan 2015. https://www.towerswatson.com/en-GB/Insights/IC-Types/Secondary-Research/2015/CFA-executive-compensation-report.
CFA Institute. Measuring and Rewarding Performance in Relation to Executive Compensation, 2014.

Costa M, Lippincott T. Enduring high-performing companies take the road less traveled in executive compensation design. Willis Towers Watson, 15 July 2014. https://www.towerswatson.com/en/Insights/Newsletters/Global/executive-pay-matters/2014/Executive-Compensation-Bulletin-Enduring-High-Performing-Cos-Take-Road-Less-Traveled-in-Exec-Pay.

Gordon S. Top managers' pay reveals weak link to value. Financial Times, 28 Dec 2014. www.ft.com/cms/s/0/0e88759a-8ac0-11e4-be0e-00144feabdc0.html.

Gumport M. A. The next, great, corporate scandal. Social science Research Network Sep 7, 2006.

Hass LH, Liu J, Young S, Zhang Z. Measuring and rewarding performance: theory and evidence in relation to executive compensation. (Report) Lancaster University Management School and CFA Society United Kingdom, October 2014.

Okun AM. Equality and efficiency: the big tradeoff. Washington, DC: Brookings Institution Press; 1975.

Piketty T. Capital in the twenty-first century. Cambridge, MA: Harvard University Press; 2014.

The Economist. Performance-related pay, 30 Oct 2009. http://www.economist.com/node/14301231.

Willis Towers Watson. Deferred shares—a particular solution to executive remuneration alignment? Towers Watson, November 2010 (report).

Willis Towers Watson. The CFA Executive Compensation Report Report. January 2015 and Calibrating Directors' Pay with GR: IN Analysis.

Wilson F. Employee equity: restricted stock and RSUs. AVC, 2013. http://avc.com/2010/11/employee-equity-restricted-stock-and-rsus/.

10

Regulation and Control of Economic Value

Abstract This chapter looks at the needs of regulation and control from a "businessman's" point of view regarding the recent crisis of trust and confidence in the financial system. It calls for the concept of "economic value" to be used as a basic metric in reporting and control to get the balance right between solvency and economic value, as the starting point for the more complex task of calculating intrinsic value. Some of the faults, mistakes and abuses of the past years are discussed, as well as new

---

An Introductory "Caveat." In looking at the regulation and control we need for measuring the economic health of a business enterprise, we do so not as qualified regulatory experts, but rather as "users" or "consumers" of financial services, and students of economics in business. We hope that our views reflect the opinions and concerns of businessmen as "economic operators", engaged in "doing business" (whether financial, industrial or non-profit), and also those of the man on the famous "Clapham Omnibus", who entrusts his savings to financial institutions. Our aim is to suggest what might be done to restore consumer confidence in the honesty and competence of financial institutions, and the professional competence of the regulatory authorities, whose purpose is to facilitate the provision of capital for business, and to protect the earnings and assets of those who save and invest. We agree with Mark Carney, the Chairman of the G20 Financial Stability Board, and Governor of the Bank of England, on the need to restore confidence, when he says, "Fundamental changes are necessary to rebuild trust in finance. Those practising in the industry must demonstrate exemplary behavior and be seen as serving end users rather than their own interests."

© The Editor(s) (if applicable) and The Author(s) 2016   **189**
M.R. Griffiths, J.R. Lucas, *Value Economics*,
DOI 10.1057/978-1-137-54187-1_10

legislation, such as the Dodd–Frank Ack, the Volcker Rule, and the EU Directives, designed to prevent those mistakes occurring again. The chapter takes a layman's view of the Cyprus and Greek sovereign debt crises, and why the "experts" were unable to prevent those crises. The question of how to calculate the economic value of financial instruments, like derivatives, is also discussed. Finally, it is suggested that the annual reporting of the regulatory authorities might cover, as well as solvency and capital adequacy, the "economic value" issues which the economy is facing, and a section on consumer trust and confidence.

10.1 Chapter Overview

What mechanisms do we need for regulating and controlling the solidity of financial institutions? Basel 3 and Solvency 2 are setting standards for measuring capital adequacy and solvency. Although these are important steps towards resolving the solvency problems of the last financial crisis, in our opinion they do not place enough emphasis on the underlying value of financial institutions in terms of the value they are creating or destroying. Information on economic value (defined as NOPAT less cost of capital) could assist the setting of "value standards" for financial institutions, and the metrics for measuring economic performance, in a way which would link capital adequacy to the economic value of financial institutions. We also see economic value as the starting point for calculating intrinsic value which takes into account discounted future profits, the value of intangible assets, and the requirements of "Triple Bottom Line Accounting" (economic, social and environmental) on which a company's future as an "ongoing and sustainable business" depends.

How are financial institutions to restore public confidence and trust in the competency and honesty of their operations? Will Dodd–Frank[1] the Volcker Rule and latest developments in the UK such as the Bank of England's "Fairness and Effective Review", be sufficient to prevent "tempests in a teapot", in the words of J.P. Morgan's Jamie Dimon, turning

---

[1] See refs. "Did Dodd-Frank work?" Jos Noceve INYT 23 July 2014 and "Wall street vampires" Paul Kingman INYT 12 May 2015.

into the "London Whale", which a US Senate report described as an operation which "piled risk on risk, ignored risk links, hid losses and misinformed the public"? Apologies from J.P. Morgan were forthcoming, but rather than being specific they focused on the need for a system for controlling the "market makers". We believe that the regaining of confidence and trust is not solely the task of the regulators, but also of financial institutions in the spirit of "physician heal thyself", which calls for internal self-regulating procedures, which could serve to reinvigorate the old City adage "my word is my bond".

In tackling these faults, mistakes and abuses, we need to learn lessons from the faults of the past, such as the rigging of Libor interest rates, and the gaming culture of the Barclays trading room. We look at a number of these examples, each of which raises questions for the regulators as to how to prevent such events happening again. The control of sovereign debt is a major problem for regulation and control. We look at the problems of controlling Euro Sovereign Debt, taking Cyprus and Greece as examples, where the ECB is limited in terms of what it can do in a market which lacks fiscal union and the ability to issue euro debt bonds, being still subject to the vagaries of 28 kinds of national debt, in spite of having a single currency.

We also consider the problems of regulating derivatives, financial instruments with no intrinsic value apart from the underlying assets to which their options are linked, and suggest that reinsurance might assist the process of putting a value on derivative options. The feasibility of this could be a subject for study by the European Market Infrastructure for Regulation (EMIR).

The complexity of present-day financial regulation calls for a new look at the emptor/vendor relationship in the provision of financial services, which we believe requires new codes of business practice for customer relationships, and for banking operations. We should like to see a joint initiative between the customers and providers of financial services in recreating that sense of reciprocal confidence and trust between the parties involved.

Finally, we look at the outlook for financial regulation and control in light of the Bank of England's "Fair and Effective Markets Review" and its proposals for banking standards and benchmarks. We believe this will require a new manual for regulatory and control procedures, which, in terms of regulatory performance, could be reported in an Annual

Regulatory Report issued by the relevant regulatory authority, and which summarizes the capital adequacy of the financial sector, the risks involved and the actions being taken to minimize them. Such a report could contain a section on the economic health of the financial sector and the economic value of individual institutions. The purpose of this would be to link capital adequacy to the underlying economic value of the financial institutions which the regulatory authority is controlling. Shareholder value is an important part of economic value, but not the only component of value which encompasses the other values inherent in the future of a business, which is now taking companies into "Triple Bottom Line Accounting" covering economic, social and environmental results. How are we to regulate and control the social and environmental aspects of economic activity?

10.2 Regulation of Economic Value

We might start by asking: how is the complex and highly volatile world of "economic value" to be controlled and regulated? Are the central financial control authorities' "due diligence" systems adequate for "valuing" financial products, as we move into the new regulatory world of Basel 3 and Solvency 2 for controlling solvency and capital adequacy? There is an uncertainty and imprecision in establishing "economic value" which arises from the fact that "value" at any one moment in time may no longer be valid the next moment, as assumptions change, and market pricing may not adequately reflect economic value. In this highly complex and unstable environment the initial financial "value" hypotheses, or conditions, may prove to be invalid, requiring a continuous real-time online analysis of variances from the initial hypotheses, which we might call a "moving target" approach to the measurement of economic value.

What valuation systems do we need to establish economic value at any specific time in the business cycle, and the target share price against which to monitor the future performance of market prices? The insurance industry uses the reinsurer to place a value on the risks it is taking in providing insurance coverage and also in pricing that coverage. We need a similar reinsurance approach to the definition and pricing of financial products, in other words third parties prepared to underwrite and price financial products which take account of their implicit and explicit "insurance" risks. Measurement of value and risk is a complex process, which needs a continuous review of the precision, or otherwise, of the assumptions and measures employed. All of these are important considerations for designing the systems the regulatory authorities need for measuring performance, financial solidity, and risk, which currently concentrate primarily on the metric of capital adequacy, rather than a metric of economic value. Basel 3 seeks to improve the ability of the banking sector to absorb shocks from financial and economic stress; to improve risk management; and to strengthen banks' transparency and disclosures. Solvency 2 seeks to define supervisory procedures for specific parameters, own funds, matching adjustments, special purpose vehicles, and internal models. Both Basel 3 and Solvency 2 call for procedures to assess the value at risk (VAR), but this needs to be linked to the economic value of a financial institution—or at least to the balance sheet net asset values and cash flows. Does regulation need to give more attention to economic value, as, for example, with the concept of "Economic Profit" used by industrial companies such as Apple, so that institutions can be held to account not only for their financial solidity but also for the economic value they are creating? Even if there are different dimensions of value, as we discussed in Chap. 8, we believe that Basel 3 and Solvency 2 should also provide guidelines for calculating the economic value of financial institutions and the related capital required for achieving their business "value" objectives.

10.3 Restoring Confidence and Trust

One of the fallouts from the last financial crisis was a crisis of confidence in both the ability and the willingness of the financial authorities to put in motion a system of regulation which will improve the transparency and accountability of financial institutions. Will the Dodd–Frank and Volcker legislation in the US and the new Financial Directives in the UK change the behaviour of respected financial institutions such as J.P. Morgan, whose CEO, Jamie Dimon, referred in April 2012 to the "London Whale" trades that had apparently lost the bank an estimated $2 billion (a figure which subsequently rose to some $6.2 billion) as "a tempest in a teapot?" Some teapot, one might say! It appeared at the time that the Office of the Comptroller of the Currency (OCC) never had a full understanding of the risks involved, and that, when bank witnesses conceded that the trades were part of a hedge that had gone wrong, it was not clear what the trades were supposed to be hedging. Jamie Dimon admitted that the strategy was "flawed, complex, poorly reviewed, poorly executed and poorly monitored". It was described as a "monstrous derivatives bet" made by Bruno Iksil, alias the "London Whale", which the US Senate report described as a "trading operation that piled on risk, ignored links on risk taking, hid losses, dodged oversight and misinformed the public".[2] These comments contain echoes of the Nick Leeson "bets" which had brought Barings to its knees in the 1990s. J.P. Morgan said "our executives believed that the facts they had at the time were true, but in retrospect the information they had was wrong, and they apologized for this". What were the changes in management procedures for preventing this kind of trading happening again, and what was the impact on the compensation of those responsible for those trading "mistakes"? This is as an example of why public confidence (in this case) in the competence of J.P. Morgan's investment management over the "London Whale" phenomenon was so badly damaged. Jamie Dimon's "tempest in a teapot" remark served only to highlight how even a proven, respected financial expert can get it disastrously wrong at times, and be out of touch with what is happening in the trading room. But it also emphasizes the complexity and risk of a financial world where the true value of new financial instruments has been difficult, if not impossible to define. It strikes at the heart of how one is to regulate and control the "market makers".

As Jamie Dimon put it, "Part of the Volcker Rule I agreed with, which is no propriet any trading. But market making is an essential function, and the public should realize that we have the widest, the deepest, the most transparent capital markets in the world. And part of this is that we have enormous market making." How to regulate and control market making is a key question for the regulators, but it has to involve the market makers themselves in a process of self-regulation, where financial experts, such as J.P. Morgan, have to provide a clear answer to the ques-

---

[2] "Senate investigation finds JP Morgan hid mistakes as losses grew" Guardian March 15, 2013.

tion: "What do you propose that market makers should do to prevent tea-cups becoming large enough to accommodate a whale?" In other words, the first rule of the game should be "physician, heal thyself", which could be the first step towards reconfirming and recreating the trust and confidence in financial institutions on the part of the public and the "man on the Clapham Omnibus", where the jury is still out on deciding whether or not the leopard has changed its spots.

10.4   Tackling Faults, Mistakes and Abuses

The outlook for restoring trust and confidence is not entirely encouraging if one considers a selection of financial headlines over the past few years, which emphasize the kind of problems the regulatory authorities need to address.

- *"From Northern Rock to Lehmans, Who Should Share the Blame?",* Martin Jacomb, *Spectator,* 20 *September 2008.* "So the problem is acute all round. And the mistakes banks have made have put them near the centre of the circle of responsibility. But governments, central banks and regulators are in there too. So are bank shareholders, who sanctioned remuneration structures which incentivized management in the wrong direction."
- *"A Boom Market in Economic Nonsense",* Ross Clark, *Spectator,* 31 *January 2009,* suggesting that the current financial crisis produced a glut of illiteracy and woolly thinking. "Anyone caught out by the credit crunch… might by reading a book on basic economics… learn that it wasn't a good idea to buy ten buy-to-lets in Newcastle on a million-pound mortgage in the belief that tenants could be conjured out of thin air and that property prices only go up." A good example of woolly thinking about "value".
- *"Smart Management Might Have Averted the Banking Crisis Without Barbed Wire Fences",* Martin Vander Weyer, *Spectator,* 6 *February 2010.* "The key, in every case, large or small, single product or financial supermarket, is laser-sharp analytical management of risk—for which legislative firewalls and barbed wire fences can never be a substitute."

- *Unravelling London's old-school bank image: "Scandals, Princely Pay and Aggressive Strategies Alter a Once-staid World", Landon Thomas, INYT,* 7 July 2012. "Long renowned as the center of global money flows, deal making and discretion, London's financial centre has become the hub to a different form of activity: Financial scandal and behavior beyond the pale. Rogue traders working out of the London offices of AIG, UBS and JP Morgan have rung up billions of dollar losses in recent years." "Greed took over", said Alexander Hoare, a managing partner of C. Hoare & Co, in commenting about the five big banks (Citigroup, J.P. Morgan Chase, Barclays, RBS and UBS) pleading guilty in anti-trust investigation (fines totally $5.6 billion for fixing interest rates and foreign exchange rates). *INYT,* 21 May 2015.
- *"Barclays Bank Had a 'Culture of Gaming'", INYT,* 17 July 2012 Scott and Castle. "There was a culture of gaming at Barclays", referring to which Andrew Bailey, head of banking supervision at the FSA, said "It had to change". A former senior Barclays executive claimed he had been instructed to report false Libor figures at the behest of British officials. Adair Turner, Chairman of the FSA, testified he was not aware of the potential Libor manipulations until being briefed in 2009. Raises the basic regulatory question of "who is in control, and of what?"
- *"Bank of England denies US (New York Fed) warned it on Libor".* There was no suggestion of fraudulent behavior, but how does one national regulatory authority relate to another? *INYT,* 18 July 2012.
- *UK bank apologizes for "skirting" regulations* in US enquiry which found HSBC helped drug cartels and terrorist organizations seeking money transfers (money laundering). $7 billion in cash from Mexico to the USA in 2007/2008. *INYT,* 18 July 2012.
- *Lord Libor Trio* (Libor broker called banks "sheep"). ICAP's controls insufficient. FT 26/9/2013. The whole scandal described as a "monstrous abuse of trust". See also steps being undertaken to overhaul the British interbank rate system. *INYT,* 11 August 2012 Mark Scott article on "Libor dealings prompt push for transparency and criminal penalties".
- *"RBS to Pay $612 Million Fine", INYT, 7 February 2013.* RBS admitted that 21 of its employees altered the firm's Libor submissions for financial gains on hundreds of occasions. Head of the US Justice Department's criminal division called the actions s "stunning abuse of trust".

- *Europeans Strike Deal on Rules for Derivatives* "Flurry of compromises leads to accord tackling risky forms of trading". Markets in Financial Instruments Directives, to be implemented in 2016. Complex, described as "a story with the detail of a Talmudic exegesis", *INYT*, 16 January 2014.
- *"Three Expensive Milliseconds"*, Paul Krugman, *INYT*, 15 April 2014. A fibre-optic cable for taking time off communication time between the futures market of Chicago (Chicago Mercantile Exchange, CME) and the stock markets of New York, which will assist the high-frequency trading discussed in Michael Lewis' book *Flash Boys*, where society is devoting more and more resources to financial wheeling and dealing, enabling finance to grow much faster than the economy as a whole. The share of GDP accruing to bankers has nearly doubled since 1980, but are we getting return for all that money? Difficult to answer after a decade when Wall Street directed hundreds of billions of dollars into subprime mortgages.
- *Five big banks (Citigroup, JPMorgan Chase, Barclays, RBS and UBS) plead guilty* in antitrust investigation (receiving fines totalling $5.6 billion for fixing interest rates and foreign exchange rates). *INYT*, 21 May 2015.
- *"Wall Street is Back, and Some Fear a Downside"*, *INYT*, 19 May 2015. Wall Street has largely returned to a state reminiscent of the go-go 2000s. Average pay per full-time worker in the securities industry was 2.2 times that of the average American worker for the 70 years ending 1999, peaking at 4.2 in 2007, and by 2013 had rebounded to 3.6 times. "While there is no doubt that a developed financial sector is important", said Luigi Zingales, President of the American Finance Association, "there is no theoretical or empirical evidence that all the growth of the last 40 years has been beneficial to society."

If the mythical man from Mars should arrive, he would read many reports of the last financial crisis such as these, and the proposed solutions now in place (Dodd–Frank and the Volcker Rule in the USA, and the EU Directives), and might conclude that appropriate actions are now in place to prevent the defects and abuses of the past from recurring. However, reading the headlines above, what would be the level of confidence and trust he would have that things will really change, and that the "experts" responsible will be able to predict and control the future any better than they have done in the past? The new regulations and financial management systems have to demonstrate that they will do so, if public confidence and trust are to be restored. To ensure that the needs and opinions of businessmen are fully considered and taken into account, there is a case for creating a trust and confidence mechanism which will, first and foremost, take account of what the consumer of financial products such as the businessman and the general public (as the expressions of consumer preferences) expect of the financial industry, and of the experts (economists, politicians and public administrators) responsible for providing the necessary economic infrastructure. An annual trust and confidence report on the part of the regulatory authorities could assist the public in understanding whether the lessons of the last financial crisis have been learnt or not.[3]

10.5 Regulatory Mechanisms for Controlling Economic Value

What mechanisms do we need to measure the solvency of a financial institution, and the value of financial products? We are now moving into the regulatory world of the Volcker Rule, and the new standards for capital adequacy required by Basel 3 and Solvency 2, but we believe

---

[3] The trust and confidence factor is also related to the "Too Big to Fail" debate which Joe Nocera discussed in his article "Did Dodd–Frank work?" (*INYT*, 23 July 2014), where the elimination of future bank bailouts was one of the aims of this legislation. The US Treasury Department was insisting the days of "Too Big to Fail" were over, with a statement by the Treasury Undersecretary for Domestic Finance that "No financial institution, regardless of its size, will be bailed by taxpayers again. Shareholders of failed companies will be wiped out; creditors will absorb losses; culpable management will not be retained, and may have their compensation clawed back." But it doesn't appear that the markets believe it. The problem relates to how the law would resolve the problem of failed institutions. Dodd–Frank requires banks to write "living wills" describing how they would wind down without causing financial catastrophe, and calls for banks to wind down through "orderly liquidation". The proof of the pudding will depend on its eating, where the complexity of regulating failed institutions raises the issue of how confident the authorities are that they can control the risks of these events occurring. Solvency requirements may be increased, but the costs of failure will also depend on whether these risks can be reinsured, and related to the economic value of the institution concerned.

that these forms of regulatory control would be more complete if they could measure economic value as well as capital adequacy. To do that we need to establish a new concept of "value in economics", which will compare economic value against the prices for equity stocks, bonds, derivatives and securitized products in terms of "under-" or "over-pricing". For regulation this could have the advantage of relating capital adequacy to underlying economic value. Econometric models can make useful predictions, but are not inherently concerned with the "economic value" of what they are predicting. We need an "ops room" approach to the pricing of economic and financial products, based on continuous "online" analysis of value at any one point in time. Regulation and control has to take account of what we mean by economic value over different time horizons, and to evaluate the "creation of wealth" not only in monetary terms, but also in terms of the value which that wealth creation is generating. In other words, regulation and control need to go beyond "book values" and "operating profits" into the dimensions of the economic and intrinsic value of a financial institution. This wider interpretation of "value" could be of use in defining the nature of the "value metrics" which the regulatory authorities need to maintain and control the economic solidity of financial institutions, which set solvency and capital adequacy in the context of the economic value which those institutions are creating.

10.6 Regulating Sovereign Debt

When the Cyprus crisis came to the fore in March 2013, it suddenly emerged that a country within the euro area had a banking system that was seven times the size of its gross domestic product. The ensuing bailout of Cyprus' financial industry was another example of public money being used to protect bank lending debt from the consequences of those lending choices, in a financial market where the rumour of recycling laundered money from Russia (through a process that was never clearly explained) only served to cast doubt on the ECB's ability to control the sovereign debt of one member of the euro area. The man in the street is right to ask where all that bailout money is going. Is it going to pay off the financial system's debt, or into industrial investment linked to restructuring and reducing public debt? The Cyprus crisis was another nail in the coffin of public confidence in the power and capability of those in charge to control and regulate financial markets. Is it impossible to define criteria for deciding what should be the relationship between the size of a country's banking system and the national economy which it supports?

In 1992, the Maastricht Treaty was signed with the intention of limiting the deficit spending of the EU members as sovereign states. However, in the early 2000s, some EU member states were failing to respect the Maastricht criteria, and turned to securitizing future government revenues to reduce the level of national debt and deficit as a percentage of GDP. This allowed the members to mask their actual deficit and debt levels through a combination of techniques, including inconsistent accounting, off-balance-sheet transactions, and the use of complex currency and credit derivative instruments. From late 2009 onwards, after Greece's newly elected government stopped masking the level of its true indebtness and budget deficit, fears of sovereign defaults in certain European states arose, leading to the downgrade of "risky" levels of government debt. Over the period 2010–12, it became clear that four out of 18 eurozone states (Greece, Ireland, Portugal and Cyprus) faced either considerable financial difficulties or a total inability to repay or refinance their government debt, without recourse to bailout assistance from the Troika (tripartite committes, EU commission, ECB and IMF). The transfer of bailout funds was performed in tranches over a period of years, on the condition that governments would implement fiscal changes, structural reforms, the privatization of public assets and the creation of funds for bank recapitalization. Of the countries Spain technically avoided a sovereign debt crisis through the receipt of financial support from the European Stability Mechanism which was earmarked to fund a bank recapitalization fund without the provision of any financial support for the government itself.

By July 2014, Ireland and Portugal had completed and successfully exited their bailout programmes through a combination of improved structural deficits and economic growth, and had regained access to markets for refinancing their future needs. By contrast, Greece failed to meet all its bailout conditions, which had originally been designed to end in 2016. In addition to the bailout programmes being implemented to combat the eurozone crisis, the European Central Bank (ECB) lowered interest rates, and provided cheap loans of more than one trillion euros to maintain money flows between European banks. In September 2012, the ECB also announced a support for all eurozone countries, involving a sovereign state bailout programme from the european stability mechanism (ESM), through Outright Monetary Transactions (OMT). The European debt crisis and austerity programmes designed to solve it has had adverse economic effects in terms of growth, with unemployment rates in Greece and Spain reaching an average of 27 percent, but being much higher among young people.

A number of factors contributed to the eurozone crisis and the difficulties of controlling the sovereign debts of the individual member states of the EU: these included, the globalization of debt finance; the easy credit conditions during 2002–08 that encouraged high-risk lending and the borrowing practices of individual EU banks; the submortgage loan financial crisis of 2007–08; international trade imbalances; excessive investment in real estate as opposed to industrial research and development; and the reduction in consumer spending. A research report completed in 2012 for the United States Congress explains, "The current eurozone crisis has been unfolding since 2009, when a new Greek government revealed that previous Greek governments had been under-reporting the budget deficit. The crisis subsequently spread to Ireland and Portugal, while raising concerns about Italy, Spain and the European banking system, and more fundamental imbalances within the eurozone." (The eurozone crisis overview and issues for congress report 29 FEB 2012). The Greek underreporting was exposed through a revision of the forecast for the 2009 budget deficit from "6–8 per cent" of GDP (no greater than 3 per cent of GDP was a rule of the Maastricht Treaty) to 12.7 per cent. Large upwards revisions of budget deficit forecasts resulting from the international financial crisis were not limited to Greece: for example, in the United States the forecast for the 2009 budget deficit was raised from the $407 billion projected in the 2009 fiscal year budget, to $1.4 trillion, and in the United Kingdom the final forecast was more than four times higher than the original. The fact that Greek debt in 2014 exceeded $400 billion (177 per cent of GDP according to Eurostat), and France held 10 % of that debt led to renewed talk of default for Greece.

Although yields on Greek 10-year government bonds reached 7 per cent in April 2010, Draghi's statement that the ECB would do all that was possible to defend the euro which preceded the introduction of Quantitative Easing, and the move towards negative interest rates, contributed to a reduction of speculation on the euro. During 2013–15 the euro declined in value against both the dollar and sterling, although it still remains above the exchange rates fixed for these currencies when the euro was introduced in 2000. The effect of current exchange rates on the euro sovereign debt levels still has to be seen, but the ECB was successful in defending the euro in a situation which is structurally weak when compared with the advantages of the Fed and the Bank of England, which have common national fiscal policies—in contrast to the 28 members of the euro. In addition, the USA and the UK are able to issue government dollar and sterling bonds, whereas the debtworthiness of the euro still depends on the cohesion between the 28 different forms of government bonds, the instability of which can be seen daily in the spreads between German bonds, and those of the other member states. The priority for the control of European sovereign debt is to move towards fiscal union and the issue of euro debt able to compete on equal terms with the government bonds of all other countries, and of the USA and the UK in particular. This need presents a key problem for the regulatory authorities in developing the structures necessary for regulating and controlling EU sovereign debt, within the context of incomplete fiscal union and the fragmentary nature of euro debt.

10.7 Controlling Derivative Values

Regulation has become increasingly difficult and complex following the development of the market for derivatives contracts, whose values depend on the performance of an underlying entity, which can be an asset, an index, or an interest rate. It is the value of these underlying entities which can cause problems in establishing the actual underlying net worth or value of a derivative. Derivatives derive their value from the performance of an underlying entity if an asset, an index or interest rate are used for a number of purposes, including insuring against price movements (hedging), increasing exposure to price movements for speculation or getting access to otherwise hard-to-trade assets or markets.

We enter the complex world of forwards, futures, options, swaps and variations of these such as synthetic collateralized debt obligations and credit default swaps. Most derivatives are traded over-the-counter (off-exchange) or on an exchange such as the Chicago Mercantile Exchange. Thus, derivatives become a separate form of financial instrument, alongside stocks and shares, and the debt instruments of bonds and mortgages. Derivatives have been the cause of unforeseen losses and in some cases accusations of mis-selling. A lack of effective regulation has led to dissatisfied customers instigating legal processes, characterized in some cases by a situations of "paying so as not to have to pay" on "future profit" bets which turned out to be impossible to realize.

The local authority in Florence, for example, in 2012 abrogated, cancelled or revoked contracts dated June 2006 with Merrill Lynch, UBS, and Dexia Crediop, who responded by taking the authority to court in London as these "toxic" contracts had been signed in the City of London, forcing the local authority to incur significant legal fees for an injudicious investment in financial products, which had negative implications for the authority's level of debt. In such a complex and introverted system of pursuing unrealistic returns, it is hardly surprising that the ratepayer feels aggrieved that he is the victim of incompetent local authority financial management.

Another derivative "horror" story has been the experience of the Monte dei Paschi bank in Italy who reported (Reuters, 6 February 2013) that losses linked to three problematic derivative trades totalled 730 million euros ($988 million), which arose from a series of derivative and structured finance deals. These trades are now being investigated in a fraud probe into the former management of the bank, and has raised questions about the role of banking supervisors and the influence of local politicians. In a *Newsnight* programme (BBC, 11 September 2012) UK-based banks were accused of massive mis-selling in Italy, where Nomura, UBS and Deutsche Bank are accused by the Italian prosecutors of mis-selling in deals in Milan worth 35 billion euros. *Newsnight* stated that the London financial watchdog was made aware of this situation by a "whistleblower" but had failed to act. This was denied, but is now the subject of civil and legal proceedings.

Between 1997 and 2007, a number of Italian cities and regions borrowed a total of some 111 billion euros from London-based investment banks whose repayments were funded by derivative swaps. Although the swaps appeared to offer attractive rates of interest, in reality the local authorities had risked taxpayers' money on complex derivative bets which ended up costing them much more than was expected. The NAPF has released a paper on the legislative initiatives in the European Union which should have a major impact on the control of derivatives. The proposed Derivatives Directive (EMIR—European Market Infrastructure Regulation) and the proposed fourth Capital Requirements Directive (CRD IV) have been developed as part of a wider international response to the financial crisis. The proposed Derivatives Directive will require derivatives to be cleared through a central counterparty (CCP) clearing house. EMIR came into effect from the end of 2012 with regulations covering reporting, clearing and risk mitigation technique for derivatives. These regulation raise issues about the safety of assets put up as collateral, which emphasizes the need for a system and procedures for valuing derivatives as alternative financial instruments.

If derivatives are a hazardous form of risk management, having no intrinsic value in themselves, the challenge is how to value the underlying assets on which they depend. The potential risk of inadequate valuation was seen most clearly in the subprime mortgage crisis, where values simply evaporated overnight. With derivatives we enter the world of structured debt, obligations and deposits, swaps, futures, options, caps, floors, collars, forwards, and various combinations of these. This was treacherous territory for both the emptor and the vendor, made even riskier by the sheer size of the market. What kind of multiple-headed hydra have we released into the financial world? In June 2011, the *Economist* calculated that the over-the-counter (OTC) derivatives market amounted to $700 trillion with a further $83 trillion traded on exchanges. To set this in perspective the total budget of the US Government in 2012 was $3.5 trillion, and the US stock market 23 trillion. World GDP was *c.* $65 trillion. Credit default swaps, which Warren Buffet described as "weapons of mass financial destruction", were $25 trillion, down from $55 trillion in 2008, which is highly volatile to say the least.

A report by Global Research (Michael Snyder, Center for research on globalization report, 27 May 2014) estimated the global derivative bubble at that time to be some 20 percent bigger than it was in 2008. In regulating this market the authorities' main task is to define how to value derivative products. Should the appropriate measure be notional value, market value, certified book (NAV) value, or economic value? If derivatives do not have an intrinsic value in themselves, but rely instead on the underlying value of their supporting assets, we need an estimate of the value of those assets. A theory for the pricing of derivative options was the basis of Black and Scholes paper in 1973, "The pricing of options and corporate liabilities". The idea was to hedge the option by buying and selling the underlying asset to eliminate the risk. If Black and Scholes can price derivative options, and we need to quantify their risk, could reinsurance assist in providing a second opinion on the adequacy of that pricing based on the economic values and risk profiles of the underlying assets?

10.8 Controlling Emptor and Vendor

We live in a financial world where it is not sufficient to believe that the principle of "caveat emptor" (the responsibility of the customer to be accountable for his decisions) should be the basic criterion of regulation and control. The principle of "caveat vendor" should be regarded as being equally important in a financial world where customer protection requires a high level of advisory competence and transparency on the part of the financial "vendor". We need to establish clear criteria for regulatory control which indicate not only how financial products are to be sold, but also how their performance is to be reported and controlled. The need for greater transparency in banking relationships has resulted in a mass of small print relating to the risks involved in banking transactions which at times is so opaque as to be distinctly "unfriendly".

We need the establishment of a Regulation Protection Agency which, like the Ombudsman, can monitor the effectiveness of regulation from the point of view not only of the sophisticated purchaser of financial products, but also of the man in the street whether he or she is, for example, a modest wage earner on the Clapham Omnibus, or an old age pensioner wondering why his pension is not what he expected it to be. It is ironic that the figure of the trusted local bank manager has been replaced by the call centre where the push button often serves only to depersonalize personal service provided by the vendor to his emptor. Ironic, that is, because it is increasingly difficult for the financial consumer to understand the mechanics and risks of financial products, where confusion or a lack of understandable information only increases the communication gap between the financial "emptor" and his "vendor". The development of "best advice" information is a step in the right direction, but it remains to be seen whether this will prove sufficient to prevent the mis-selling of fraudulent Ponzi schemes, or pension provision. The International Organization of Securities Commission (IOSCO)'s "Regulatory Principles for Corporate Financial Disclosure and Transparency" needs to give clear guidelines for managing the "vendor/emptor" relationship between financial institutions and their customers, and for reporting on market abuse, with particular reference to the level of customer satisfaction as measured by indices of customer loyalty compared with the incidence of customer complaints and disputes.

10.9   Outlook for Regulation and Control

So, following the introduction of the Dodd–Frank law and the Volcker Rule in the USA, and the new banking regulations in the UK, are things really going to change in terms of more effective regulation and control? How does one prevent that "risk oversight" which J.P. Morgan admitted at the time of the "London Whale" when the bank admitted that "we were not aware at the time of all the deficiencies in the risk organization of the trading group"? It appeared that traders had been interfering with risk measures and valuations with the result that the bank gave incorrect information to the regulator and made misleading statements to both shareholders and the public.

Risk management systems are not simple, but today we have the information technology to calculate on a continuous real-time basis whether the initial conditions and hypotheses regarding the risks we are taking are changing. We need to know the initial hypotheses which a trader is using, and to be able to evaluate whether or not those hypotheses remain valid. And how are we are to eliminate the "gaming culture" which characterized activities such as the Barclays Libor scandal? Traders need to be subject to the rigour of a system which can identify unacceptable risk taking or malpractice. Will the use of "big data" technology enable financial institutions to pinpoint malpractice in the trading room? And, in a broader context, how do we prevent banks from making bets for their own profit using customer deposits, and taxpayer-backed money? Will the Volcker Rule be able to do this?

Regulatory authorities need to be answerable for the validity of the regulatory and control systems in light of the principle of "quis custodiet ipsos custodes". The regulator, whether the external authority or the internal auditor, sets the rules, but rules require controllers or auditors who are at arm's length from the rule makers. Financial regulation and control has become so complex that the regulatory experts need a mechanism to ensure that they themselves are subject to procedures for compliance and audit, which requires an independent audit of their operations. The recent attempts in the UK to improve bank regulation caused some acrimonious comment and debate. The parliamentary commission criticized the government's proposal for the regulator to review the strength of ring-fencing—barriers to segregate retail banking units from banks' riskier investment banking operations—as being "wholly inadequate", since legislation does not include statutory provision to force the separation of retail and investment banking across the industry.

In the words of Andrew Tyrie, the chairman of the Parliamentary Commission on Banking Standards, commenting on the commission report: "We have just had a shocking Libor scandal, we have had the rigging of wholesale markets and we have seen the equally shocking rip off of customers in the P.P.I. scandal and of small business in the interest-rate swap scandal. These and other revelations which have also included sanctions-busting and money-laundering reflect deep-seated problems of standards in banking." The Bank of England's "Fair and Effective Markets Review", assisted by the Market Practitioners Panel, has been looking at the codes and standards for a new "FICC Market Standards Board" (dealing with the Fixed Income, Currencies and Commodities markets) based on principles for Fairness and Effectiveness. These principles cover the use of benchmarks for measuring performance, and the possibility to derive meaningful information and insights in real time able to control the split second timing of electronic trading.

We are in the midst of a radical rethinking of financial standards, where price benchmarks are to be the references to calculate the value of single financial instruments or positions. But are price benchmarks sufficient for indicating the solidity of financial institutions if they are not related to the underlying economic value? The review talks of aligning compensation to business standards designed to improve the fairness and effectiveness of financial institutions. In the end, however, fairness and effectiveness have to be measured in terms of the economic value they create, which is why business standards must include "economic value" standards. Regulation is still grappling with the problem of compensation with the US Securities and Exchange Commission, for example, proposing a rule to claw back bonuses when financial results do not meet the objectives on which "incentive-based compensation" was based. How is one to remove the risk that executives may be motivated to cash out quickly, regardless of whether future performance fails to deliver the results on which bonuses were paid out? The rule required by the Dodd–Frank legislation to achieve greater corporate accountability "targets", in the words of Kara Stein, a Democratic Commissioner at the SEC, aims to correct "the lack of accountability and inflated compensation that helped contribute to excessive risk-taking in the run up to the financial crisis".

At present, the SEC and banking regulators are working together on compensation rules for pay at financial institutions. It is to be hoped that the metric of economic value will be incorporated into these rules. A latest twist to the regulation debate concerns the so-called "shadow banking" system involving unregulated financial institutions and the question of leveraged lending associated with buyouts by private equity firms to purchase public companies. In this system investment banks are not subject to the limits on leveraged loans set by the Federal Reserve, the OCC, and the FDIC, which classified any loan above six times a company's EBITDA (earnings before interest, taxes, depreciation and amortization) as being too risky (see Steven Davidoff, "In Regulation Game, Shadow Lenders Win", *INYT*, 9 July 2015). One might well question, if banks losing out to shadow banks as private equity seeks a way to avoid the new

EBITDA norms, is a good or a bad thing for the economy. Another area for new economic thinking?

The Bank of England's "Fair and Effective Markets Review" emphasizes the complexity of regulation and control, and lays out the standards for measuring the solidity of financial institutions. Basel 3 and Solvency 2 are concentrating on the area of capital adequacy, but the Bank of England Review is taking regulation into the world of standards and benchmarking, and the related areas of consumer preferences and protection. However, the bedrock of standards for regulation and control has to be the creation of value, which takes us on to the question of how we define the economic value of a financial institution. Capital adequacy is, of course, an essential metric for regulation and control, but it needs to be set in the context of the "economic value" which this capital is creating as the basic metric for assessing the solidity and health of financial institutions. The Fairness and Effective Market Review is making detailed recommendations about all aspects of banking operations. The challenge will be to implement them in practice and this will require actions on the part of the regulatory authorities to produce a revised manual of regulatory and control operating procedures for fairness and effectiveness.

The authorities need to propose a system for reporting on their operating performance. This might take the form of an Annual Regulatory Report, which would assess the capital adequacy of financial institutions, and evaluate the risks facing the financial sector, and the actions being taken to control and minimize them. If the argument for giving more emphasis to economic value is accepted, then this Annual Regulatory Report could include a section on the creation of economic value by economic sector, in order to emphasize the importance of value creation in the national economy, and the metrics for measuring that value, discussed in Chap. 8.

Concluding Note

There is at present plenty of activity in trying to improve regulation and control, but the man on the Clapham Omnibus may still have doubts about the extent to which things are actually going to change. As Hancock and Zahawi state in their book *Masters of Nothing*, things are unlikely to do so, unless there is a change in the way people behave, which becomes the future leitmotiv (or, to use a phrase from Italian opera, the "motivo conduttore") for the entire financial community. If Eliza Doolittle joins the man on the Clapham Omnibus in talking about regulation and control she would be right to repeat her refrain from *My Fair Lady* "Words, words, words! I'm so sick of words... Show me... Show me..." So, the ball is in the court of the regulatory authorities and the institutions which they regulate; it is up to them to show that the fundamental changes hoped for in Mark Carney's quote given at the beginning of this chapter become a reality in demonstrating "exemplary behaviour in serving end users rather than their own interests."

References

New Regulation Following the 2008 Crisis

Bank of England "Fair and Effective Markets Review": http://www.bankofengland.co.uk/markets/Pages/fmreview.aspx.
Basel 3 and Solvency 2, "A new regulatory world" (solvency and capital adequacy).
Dodd–Frank Act (financial regulation in the USA).
ECB Regulation (reporting of supervisory financial information).
Guide to European Market Infrastructure Regulation (EMIR). Linklaters November 2013.
The Volcker Rule (speculative and propriety trading in the USA).
UK Banking Directives (creating the FRA and FRC).

Specific Regulation Issues Arising from the 2008 Crisis

Clark R. A boom in market and economic nonsense. The Spectator, 31 Jan 2009. http://new.spectator.co.uk/2009/01/a-boom-market-in-economic-nonsense/.
Controlling Derivative Values (toxic contract experiences, and the new EMIR and CRD regulations).
IOSCO Regulatory Principles for Corporate Financial Disclosure and Transparency (managing the vendor/emptor relationship).

Jacomb M. From Northern Rock to Lehman: who should share the blame? The Spectator, 20 Sept 2008. http://new.spectator.co.uk/2008/09/from-northern-rock-to-lehman-who-should-share-the-blame/.

Kingman P. "Wall street vampires" INYT 12 May 2015.

Nocera J. "Did Dodd-Frank work?" INYT 23 July 2014.

Regulating Sovereign Debt, the Cyprus and Greece crises.

Scott and Castle, Barclays had a culture of 'gaming'. International New York Times, July 2012.

The "London Whale" experience (how hedging trades led to a $2 Billion loss for JP Morgan).

Thomas L. Sandals, princely pay and aggressive strategies alter a once staid world. International New York Times, 7/2012.

Restoring Confidence and Trust

Dombret A. Restoring confidence in the financial system. Deutsche Bank, ECB Speech, 21 Nov 2012. http://www.bis.org/review/r121122c.pdf?frames=0.

Llewellyn DT. Reforming the culture of banking: restoring trust and confidence in banking. J Financ Manag Market Inst. 2014;(2):221–36.

Springford J, editor. A confidence crisis? Restoring trust in financial services. London: Social Market Foundation; 2011.

Taft JG. How to fix financial capitalism? Focus on ethics. Harvard Business Review, 5 July 2012. https://hbr.org/2012/07/how-to-fix-financial-capitalis.

11

Corporate Social Responsibility and Business Ethics

Abstract Corporate social responsibility (CSR) emphasizes that companies need to be accountable not only for the economic results of their activities, but also of the social and environmental results of those activities, which has introduced the concept of "Triple Bottom Line Accounting," and the idea of a Social Balance Sheet (SBS), or Sustainability Report (SR) which complements the economic performance accountability of the statutory accounts. While such reports are now produced by many companies, and contain much important CSR information regarding also the future sustainability of a company, they sometimes remain of secondary use for the investment analyst, who, in making his share price buy or sell recommendations, tends to concentrate on the hard financial figures, rather than on the softer statements of social mission and results. But this should not detract from the importance and value of the SBS or SR for the economic education of employees and the other stakeholders, including details of the company's ethics for doing business expressed in a Code of Business Ethics.

© The Editor(s) (if applicable) and The Author(s) 2016   **213**
M.R. Griffiths, J.R. Lucas, *Value Economics*,
DOI 10.1057/978-1-137-54187-1_11

11.1 Chapter Overview

This chapter looks at issues regarding the corporate social responsibility (CSR) of business and business ethics. It discusses the requirements set out in the European Directive for CSR, and the ISO 26000 CSR standards, which recommends principles—such as accountability, transparency and ethical behaviour—and procedures for corporate governance, human rights, labour practices, consumer issues and the environment. These standards have been summarized in the trilogy of "People, Planet and Profit", covering the management of human and natural (the environment), capital, and the profitability of business in terms of economic value added, and how it is distributed between stakeholders, where we take as an example BP's approach to EVA reporting.

The Global Reporting Institute (GRI) suggests standards, which also cover sustainability procedures for such things as environmental social governance (ESG), ecological footprinting, and environmental cost accounting (EFCA). This has led to the development of ecocapitalism, which concerns itself with the "green" economy, and concepts such as the "Cradle to Grave" analysis of products from their inception, through production and distribution to final disposal. Today, there are about 7500 companies using these guidelines according to the GRI.

Social accounting, which has led to the concept of "Triple Bottom Line Accounting" (economic, social and environmental), today uses the Social Balance Sheet (SBS), or Sustainability Report (SR) to report results in the context of a company's corporate identity (expressed in its mission, strategy and business model), its financial results, and relations with all its stakeholders. We include an example of how an SBS, or Sustainability Report can be structured, which can also contain a description of a company's code of ethics and rules of conduct, for which we also include an example of how such a code can be structured.

Finally, we look at the link between CSR and economic education as the instrument for increasing the awareness of stakeholders, particularly employees, of a company's financial and social results, which we divide into five main elements: communication of the statutory accounts; communication of these "Social" reports; communication of the Code of Business Ethics; an annual compensation (direct and indirect) statement for each employee; and an annual statement of the company's economic value, and how it is distributed. In this context CSR can emphasize the social role of business and the concept of "shared value", which was well expressed by Porter and Kramer in the *Harvard Business Review* when they stated that "Companies could bring business and society back together if they redefined their purpose as creating "shared value"—generating economic value in a way that *also* produces value for society by addressing its challenges. A shared value approach reconnects company success with social progress." A similar view was expressed by Stuart Thorn, the Chief Executive of Southwire (in Eduardo Porter, "Limits of Social Action", *INYT*, 10 September 2015), when he said, "If you are creative, you can find ways to create economic value and social value simultaneously".

The chapter takes a more pro-active view of the importance and value of CSR, than that expressed by Crystia Freeland of Reuters in an article (July 2013) on BP's CSR when she states that "Corporate social responsibility sounds as unobjectional as motherhood and apple pie—and it would indeed be crazy to object to rich companies writing big checks for good causes. But we shouldn't let that distract us from the fact that the chief corporate social responsibility of government is to be sure that perfectly proper corporate greed is channeled and constrained for the greater good of us all."

11.2 CSR and Social Accounting

The European Union expressly defines CSR in its Directive "Corporate Social Responsibility in the EU" as follows: "Corporate social responsibility refers to companies voluntarily going beyond what the law requires to achieve social and environmental objectives during the course of their daily business activities."

ISO 26000 is the recognized international standard for CSR, which is used by public sector organizations such as the United Nations, and includes standards for "Triple Bottom Line Accounting" (TBL) reporting, although there is no formal obligation regarding its use. ISO 26000 provides guidance on how businesses and organizations can operate in a socially responsible way, which, in terms of ethics and transparency, contributes to the health and welfare Eudaimonia of society. It provides guidance rather than statutory standards through the sharing of best CSR practices, which however cannot be certified unlike other ISO standards. The standard for CSR was launched in 2010 following five years of negotiations between different organizations across the world, including government, NGOs, industry, consumer groups and labour organizations.

It articulates seven key CSR principles:

- Accountability.
- Transparency.
- Ethical behaviour.
- Respect for stakeholder interests.
- Respect for the rule of law.
- Respect for international norms of behaviour.
- Respect for human rights.

In addition, it indicates the organization and procedures which the implementation of CSR should address:

- Corporate governance.
- Human rights.
- Labour practices.
- Environment.
- Fair operating practices.
- Consumer issues.
- Community involvement and development.

There are a number of standards and guidelines relating to these questions such as those issued by the ILO and the OECD, as well as the ISO 14001 standards for the environment and SA 8000 for human rights.

However, CSR and social accounting has a number of critics, who echo Milton Friedman's assertion that "There is one and only one social responsibility of business, which is to use its resources and engage in activities designed to increase its profits" and is reflected in the Reuters quote given at the start of this chapter. To take this as justification that

CSR is a cost which serves only to reduce profits is irrational in today's economic world, where shareholder value depends on investment in such things as environmental protection and control, as shown by the experience of the BP DeepWater Horizon disaster. The costs of CSR are now considerable and it is estimated that the largest firms in America and Britain together spend more than $15 billion a year on CSR (Economic Policy Group (EPG), a London based economic consulting firm, estimate). Companies need systems which account for the costs and benefits of CSR expenditure on social and environmental requirements. "Triple Bottom Line Accounting" has now arrived to account for the economic, social and environmental elements of economic activity. The triad of "People, Planet and Profit" has been used to describe TBL reporting (see the title of Shell's first sustainability report in 1997).

"People" relates first and foremost to a company's investment in the human capital represented by its employees, but it also relates to all the other stakeholders who compose what has been described as the reciprocal social structure of society. (See a vast bibliography covering a range of thinkers, from Marx, Althusser, Weber, Durkheim and Habermas through to Anthony Giddens' *The Runaway Society*.)

We talk today of the "upstreaming" of profitability deriving from the marketing of finished goods back to the original producer of raw materials—for example, a farmer in a fair trade agricultural agreement. A TBL business may also seek to "give back" by contributing to the strength and growth of its community—for example, in the areas of health care and education. The quantifying of this bottom line is relatively new, problematic and often subjective. The Global Reporting Initiative (see below) has developed guidelines to enable corporations to report on the social impact of business in terms of "fair trading" and local community involvement.

"Planet" (natural capital) refers to sustainable environmental practices. A TBL company endeavours to reduce or eliminate the negative effects of its operations on the environment. We talk now in terms of ecological footprints resulting from the consumption of energy and controls over the manufacture of toxic waste. We also have the "Cradle to Grave" concept where companies make a life cycle assessment of products to determine the environmental costs, ranging from raw material extraction through material processing, manufacturing and distribution of products in terms of use, repair, maintenance, disposal and or recycling. Who should pay, for example, for the cost of disposing of non-degradable or toxic products? The State or the company? The management of "natural capital" also covers ecologically destructive practices, such as overfishing or other depletions of resources. The costs of environmental sustainability are now part of social accounting, where the reporting metrics are better quantified and standardized for environmental issues than for social ones. A number of organizations to promote these objectives now exist, including the Global Reporting Initiative and CERES (the non-profit organization for the development of a sustainable global economy). The result of all these developments has led to the idea of ecocapitalism, and the development of environmental cost accounting (ECA) as an aspect of social accounting, which has now resulted in demands for the protection of the "green" economy (See "The "Greening of Capitalism?" by Heather Rogers, 2009).

"Profit" for TBL is the economic profit of a company after deducting the costs of all inputs relating to social and environmental factors, including the cost of capital. It extends the traditional accounting definitions of profits to take account of all the costs incurred by a company in operating in a specific social environment. To calculate profit in this way is a challenge for traditional accounting, and raises the question of how to calculate and report on economic value discussed in Chap. 8.

The **Global Reporting Initiative** (GRI) is an international independent standards organization that aims to set standards relating to climate change, human rights and corruption. It produces standards for sustainability, such as ecological footprint reporting, environmental social governance (ESG) reporting, triple bottom line (TBL) reporting, and corporate social responsibility (CSR) reporting. By 2015, 7500 organizations were using GRI guidelines for their sustainability reports.

This indicates the way in which sustainability reporting is gaining in importance and becoming a part of new economic thinking. As the complexity of economic compliance has led to the creation of dedicated Compliance Officers, the function of such officers could be extended to include compliance in the areas of social and environmental regulations, with the intention of submitting an annual report on these areas in a Social Balance Sheet, or Sustainability Report (Discussed in the next section of this chapter.) How are we to report on the social value delivered to society arising from a company's operations? For example, BP state clearly that "we believe societies and communities where we work should benefit from our presence", which implies that the company sees itself as creating social value when its projects and operations create job opportunities for local suppliers and generate tax revenues. BP expressly states that when it moves into a new area it looks for opportunities to create a positive impact in supporting communities' efforts to increase income and improve standards of living.

In 2014 the economic value of BP was stated to be $359.8 billion (see BP Sustainability Report 2014), of which $311.6 billion was distributed to suppliers and $8 billion was paid to the government in taxes. For suppliers this value includes purchases from suppliers, contractor costs, and production expenses. For governments, the economic value arises from taxes deriving to economies around the world and taxes collected on BP products and services. This is an example of how BP thinks not only in terms of the creation of economic value, but also how it is distributed. In 2015 BP economic value declined to $227.9 billion, which emphasises the importance of economic value as a metric of value (discussed in Chap. 8) and the effects an environmental disaster can impact on economic value.

11.3 The Social Balance Sheet and Sustainability Report

The purpose of the Social Balance Sheet, or Sustainability Report as part of the system of social accounting suggested by ISO26000 for CSR reporting, is to complement the statutory accounts by providing information on the social achievements of a company within the context of its profitability and investment return for its shareholders. In this way, these reports are important social documents for describing how the company is satisfying the requirements of all its stakeholders in terms of their needs, wants and objectives. In that sense they can be regarded as an "open letter" to all of the parties involved in its activities. There is no agreed or prescribed format for a social balance sheet, but in Appendix 1 we present an example of how a Sustainability Report can be constructed, covering a profile of the company, its corporate identity, and sustainability indicators.

Corporate Identity covers the **Vision** of the company, its **Mission**; its **Values**; its **Business Model**; and its **Strategy** in terms of quality and service as a responsible TBL business.

Sustainability Indicators include economic performance (in terms of profitability and financial solidity) and the economic value created and how it is distributed between all the stakeholders.

There are many examples of social accounting and reporting, which, even if not presented in a formal and separate social balance sheet, can be detailed in specific sustainability reports—see, for example, the reports of oil companies such as BP, Shell or Exxon Mobil. The level of expenditure on the environmental requirements for these companies is significant, and illustrates how shareholder value today has to include "social and environmental" expenditure and investment, which contribute over the long term to the creation of increased profits expressed in Milton Friedman's "sole purpose" objective for business. TBL accounting is now becoming an important part of business reporting which emphasizes the social contribution of business where the notions of "People, Planet and Profit" are combined to create value which can be "shared" by all members of the stakeholder community.

11.4 Codes of Business Ethics

The concept of TBL has implications for the tripartite nature of business (economic, social and environmental) in deciding how the company intends to operate and "behave" expressed in terms of a Code of Business Ethics Business and Rules of Conduct. Ethics take us into the area of identifying the values which drive the way we do business, covering a range of ethical values, such as freedom of choice, equity, equality, professional diligence, honesty, transparency, confidentiality, loyalty, impartiality, respect for the law, environment care, health and safety protection, and respect for the "other" in the widest sense of human rights, each of which needs to be expressed in specific rules of conduct. The challenge is how to prevent these values becoming "motherhood" statements to which only "lip service" is paid, and to ensure that they are expressed in practical guidelines for business behavior and rules of conduct.

Appendix 2 contains an example of the content and structure of a Code of Business Ethics which illustrates the detail of the Code and the related Rules of Conduct. Once designed, these codes require an organization to implement them, so that they are related to specific functions and job descriptions, which, in addition to the task of communicating the principles and rules of the codes, require definition of how the rules of conduct are related to the specific responsibilities of jobs—from the board down to the shopfloor. The implementation of ethical codes need to be supported by an Ethics Committee and/or an Ethics Officer responsible in conjunction with personnel management for diffusion and communication of the Code to all departments and employees, and available for answering questions, dealing with ethical problems as they arise, and taking the necessary remedial actions in collaboration with departmental heads. Annual reporting on business ethics can become a part of "social" reporting where issues and problems, which have arisen and how they have been handled, can be discussed. Ethical reporting in this sense can also include the levels of employee and customer satisfaction, and compliance in meeting regulatory requirements covering internal auditing, and the systems for dealing with corruption, such as bribery and money laundering.

11.5 Economic Education

The Social Balance Sheet (SBS) and Sustainability Report can be a useful instruments for the economic education of employees, and communication between the company and all its stakeholders.

For employees, such economic education could be structured with the following elements:

1. *Annual presentation of the Statutory Accounts* to all employees explaining the company's economic performance and distribution of economic value to all stakeholders.

2. *Annual presentation of the SBS or SR* to all employees and other stake-holders reviewing the values, mission and strategy of the company, and results in term of social and environmental performance.

3. *Communication of the Code of Ethics* to all employees, and other stake-holders, explaining the principles and rules of conduct, with an annual report in the SBS or SR of company ethical issues and how they have been handled.

4. *An annual compensation statement* to each employee summarizing annual remuneration, and the value of direct benefits, ie, pension contributions, and indirect financial benefits, ie, employees' services, and participation in professional development programmes. Also, any participation in profit sharing and allocation of shares if applicable. The purpose is to provide each employee with a statement of the "total value" of their annual compensation package (both direct and indirect).

5. *An annual statement of the company's economic value* at the end of year divided between all stakeholders, including State taxes, and contributions for social and philanthropic purposes. The purpose of such a statement is to increase employee awareness and understanding of the company's social objectives and achievements.

Education of employees is an important part of CSR, and requires policies and procedures for doing this, in terms of relating CSR to the definition of job functions, and to the wider implications of participation in decision-making and in the economic value of the enterprises for which they work.

Appendix 1: Structure of a Sustainability Report (Example Mediolanum Group)

Introduction

– Letter to stakeholders
– Methodology of the report

Profile

– Highlights of financial performance
– Corporate structure
– Historical development

Corporate Identity

– Vision, mission and values
– Business model
– Stakeholder engagement
– Governance, risk management and compliance

Sustainability Indicators

– Financial solidity and stability
– Personalisation, security and innovation
– Multichannel banking and digitalisation and the Family Banker network
– Development of skills and knowledge
– Responsibility to the community

Source: Mediolanum Group Sustainability Report 2015

Appendix 2: Code of Ethics and Code of Conduct (Example Mediolanum Group)

Rules of Conduct

The *Code of Ethics* and *Code of Conduct* express the rules adopted by the Group.

Code of Ethics

Since 2002, Group companies have adopted a *Code of Ethics*, that is, a set of internal rules aimed at mitigating operational and reputational risk as well as promoting a widespread culture of internal control. The

Code also plays a role in the prevention of crimes covered by Legislative Decree 231/2001, as it contains a series of corporate ethics principles recommending, promoting or forbidding specific behaviour, regardless of regulatory provisions. The *Code of Ethics* is the result of active consultation and participation by the various stakeholders. Updated in September 2013, it is aimed at disseminating ethical values that reflect the Company's principles, as well as providing a concrete response to its stakeholders: employees, suppliers, customers, partners, local communities and institutions, indicating specific commitments in their regard in terms of the principles of conduct and control. The Group's stakeholders, however, are also requested to respect such values, creating a reciprocal relationship. The Code is divided into two sections. The first focuses on the values of *freedom, excellence, respect, transparency, integrity and fairness*, while the second identifies rules of conduct representing specific and mandatory commitments for every employee, helping to build a business culture consistent with our underlying values.

The approach is designed to underscore the key values underpinning the business of Banca Mediolanum S.p.A. and Group companies, as well as the rules through which our values are put into practice on a daily basis. These key ethical values reflect the entrepreneurial spirit that has always been central to the Group: *"To believe success is possible while at the same time helping people"*.

The principles of conduct and control concern:

1. Business relationship management
2. The conduct of employees and contract workers
3. Socially responsible behaviour
4. Occupational safety
5. Environmental protection
6. The role of the internal control system

There are also rules on:

- Implementing and promoting the Code;
- Dealing with reports of alleged violations; and
- Imposing sanctions for proven violations.

The Code was drafted by a working group made up of representatives from all departments overseeing the principles of conduct and control imposed by the Code. In 2013 an independent Ethics Committee was appointed at the parent company of Mediolanum Group, tasked with promoting and updating the Code. Since its establishment, the committee's members have included the heads of corporate departments that play a key role in the internal control system as a whole. Those departments include:

- Internal Auditing;
- Compliance;
- Risk Management;
- *Sales Network* Inspectorate;
- Human Resources; and
- *Sales Network.*

Reports of alleged violations of the principles contained in the Group *Code of Ethics* can be addressed by e-mail to *codiceetico@mediolanum. it*, or otherwise to the company's e-mail address, to the attention of the Ethics Committee.

The updated *Code of Ethics* of Banca Mediolanum, approved by the company's *Board of Directors* in September 2013, is available on the website www.bancamediolanum.it.

Code of Conduct

The *Code of Conduct* of Banca Mediolanum S.p.A. (updated in 2012) and the *Code of Conduct of* Mediolanum Gestione Fondi S.G.R.p.A. (updated in 2014) set forth more detailed rules which all Group employees are required to follow in the ordinary performance of their tasks and duties.

The key regulations are set out below:

1. Confidential or insider information, whether verbal or electronic, shall not be disclosed.
2. Confidential or insider information received from third parties, or by virtue of a position held, shall not be used for personal dealings, including via third parties.

3. Speculative investments are prohibited during working hours. Intraday trading is prohibited, that is, the purchase and sale of the same share on the same day.
4. Personal dealings—including in the name or on behalf of third parties—in trading derivatives, other derivatives (futures, options, or swaps), short selling, as well as dealings with a frequency that suggests speculative purposes other than those associated with normal investment transactions, are prohibited during working hours.
5. Any activity or transaction in which Group employees may have significant personal interests or interests which may be in conflict with those of the company, of existing/prospective customers and/or managed assets, shall be fully disclosed.
6. Any gift that, due to its nature or value, may potentially lead to behaviour in conflict with the interests of investors or the company may not be accepted.

Source: Mediolanum Group Sustainability Report 2015

References

Armstrong MB. Ethical issues in accounting. In: Bowie NE, editor. The Blackwell guide to business ethics. Oxford: Wiley-Blackwell; 2002.

Dobson J. Finance ethics: the rationality of virtue. Lanham, MD: Rowman & Littlefield; 1997.

Hoffman MW, Moore JM. What is business ethics? A reply to Peter Drucker. J Bus Ethics. 1982;1(4):293–300.

Machan TR. The morality of business: a profession for human wealthcare. New York: Springer; 2010.

Porter M. Creating shared value: redefining capitalism and the role of corporation in society. Paper presented at the FSG CSV Leadership Summit, Cambridge, MA, 9 June 2011.

Rogers H. The Greeting of Capitalism? International Socialist Review article of talk at conference Oct 2009 in New York.

Sullivan ET, Hovenkamp H, Shelanski HA. Antitrust law, policy and procedure: cases, materials, problems. Newark, NJ: LexisNexis; 2009.

12

Philosophy of Economics and Business Ethics

Abstract This chapter looks at some of the rational principles of economic philosophy covering consideration of the "other", which we call the "alteritas" principle; cooperation and facilitation (as service); money as "encapsulated" freedom of choice; business as a non-privative activity; and the uncertainty and indeterminacy of economic activity, all of which can be used in the design of practical codes of business ethics and codes of conduct.

In asking the question, "Will things really change?" in business behaviour following the last financial crisis, it looks at two examples of what Dutch and German banks are doing to implement cultural change in the way they operate. The creation of economic value as a philosophical principle of economics is examined, and how this relates to what we call the ethical "excellence" or "virtue" of a businessman as Economic Man, as a measure of his performance in achieving the economic, social and environmental objectives of business management. Finally in looking at the traditional theories of economic philosophy, such as rational decision theory, the chapter makes a plea to avoid the danger of "econospeak" in the language of economic theory when

© The Editor(s) (if applicable) and The Author(s) 2016   **227**
M.R. Griffiths, J.R. Lucas, *Value Economics*,
DOI 10.1057/978-1-137-54187-1_12

communicating with the business world, and to involve the business-man more in economic theorizing, and in setting the assumptions for econometric modelling.

12.1 Chapter Overview

The philosophy of economics is concerned with investigating the ratio-nality of economic activity and the principles for the organization and management of economies at both the macro and micro levels. In this context the chapter investigates the kind of philosophical principles on which business ethics need to be based to restore that civic sense called for by Jeffrey Sachs in his book *The Price of Civilisation* when he remarks that "At the root of America's economic crisis lies a moral crisis: the decline of civic virtue among America's political and economic elite. A society of markets, laws and elections is not enough if the rich and powerful fail to behave with respect, honesty and compassion toward the rest of society and toward the world."

In *Ethical Economics* we attempted to dispel the false images of Economic Man as a self-interested profit maximizer and to see him not as a selfish manipulator but as a facilitator of wealth creation and service for all stake-holders in a business enterprise and society in general. In a redefinition of his role, we argued that it is rational to see business activity also in terms of five guiding philosophical principles: the "alteritas" principle or consid-eration of the "other" in all business relations; cooperation and facilitation (service); money as "encapsulated" freedom of choice for the satisfaction of consumer preferences; business as a non-privative activity for the cre-ation of economic and social value where shareholders are part of a wider constituency of stakeholders; and the uncertainty and indeterminacy of business activity and its economic outcomes. These principles have fun-damental implications, not only for business ethics, but also for business management and organization. In this chapter we consider how these five principles can be expressed in a philosophy of economics which could provide a basis for practical codes of business ethics. We try to do this in a way which is comprehensible and useful for the businessman by consider-ing two examples of "cultural change", and in a way which will avoid the danger of "econospeak" in discussing the philosophy of economics, which can leave the businessman out of the debate by concentrating too much on academic theory, and too little on the management and organizational needs of running a business. With this in mind, we look at the competency of "management excellence", which we call the "virtue" of the businessman, necessary for success in business, and for the way we design practical codes of business ethics, which set the guidelines for how "we do business".

To do this, and in an attempt to answer the question, "Will things really change after the last financial crisis?", we consider two examples of how Dutch and German financial institutions are tackling the problem of achieving "cultural change" through the promotion of codes of business ethics, as an input for deciding how philosophical principles can provide criteria for a definition of economic justice. We set this discussion of economic philosophy and its related codes of ethics in the context of the "economic value" created by businesses, and the need to use this as the basic metric for measuring "management excellence" in the achievement of business objectives which combine "profits" and "ethics".

The chapter also proposes that philanthropy is one aspect of seeing business as a non-privative activity, and that a philosophy of economics needs to include philanthropy as one of its rational principles to be expressed in a Charter to encourage this "giving back" aspect of business activity. That philanthropy is a live and active part of present-day economics was expressed in a CNN Press Release which said, "Ten more billionaires are pledging to give away at least half of their fortunes to philanthropic causes". They signed the *Giving Pledge*—an effort started in 2010 by Warren Buffett and Bill and Melinda Gates—to encourage billionaires to commit to giving away most of their money either during their lifetimes or in their wills".

12.2 Rational Principles

At the outset we propose five rational principles for economic philosophy, which we investigated in "*Ethical Economics*" and which we shall use as guidelines for looking at economic philosophy and business ethics in this chapter.

1. *Consideration of the "Other"*. This is the principle which gives primary importance to empathy in understanding the "Other" in terms of the interests, wants and needs of all stakeholders in a business, including society in general.
2. *Cooperation and facilitation*. The principle for managing relations with all stakeholders, with particular reference to employee participation in decision making and profitability, and to customer service and feedback.
3. *Money as "encapsulated" freedom of choice*. The principle of money not as an inert immaterial substance, but as the means for exercising a freedom of choice in satisfying the wants and needs of consumer preferences; which determine economic policies for managing the demand and supply of money in balancing the needs of consumption and investment.
4. *Business as a non-privative activity*. The principle of seeing business not just as the privative property of the owners, but as a non-privative activity where shareholders are part of a wider constituency of stakeholders, all of whom share in one way or another in the "economic value" of a business enterprise. This does not diminish the centrality of the "shareholder" in seeking to maximize the return on his investment, but places greater emphasis on how the "cooperators' surplus" is distributed amongst all the stakeholders.
5. *Indeterminacy of outcomes*. The uncertainty and unpredictability principle of economic activity, which places a high premium on the competencies for financial planning (valid assumption setting), for risk management, and for the creation of economic value.

Risk management is a vital competency for managing the uncertainty and indeterminacy of economic activities; the predictive modelling techniques of economics are important tools for the assessment of business risks. Risk management requires a close working relationship between the businessman and the economist in the setting of assumptions which need to be firmly based on the specific microeconomic experience of individual business sectors combined with the macroeconomic skills of the economist. The assumptions for national econometric modelling need to draw on, for example, the experience of the Fortune Top 500, in setting and testing the validity of these national economic modelling assumptions. This could also help to strengthen the working relationship between the national economist and the businessman that we discuss later in this chapter.

If we agree that the points raised above are rational philosophical principles for doing business, we have criteria for designing business models, the operating procedures for implementing them and for the design of practical codes of business ethics. If codes of ethics are going to influence business behaviour in the real-world complexity of any specific market environment, they need to be based on the specific an individual operating needs of the business model under consideration. In other words, the five principles above have to be related directly to the competencies required for performing the functions of particular jobs. To take just one example, the job description of a sales manager will need to specify who are the "others" with whom he has to deal, how he cooperates with them, what is the nature of the money relationship he has with his staff and his customers, how he participates in creating, and possibly sharing in, the profitability of his department or division, and how he can contribute to the identification of risks in setting and achieving his sales objectives.

12.3 Danger of "Econospeak"

In discussing the philosophy of economics for the businessman we need to bridge the gap which can exist between academic theory and the need for the businessman to have a practical philosophy which can assist him in creating a business model for his organization and the way in which it will be managed. If traditional economic philosophy is concerned with (a) the concept of rational choice, (b) the way in which we evaluate economic outcomes, and (c) the nature of economic phenomena, these "economic factors" need to be presented in a way which are comprehensible for the businessman in deciding what actions he needs to take in "doing business", and what are the ethical implications of what he is doing. It was argued in Chap. 2 that economics should be seen as a moral, as well as a mathematical, science, which considers the normative ("ought") implications of "economic facts", which econometric models analyse and quantify. As a moral science economics looks at how people behave when making economic decisions; as a mathematical science it is concerned with verifying the scientific and logical validity of its analysis of economic phenomena.

Let us consider the "state of the art" in studies of economic philosophy. The book *Philosophy and Economic Theory*, edited by Frank Hahn and Martin Hollis, and published by the Oxford University Press in 1979 made a useful contribution to the subject, but also highlighted the problems of how to make the philosophy of economics of practical use to the businessman in influencing the way he "does business". The book proposes that economic theory rests on propositions about the actions a businessman needs to take in organizing his business and managing the resources he employs. Classic economic theory asserts that Economic Man is a rational egoist who makes economic decisions which are in his own interest. If that is the case, how do we distinguish between rational and irrational actions and decisions in the way those decisions are taken? How do we manage economic activities where many of the outcomes are indeterminate and contradict those deterministic theories of economics, which assert that it is possible to predetermine how people are going to act.

The book discuss the concept of competitive equilibrium through the Pareto-efficient allocation of resources (an equilibrium arising from an allocation of resources where the maximization of one person's interests does not impact negatively on someone else's interests). Pareto efficiency is a basic tenet of the classical economist, but in practice it is often impossible to realize this "efficiency" in the relentless economic process of trade-offs between different sets of interests and objectives. This requires a businessman to have a high level of competence in negotiating skills, which are important for business when operating in an indeterminate—and often unpredictable—environment. Hahn and Hollis proceed to a discussion of the rationality of collective action described in Arrow's "Independence of Irrelevant Alternatives" which claims that if we allow any preferences in an "unrestricted domain" and require non-dictatorship, the Pareto condition and the Independence of Irrelevant Alternatives, then a social preference cannot be constructed from the preferences of individual agents. This is the kind of "econospeak" which gives the businessman every right to say "So what?", and "What relevance does this have for my own individual decision making?" We take this as an example to illustrate the kind of "communication gap" which can exist in the dialogue between the economic theorist and the businessman, which is crucial to acknowledge if businessmen—as individual economic operators—are to buy in to the relevance for them of this kind of economic theorizing.

An important starting point for this dialogue concerns the way in which we consider the rationality of consumer preferences, what they are and how they are determined. The identification, satisfaction and management of consumer preferences is the daily task of any businessman. The skills and methodologies for identifying and managing consumer preferences is another essential competence for the businessman. Competence in achieving what one is responsible for, e.g, customer service management, is an aspect of business philosophy, which provides the businessman with a set of criteria for defining the competences he requires in managing his business, and the ethical standards required for putting those competencies into practice, for example the ethical standards for customer service. Consumer preferences take us into the area of social worth and welfare economics which raise complex questions for determining the rationality or irrationality of consumer choice. Classic economic theory does not admit that preferences may be irrational, and Hahn and Hollis are right to conclude that there is no "correct" definition of rationality, and that different applications of economic theory call for different definitions, each leaving a "fringe of actions" whose rationality is unpredictable and indeterminate.

It is in this indeterminate area where economists can enter in to the world of "econospeak" when statements like this are made. "The rationality postulate cannot be construed as a tentative empirical postulate which experience confirms in particular areas; nor is it incidental that what it postulates happens to be labelled "rationality". The rationality of economic decision making is a key area for economic theory, but it needs to be liberated from economic jargon, and to base its theory on the practical reality of how different businesses design their business models in order to satisfy consumer preferences, whether they be General Motors, General Electric, Kraft General Foods, DuPont, Coca Cola or

Apple. If economists are to gain the trust and respect of businessmen they have to demonstrate that their theories take account of the individual economic profiles and experience of businesses such as these, whose business models have to respond to a wide range of different consumer preferences. Economic theory has to use inductive reasoning (based on individual business experiences) in setting assumptions for econometric modelling—something that is particularly important at the microeconomic level composed of individual companies and consumers. In this area we need mechanisms for improving the dialogue between the professional economist and the businessman.

Finally, in defining the philosophical nature of "Economic Man" it is necessary to see him in the social setting in which he operates, and Hahn and Hollis are right to use Rousseau's theory "Men as they are, and laws as they might be" in seeing how economic laws and theories work out in practice in diverse market environments, which, as we proposed in *Ethical Economics*, are indeterminate in the way they adapt themselves to the time, place and circumstance in which they find themselves. This confirms the importance of the indeterminacy principle when we try to define a philosophy for economics, which must be relevant for the tools of business management, such as cost–benefit analysis, and the evaluation of risk and uncertainty.

The introduction to *Philosophy and Economic Theory* proposes that it can be useful to look at economic philosophy from three distinct points of view: (1) **Explanation**, drawing on, for example, Milton Friedman's essay *The Methodology of Positive Economics*; (2) **Rationality**, such as Simon's "From Substantive to Procedural Rationality"; and (3) **Questions of Value**, drawing on contributions such as Rawls's *A Theory of Justice* and Arrow's "Values and Collective Decision Making". Again here is an example of the risk of falling into the language of "econospeak", where the economic theorist and the businessman may part company. We need to draw the big oblong words of Explanation, Rationality and Questions of Value into the reality of what they mean for "doing business".

We can make a start by distuiguishing between "values" and "value". Values, which we can also call philosophical principles, are those beliefs and convictions which determine the way we behave. Values cover not only the principles of honesty and fairness, but also the need for a "level playing field" as a prerequisite for economic efficiency, which require rules and ethical regulations to create and maintain such a "field". Value is the worth, both monetary and not, we put on the outcomes of economic activity, where we need to define and agree the monetary measures we use for putting a "value" on the different dimensions of value discussed in Chap. 8. This means that any philosophy of economics should be based on a theory of what we mean by the creation of "economic value", as the metric we can use for quantifying and measuring the outcomes of economic activity. In other words, we need a rational theory of economic value which provides criteria for deciding how to allocate resources between private and public consumption and investment, supported by an analysis of the monetary values of each sector, and also for the allevia-tion of global social problems, such as poverty, inequalities of per capita incomes, health, education, and environmental protection. Thus, the "creation of value" becomes a key principle of economics philosophy, as it is the purpose of any economic activity to create value, which no busi-nessman or economic operator should have a problem of "buying-into". How we create value is a key question, since it is the responsibiity of any economic operator to explain what value he or she is creating, and how it is measured in both monetary and non monetary terms.

We need to look at the "value creation"experiences of economic opera-tors of which there are many examples, for example Apple's concept of "economic profit" which they call economic value added, and define as NOPAT less the cost of capital in measuring the economic value created.

However, today a theory of the creation of economic value has to take account of the principles of "Triple Bottom Line Accounting (TBL)" which values economic activity also in terms of its social and environ-mental results. In this way econokmic value becomes the starting point for calculating the intrinsic value of an economic activity, and its capabil-ity to continue as a sustainable business in the future discussed in chapter 8. The important conclusion is that the philosophy of economics needs to be based on a rational theory of "value creation", as an input for a theory of economic justice discussed in Chap. 13.

12.4 Management Excellence

In looking at the way a philosophy of economics can provide the basis for codes of business ethics it is necessary to determine the nature of the tasks and competencies of the job that an employee is being asked to do. Codes of ethical behaviour need to be related to the tasks specified in specific job descriptions, covering a number of areas: responsibilities and accountability; the competencies required in terms of technical and managerial skills (such as professional and trade know-how); negotiation and communication ability, and the capacity to identify and manage consumer preferences. These requirements require us to decide what we mean by "management excellence" in evaluating performance in achieving the objectives for a specific job.

The Baldrige Model, launched by the US Government, and also known as "The Criteria for Performance Excellence", specifies a number of management competencies for business organization, and outlines the criteria for evaluating performance. The Baldrige model consists of practices that are incorporated into seven Approach categories consisting of:

- Leadership.
- Strategic Planning.
- Customer and Market Focus.
- Measurement, Analysis, and Knowledge Management.
- Workforce Focus.
- Process Management.
- Business Results.

There are some similarities here with Michael Porter's five forces that influence competitive strategy and advantage defined as direct competitors, suppliers, customers, alternative products and potential new entrants, which has led him recently into analyzing competitive advantage in relation to CSR and his work with Kramer in the area of creating shared value. See References.

Neither of the approaches goes into the question of how to measure economic value, which is an excellence to which all these competencies aim. In the end excellence has to be measured in terms of how successful a company is in creating economic value for all its stakeholders.

"Excellence" is a good word for describing how successful a businessman is being in achieving his objectives of value creation, which we might also call the "virtue" of a businessman. The competency and skills for achieving business objectives are the "virtues" or "excellence" of business in the arête (virtue) concept of classical Greek philosophy, which in its original sense meant something or someone performing their essential function, or end (telos), in an efficient manner: For example, "sharpness" is the virtue of a knife, "military prowess" the virtue of a soldier, and "moral rectitude" the virtue of a human being. In that sense we might say the virtue of a businessman is the "creation of value", with all that implies in economic and social terms. The ethical implications of these "excellences" find their expression in the "behavioural qualities" of honesty, fairness, magnanimity, and respect for the law (in the general sense, but also in the sense of professional standards), and in relationships with all the stakeholders with whom any manager or employee is involved; all of which are the ethical qualities we look for in the way a businessman as an economic operator, "behaves" in performing his job.

The "Excellence" of Honesty

Honesty is one of the ethical qualities most people would claim to have, but it is one of the qualities most open to self-deception. As Groucho Marx said: "There's one way to find out if a man is honest: ask him. If he says 'yes' he's a crook."

One of the best discussions on the subject is a book by Dan Ariely (2012), "The (Honest) Truth about Dishonesty". On the presumption that almost everyone is dishonest for personal gain given the opportunity, the book discusses the factors which motivate people to cheat, what drives altruistic honesty, and how to encourage other people to tell the truth, or lie to you, using some innovative experiments and case studies, including a friend who worked as a consultant for Enron, and explaining how the Simple Model of Rational Crime (SMORC) was born. However, the good news with which the book ends "is that we are not helpless in the face of our human foibles (dishonesty included). Once we understand what really causes our less-than-optimal behavior, we can start to discover ways to control our behavior and improve our outcomes. That is the real goal of social science."

12.5 Ethical Codes

A MORI research project in 2012, conducted in the wake of the last financial crisis, identified three central ethical concerns among the general public: executive pay; corporate tax avoidance; and bribery and corruption. These are all concerns which business has to tackle "head on" if the public is not to believe even more firmly in Adam Smith's famous statement: "People of the same trade seldom meet together, but the conversation ends in a conspiracy against the public, or in some contrivance to raise prices."

Since basic principles of business ethics concern the way in which a company intends to implement its philosophy of business expressed in terms of its mission and corporate objectives, ethical codes have to involve everyone from the boardroom to the shopfloor, and should cover all levels of responsibilities and accountability within the organization. A code of business ethics sets out the standards for how a company wishes its employees to behave. Appendix 2 of Chap. 11 contains one such example of the content and structure of a Code of Ethics, and Code of Conduct.

The problem then arises as to how these codes are to be managed and controlled to avoid the danger that there is a "disconnect" between a company's code of ethics and its actual management practices. This requires an organizational structure involving all aspects of compliance (legal, fiscal and ethical) and the appointment of a Compliance or Ethics Officer, or Committee, responsible for compliance on the part of employees, but at the same time for providing training, education, advice, and achieving the resolution of ethical problems. The system for ethical feedback and control needs to be fully understood by all concerned. For example, customer feedback is an important indicator of how a business is seen in terms of the honesty and fairness of its service, the results of which can be reported in the Social Balance Sheet, as discussed in Chap 11. The important thing is to have a reporting system which comments on the performance of business in adhering to its code of ethics.

There are many examples of codes of business ethics (or codes of conduct as some companies call them) which can be found and consulted on Wikipedia, including companies such as Morgan Stanley, Colgate Palmolive, Esso, Coca Cola, DuPont, KGF and also organizations such as the Institute of Internal Auditors.

12.6 "Taking the Oath"

The recent economic and financial crisis resulted in an angry mistrust of those experts and authorities considered to be responsible, and calls for the introduction of new standards for business ethics.

In responding to the need to restore public confidence in the financial system, the Dutch authorities have gone so far as to ask bankers to take an oath on the ethics of how they do business. The Dutch experiment requires bankers to take the Banker's Oath (*INYT*, 13/14 December 2014), which raises questions about how to make business ethical codes of business effective, and to avoid the danger of them being seen as window dressing. In promoting the Banker's Oath campaign, Chris Buijink, Chairman of the Dutch Banking Association said "we are renewing the way we do business from top of the bank to the bottom. Seeing your clients as Muppets (as a former Goldman Sachs banker is said to have described the bank's customers) "would not be in conformity with the oath."

But will such moral initiatives succeed in recreating public confidence in the banking industry scarred by incidents like the fine of $3 billion levied on some of the world's largest banks in the USA, the UK and Switzerland for conspiring to manipulate foreign currency markets? Small wonder that the man on the Clapham Omnibus might ask "What on earth is going on?" In the Netherlands the Dutch Banking Association initiative is aimed at recreating trust in banking in a country where the Rabobank Group was involved in a scandal in which traders were rigging global benchmark interest rates, and which resulted in a fine of $1 billion and the resignation of the group's chairman. ABN Amro, the ING Group, and Rabobank were involved in a series of scandals which cost Dutch taxpayers more than $140 billion in bailouts. The oath, as Mr Buijink said, will only be meaningful if there is "real cultural renewal" and the Dutch Finance Minister also remarked: "The truth is we don't know, if the oath will have that effect". Or, in the words of Philip Bond of ResPublica (an independent think tank), "If you have a culture that is bad, no amount of regulation or punitive sanctions will shift it to favor the idea that people need to be to be held individually accountable". To make ethical codes work, "you have to have an intense internal dialogue with the employees who say, yeah, I read the code, but what does it mean for me, and what does it mean exactly to act in the client's interests?", as Mr Timmermans, vice chairman of the ING board, said.

In the end we are faced with an issue of business culture, where we have to agree what are the values on which such a culture should be based. In the end ethical codes have to be judged by how successful they will be in preventing the abuses discussed in Chaper 10.

12.7 The Deutsche Bank Code of Ethics

In describing the issues involved in introducing practical and effective codes of business ethics, an article in the *INYT* (20 May 2014) described Deutsche Bank's promise to put ethics first in an attempt to summarize the ways in which employees could avoid future scandals (such as those that have occurred in the past) by distributing a code of ethics, consisting of 18 bullet points, with the aim of prioritizing long-term success over short-term gain. How real and effective will these ethical principles be in the cut-throat global investment market in which Deutsche Bank operates? Interestingly, this attempt to reform the bank in terms of ethical behaviour goes hand in hand with its plan to increase capital by eight billion euros in order to reduce its dependence on borrowed money and to strengthen its reserves and make it more resilient against future financial shocks. This emphasizes that business ethics cannot be removed from the reality of how an investment bank can avoid the dangers of manipulating interest rates or rigging currency markets in order to maximize trading profits. General motherhood statements about transparency, honesty and fair dealing will achieve little unless they indicate how people should behave in an environment which places a premium on short-term results, and in which greed may take precedence over ethics. Deutsche Bank declares that it is changing the way it promotes and compensates people, but these policy changes have to demonstrate that they will have an impact on individual behaviour. Personal integrity is a noble objective but has to be connected to the professional competencies that have to be possessed by any incumbent of any function in the carrying out of his or her responsibilities. As we have said above, codes of business ethics have to become an integral part of "how we do business". In this case what are the challenges and organizational requirements of investment banking for Deutsche Bank—where 10 percent of the bank's 97,000 employees account for nearly half of revenue? What are the ethics required of this business, and how are the principles of transparency, honesty and fair dealing to be expressed in the practical day-to-day operating needs of investment banking?

12.8 Will Things Really Change?

Hancock and Zahawi's *Masters of Nothing*, which analysed the reasons for the last global financial crisis, and what should be done to prevent it recurring, provides another input for answering the question as to whether things will really change. In one of the chapters in their book, "The Dangers of Business as Usual", the authors refer to an article in the *Financial Times* in July 2010 entitled "Financial Leaders Pledge Excellence and Integrity", which was signed by a number of business leaders, including Win Bischoff, Marcus Agius, Mark Garvin, Chris Gibson-Smith, and the heads of the leading accounting firms. This has led in the UK to changes in corporate governance for financial institutions, and guidelines for ethical behaviour, but, as Hancock and Zahawi observe, things are unlikely to change unless there is a change in people's behaviour. The challenge is to convince people that the UK financial community can regain the moral initiative which it lost as a result of the failures of people like Fred Goodwin of RBS and Bob Diamond of Barclays. Codes of ethics can set the guidelines for the change in business behaviour and be an instrument for moving in that direction, but they have to be supported by regulation, or the "rules of the game", which have to keep pace with market and product developments. As Martin Vander Weyer wrote in the *Spectator*, "We found ourselves in a situation where bankers were dealing with products they did not fully understand, and which were not sufficiently regulated." The deregulation of financial services was the theme of the last quarter of the twentieth century. Although it may have been the correct response in terms of introducing market freedom to the sector, it went ahead without sufficient controls on the value of the deregulated financial products. So we return to the ethics of business in the way it controls the value of what it is doing, and, first and foremost, in ensuring that the risks, as well as the advantages, of its product offering are understood by all. The rest of this chapter discusses how ethical codes can be related to a number of rational philosophical principles aimed at achieving that behavioural change, which Hancock and Zahawi called for in *Masters of Nothing*, if things are really going to change.

12.9 Postscript to the UK Experience

In considering the aftermath of the last financial crisis, it is important to understand that one of the main causes was a failure of financial and regulation management. When the minutes of Bank of England meetings from the time, as reported in the *INYT* (8 January 2015) were released, they revealed that the regulators misjudged the magnitude of the crisis and were short of tools to address it. In September 2007, the chairman of the FSA saw the problems in the market as "ones of liquidity not of institutional insolvency", emphasizing "that the UK banking system was sound and that there was scope for bringing back onto balance sheets items that needed to be dealt with". The governor of the Bank of England remarked that the crisis of confidence had shaken "the unusual serenity of recent years but that if managed properly it should not threaten our long-run economic stability". Days later, Britain witnessed its first bank run since 1866 on the mortgage lender Northern Rock, which was subsequently nationalized.

The following year the government spent £45 billion to buy more than 80 percent of the Royal Bank of Scotland, and £20.5 billion bailing out Lloyds TSB Bank. In the words of Andrew Tyrie, chairman of the Treasury Select Committee, "the minutes show that during the crisis the Bank of England was unable to obtain the market data to make the decisions it was making. The so-called tripartite system for sharing responsibility for financial among the FSA, the Treasury and the Bank of England became discredited, with the Governor of the Bank stating that the arrangements were "not sufficiently workable" or relevant to "managing a crisis".

The system has now been restructured, with new regulatory powers assigned to the Bank of England, and a new agency, the Financial Conduct Authority, given responsibility for a large part of the market. Following the collapse of Lehman Brothers the Bank pressed for a recapitalization of the banks, including partial and temporary guarantees to jump-start financing and the provision of central bank liquidity to ensure the stability of the banking system, which, after meetings of the IMF, the US also adopted such a plan. As a result, the board of the Bank of England was revamped and is now run by a non-executive chairman.

The phenomena and difficulties of these recent years indicate that mission statements of business philosophy and codes of business ethics are unlikely, by themselves, to "manage the future" any better, unless they are accompanied by improved systems and procedures for calculating economic value, and managing extraordinary risks (indeterminacy management), with a risk assessment paragraph included in the statutory accounts. The regulatory authorities could also call for "future sustainability" reports for financial institutions as many major industrial companies provide today. And, finally, the mismatch between short- and long-term compensation systems needs to be addressed within the context of new systems for measuring and rewarding the creation of long-term "economic value", which we discussed in Chap. 9.

12.10 Putting Philosophical Principles to Work

In concluding this discussion on the philosophy of economics and codes of business ethics, we discuss how the five philosophical principles (which we might call "ethical rationalities") discussed in this chapter can be worked out practically in a company's "business model".

1. *The ethical rationality of recognizing and responding to the needs and interests of the "Other" (the "alteritas" principle)*. This requires an analysis and definition of the needs and interests of all stakeholders in the business in the form of a Business Charter specifying how the company intends to respond to these needs and interests at each stakeholder level, and outlining the ethical standards involved.

2. *The ethical rationality of seeing business as a cooperative and facilitative activity.* Customer service and employee relations will be key elements for defining the management procedures for satisfying the "preferences" of these two basic "stakeholder" constituents of any business. These procedures need to include the "feedback" procedures in terms of customer and employee satisfaction and indicate the ethical standards for cooperation and facilitation, including the resolution of conflicts of interest which may arise in managing customer and UK employee relationships.

3. *The ethical rationality of seeing money as "encapsulated" freedom of choice in satisfying consumer preferences* This will require a clear analysis of the company's cash flow profile, indicating clearly where money is coming from and where it is going, visually expressed in the traditional "pie " analysis. It will need to be broken down into each element, based on the statutory classifications of the balance sheet, and will serve, among other things, to analyse the nature and source of customer income and the nature of employment expense, broken down by sub-element—that is, salaries, performance-related pay, pension contributions, financial benefits, training and development. Each element of cash flow places a monetary value on the economic "choices" of the company "in doing business", and in each case can be related to the ethical standards for each element of the profit and loss account. In this way a code of ethics can be related to the individual job descriptions, so that each incumbent can see how the basic principles of honesty, fairness and transparency apply to his or her specific function.

4. *The ethical rationality of seeing business as a non-privative activity.* This will require the company to draw on the profile analysis of stakeholders (see point 1 above) in putting a monetary value on what each stakeholder receives from the company, starting with the shareholders in terms of the return on their investment (dividends and capital growth), and then moving on to the employees, which will cover all forms of compensation, i.e., cash remuneration, profit sharing; bonuses; stock participation in the form of stock options and possibly deferred shares. Participation and sharing are important rational principles of business as a non-privative activity.

These stakeholder profiles will cover all the other stakeholders, that is, suppliers; the State, in terms of taxation and social contributions; the local community; and social or research institutions or organizations in the form of donations and contributions, either directly or through company trusts or foundations.

Philanthropy is a result of seeing business not solely as a "privative" activity, where successful businessmen "give back" part of their personal wealth, as many philanthropists like Carnegie, Rockefeller Ford and Cadbury have done in the past, and today in initiatives such as the "Giving Pledge" of Bill Gates and Warren Buffett, and Tim Cooke of Apple, who has declared that he is to gift $800 million of his personal wealth to charitable causes. We need a Philanthropists' Charter, assisted by organisations like the Council of Foundations in the USA, and the European Foundation Centre (EFC) which sets standards and procedures, including disclosure, for philanthropy. This might also provide information for an annual Government Report on the levels of giving (the Giving Institute in the Usa puts this at $373 billion in 2015), which would also report on the cost of fiscal incentives for philanthropy and charitable giving. In terms of communication to the general public such a Report could also be included in a national budget for the income, costs and benefits of philanthropy. The Appendix at the end of this chapter includes a list of some of the major individual bequests.

5. *The ethical rationality of the "indeterminacy" principle.* It may not be immediately apparent how business ethics are related to the "indeterminacy" principle, but business ethics are closely related to a business's operating procedures. The "indeterminacy" principle requires clear operating procedures and skills for managing an indeterminate and unpredictable environment, e.g. risk management; economic forecasting; scenario testing (business assumptions); cost–benefit analysis; capital allocation; and investment in tangible and intangible assets. The ethical implications for "good management" in these areas are reflected in the competencies required by those responsible for these activities, and the commitment to the professional and technical standards required for performing these business functions. The Enron experience showed the results of management procedures being manipulated

in a fraudulent way, that is, dishonesty in the use of statutory accounting and reporting procedures, which put management in the dock and a professional accounting firm out of business. Codes of business ethics need to specify standards for all the operating procedures of a business, which in recent years have placed greater emphasis on the functions of audit, control and compliance in managing the responsibilities of "Triple Bottom Line Accounting".[1,2]

Appendix: Major Philanthropic Giving: Individual Bequests (Nominal Values)

- $31 billion from Warren Buffett to the Bill and Melinda Gates Foundation (initial value of the gift)
- $9 billion from Chuck Feeney to Atlantic Philanthropies
- $2 billion from Azim Premji to the Azim Premji Foundation in 2010
- $1 billion from Ted Turner to the United Nations

---

[1] Implications for ethical education and training: In looking at business ethics we believe it is appropriate to look at the "virtues" of a businessman in terms not only of the moral virtues of honesty, fairness, alteritas (consideration of the Other), respect for legality, and magnanimity, but also of the management virtues of technical competence, negotiating skills, leadership, profitability and sustainability, where codes of ethics need to set standards for both moral and management "excellence". We need a process for ethical education in this wider sense where we take account of the "eudaimonia" (human welfare) and "empathy" qualities set out in Aristotle's *Nicomachean Ethics*, and Adam Smith's *Theory of Moral Sentiments*, as the basis for education in skills for managerial competence, responsibility, accountability and the creation of economic value. Each of these management competencies has an ethical dimension for the ways in which those competencies are to be exercised.

[2] Academic discipline: As an academic discipline, business ethics emerged in the 1970s. Since no academic business ethics journals or conferences existed, researchers published in general management journals, and attended general conferences. Over time, specialized peer-reviewed journals appeared, and more researchers entered the field. Corporate scandals in the earlier 2000s increased the field's popularity. As of 2009, 16 academic journals devoted to various business ethics issues existed, with the *Journal of Business Ethics* and *Business Ethics Quarterly* considered the leaders. The International Business Development Institute (IBDI) is a global non-profit organization that represents 217 nations and all 50 US states. It offers a Charter in Business Development (CBD) that focuses on ethical business practices and standards. The Charter is directed by Harvard, MIT, and Fulbright scholars, and it includes graduate-level coursework in economics, politics, marketing, management, technology, and legal aspects of business development as it pertains to business ethics. IBDI also oversees the International Business Development Institute of Asia which provides individuals living in 20 Asian nations the opportunity to earn the Charter.

- $500 million from T Boone Pickens to Oklahoma State University
- $500 million from Walter Annenberg to public school reform in the United States
- $350 million ($7 billion in modern terms) from Andrew Carnegie in 1901 who distributed most of his wealth to philanthropic causes, including the building Carnegie Hall New York City
- $424 million from managers of the *Reader's Digest* fortune to the Metropolitan Museum of Art
- $350 million from Michael Jackson who distributed most of his wealth to philanthropic projects, and who supported over 39 charity organizations. He was listed in the *Guinness Book of World Records* for the "Most Charities Supported By a Pop Star"
- $350 million from Yank Barry and his Global Village Champions in food, education and medical supplies to the needy around the World from 1990 to the present
- $225 million from Raymond and Ruth Perelman, parents of Ronald O. Perelman, to the University of Pennsylvania School of Medicine in 2011
- $200 million from Joan B. Kroc to National Public Radio in 2003
- $100 million from John D. Rockefeller to the Rockefeller Foundation 1913–1914
- $100 million from Henry and Betty Rowan to Glassboro State College. Source: Wikipedia.
- $220 million from Phil Knight (founder of Nike) and Penny Knight to Oregon Health & Science University
- $100 million from Mark Zuckerberg to his foundation Startup: Education
- £8 million from Sir Paul Judge to the Judge Business School in Cambridge, UK
- $400 million from Oprah Winfrey for educational causes
- $138 million from Mike Lazaridis to the Perimeter Institute for Theoretical Physics, Waterloo, Ontario
- £50 million from The Hunter Foundation in Scotland for Projects in education, international development, and entrepreneurship

References

Arrow KJ. Values and collective decision making. In: Laslett P, Runciman WG, editors. Philosophy, politics and society. Oxford: Basil Blackwell; 1967. p. 215–32.

Berman, H., The Influence of Carnegie, Ford, and Rockefeller Foundation on American Foreign Policy, the Ideology of Philanthropy. Albany, NY, SUNY Press.

Dworkin R. Sovereign virtue: the theory and practice of equality. Cambridge, MA: Harvard University Press; 2002.

Friedman M. The methodology of positive economics. Cambridge: Cambridge University Press; 2009.

Griffiths and Lucas, Ethical Economics. Macmillan; 1996.

Hahn F, Hollis M. Philosophy and economic theory. Oxford: Oxford University Press; 1979.

Hancock M, Zahawi N. Masters of nothing: how the crash will happen again unless we understand human nature. London: Biteback; 2011.

Lucas. On Justice. Clarendon Press; 1980.

Lucas. Responsibility. Clarendon Press; 1993.

MacIntyre A. After virtue: a study in moral theory. Notre Dame, IN: University of Notre Dame Press; 2007.

Mackie JL. Ethics: inventing right and wrong. London: Penguin; 1977.

Porter, M. Competitive Advantage, creating and sustaining superior performance. New York: Final Press; 1985.

Porter and Kramer. Strategy and society, HBR; Dec 2006.

Rawls J. A theory of justice. Cambridge, MA: Harvard University Press; 1999.

Sen A. On ethics and economics. Oxford: Wiley-Blackwell; 1989.

Simon HA. From substantive to procedural rationality. In: Kastelein TJ, Kuipers SK, Nijenhuis WA, Wagenaar GR, editors. 25 years of economic theory. New York: Springer; 1976. p. 65–86.

Susan Senior Nello, *The European Union: Economics, Policies and History* (McGraw-Hill, 2012).

Zunz, O., Philanthropy in America, Journal of Personality and Social Psychology, 2011. Princeton University Press.

The bibliography for economic philosophy and business ethics is vast, as the Wikipedia listings indicate. Some of the more general sources which can be useful are:

1. *The Stanford Encyclopedia of Philosophy* with specific sections on Philosophy of Economics; Economic Justice; Business Ethics and Ancient Ethics (eudaimonia).
2. Professional journals, such as *Business Ethics: Magazine of Corporate Responsibility* and the *Journal of Business Ethics* (Springer).
3. For Codes of Business Ethics, useful references include the following: Berkshire Hathaway, Morgan Stanley, Colgate Palmolive, Esso, Coca Cola, DuPont, KFG (Kraft Foods Group) and the Institute of Internal Auditors.

13

New Economic Thinking and
Economic Justice

*The ideas of economists and political philosophers, both when they
are right and when they are wrong are more powerful than is
commonly understood. Indeed, the world is ruled by little else.
Practical men, who believe themselves to be quite exempt from any
intellectual influences, are usually slaves of some defunct economist.*

John Maynard Keynes

Abstract The purpose of *Value Economics* has been to examine some of
the issues facing economic theory and practice, with particular emphasis on economics as a moral science, and on the creation of economic
value in relation to economic justice. It is proposed that the creation of
economic value is a basic principle of economic justice, as it provides a
measure of the monetary wealth (NOPAT less cost of capital) available
for distribution between the stakeholders in an economic enterprise. In
other words, it provides a monetary quantification on which decisions
can be made for the distribution of this wealth according to the principles
of economic justice regarding the creation of this wealth in a given situation. The chapter looks at some recent developments in distributive and
fiscal justice in the work of the OECD's project Base Erosion and Profit

© The Editor(s) (if applicable) and The Author(s) 2016   **251**
M.R. Griffiths, J.R. Lucas, *Value Economics*,
DOI 10.1057/978-1-137-54187-1_13

Sharing (BEPS), the Tax Justice Network, and the Center for Economic and Social Justice (CESJ). It summarises the key issues and questions raised by *Value Economics*, and proposes two "economic value" projects to provide information for answering five strategic questions for new economic thinking. It concludes with some final considerations on how economic value relates to economic justice in responding to the demands of consumer preferences, and the needs of human welfare (eudaimonia).

13.1 Chapter Overview

The chapter opens with some considerations about how economic justice relates to the concept of seeing business as a participative, non-privative, and "shared value" activity, rather than a zero-sum game which only exists to maximize the return to the share holders. This means that the objectives of the shareholders have to be modified in light of the objectives of the other stakeholders, particularly the employees in terms not only of remuneration, but also of participation in the profitability of an enterprise. This requires a new look at organizational theory as it relates to of economic justice, which Nicholas Rescher in *Distributive Justice* proposes should be: "To each according to his need. To each according to his worth. To each according to his merit. To each according to his work. To each according to the agreements he has made." Sources for a more detailed analysis of economic justice are identified and briefly discussed, including the work and theories of Locke, Hume, Mill, Rawls, Hayek and Nozick.

The chapter considers some of the recent developments in distributive (participative) and fiscal justice in the work of the OECD's project Base Erosion and Profit Sharing (BEPS), which specifies actions for international taxation; the Tax Justice Network in relation to the work of the UK All Party Commission on Tax; and the Center for Economic and Social Justice (CESJ) looking at ways for creating a "just global economy", and tackling the difficult question of knowing what is "due" to all the stakeholders in an economic enterprise. Fiscal justice, where the existence of tax havens, and practice of "inversions" have emerged as the result of globalisation and the opportunities to minimise taxation in a global economy without global tax harmonization, has to answer the questions of what is "due" from or to "whom", and where (geographic location).

The chapter discusses the key issues and questions raised by *Value Economics*, and proposes two "economic value" research projects for studying the economic experiences of the financial crises of the past 25 years and those of individual economic sectors and companies during this period. We set these in the context of providing information for managing the business cycles for both the private and public sectors of national economies.

An important result of this research would be to provide the information for defining a set of strategic questions for new economic thinking, covering the correlation of economic value with the key performance indicators of growth, productivity, inflation, investment, debt and currency values. These correlations would provide the information necessary for setting objectives and targets for national competitiveness, capital and liquidity requirements, and sovereign debt levels as they relate to the creation of economic value. In this way, economic value becomes a metric for defining the levels of economic justice which are being achieved in national economies, and provides an economic criterion for defining objectives for the realization of economic justice in those economies.

The chapter concludes with considerations on the relationship between economic value and economic justice, which relate to the participative, non-privative, and "shared value" nature of business, and to the interface between the privative and public sectors of an economy, and the need for greater transparency in the communication of private and public wealth. The publication of private tax returns which distinguish between gross and net income could assist in reinforcing the "giving back" aspect of philanthropy and donational activities by revealing how wealth at both the public and private level is not only being created but also distributed. A national balance sheet of private and corporate "giving" could be a good thing if it starts first with a statement of gross income and tax paid to highlight net income and how this is being used for philanthropic and social giving in the distribution of private and corporate net worth. What are the economic and social values of this wealth, and the resulting economic justice of the way that wealth is being distributed?

13.2 Economic Justice Considerations

Value Economics has argued that freedom of choice; consideration of the "Other's" needs, wants, values and self-interests (the "alteritas" principle); and the creation of economic and social wealth, are rational principles for economic justice. See Chap. 3, Sect. 3.4, and Chap. 5, Sect. 5.3. How these principles may be worked out in practice was discussed in Chap. 12, with particular emphasis on seeing business as a participative, non-privatative, and "shared value" activity, where the privative interests of the shareholders are modified in light of the self-interests of the other stakeholders. However, we need to recognise another aspect of economic justice, which we call "competency" discussed in Chap. 12, in terms of "management excellence" in creating economic and social value, through the successful management of the uncertainty and indeterminacy of economic outcomes, in order to ensure the sustainability of a business as a viable "on-going" concern, which provides the economic wealth and resources on which the realisation of economic justice depends.

A successful business needs to draw on the experience and econometric know-how of the economist, which is why we chose as an opening quote for this chapter Keynes's warning of the danger that the "practical" man, pace the businessman, can become beholden to outdated economic theories. If that is the case, new economic thinking needs to consider how economics should revisit and renew its theories regarding the management of economic activities. As we asked in Chap. 5, when examining the experience of economics since Bretton Woods, are we about to see a new synthesis between the theories of the Keynesians and the Friedmanites, (which Paul Krugman discussed in an article in the *INYT* (July 24 2015) on the MIT gang), in taking a new look at the debate between the pro- and anti-austerity proponents?

The principles of justice have been much discussed. It has been the purpose of Value Economics to identify those rational principles of economic activity, which can contribute to defining the criteria for assessing the level of economic justice being achieved in a specific economy. In defining these criteria we refer to the five principles proposed in Nicholas Rescher's book "Distributive Justice", namely need, merit, worth, work performed and respect for agreements. How these principles can relate to business practice and ethics are illustrated in Chap. 11, Appendix 1 "Structure of a Sustainability Report", and Appendix 2, "Code of Ethics and Code of Conduct".

As references for a more detailed study of economic justice we list some of the key sources in the footnote below.[1]

For a full discussion on *Distributive Justice* we would refer readers to the article by Edmund Phelps in the *New Palgrave Dictionary of Economics*. More recent developments can be found in the work of the OECD with its project Base Erosion and Profit Sharing (BEPS) to reform international tax, the Tax Justice Network, and the Center for Economic and Social Justice (CESJ).

The OECD (BEPS) report seeks to reform tax strategies that exploit gaps which enable profits to be artificially shifted to low- or non-tax areas, the trend towards "inversions" which transfer profits to tax havens where those profits have not been generated. The BEPS programme specifies actions regarding such areas as the digital economy, control of foreign companies, transfer pricing, and disclosure. About 100 countries are now involved in implementing the BEPS recommendations.

---

[1] Sources for defining principles of economic justice

1. *The New Palgrave Dictionary of Economics*, including the article on "Distributive Justice" by Edmund Phelps.
2. The Stanford Encylopedia of Philosophy "Economices or Economic Justice.
3. J.R. Lucas, *On Justice*, which examines the nature of distributive, economic, commutative and fiscal justice.
4. F.A. Hayek, *The Constitution of Liberty*, which puts the case for classical liberalism (free markets and minimum State control).
5. J. Rawls, *A Theory of Justice*, J. Rawls, which discusses Justice as "fairness", the concept of "civility", and the relationship between freedom and equality.
6. R. Nozick, *Anarchy, State and Utopia*, a libertarian approach to economics with "minimal State involvement".
7. J. Locke, An Essay Concerning Human Understanding, the precursor of the USA's Declaration of Independence "Life, Liberty and the Pursuit of Happiness" with its case for the Social Contract, separation of powers, and freedom of conscience.
8. J.S. Mill, *On Liberty*, J.S. Mill, with its defence of free markets and concept of "trade as a social act".
9. D. Hume, *A Treatise of Human Nature*, the empiricist, who sees "passion not reason as governing human behaviour", and the self as "a bundle of perceptions" without a cohesive quality, where we cannot logically induce an "ought" from what "is".

The Tax Justice Network is an independent non-profit organisation started in 2003, which looks at a wide range of tax issues including the work of the UK All Party Parliamentary Group on Tax which investigates the need for a more responsible global tax system. The Network is also pushing for ways of doing away with tax secrecy to restore public confidence in the integrity of international tax systems.

The CEJS, an independent organisation established in 1984, is calling for what it calls a More Free Market and Just Global Economy in facing up to the problem of how one decides what is "due" in giving people what they are "due". It has produced a wide range of reports on participative, distributive, and social justice, such as "The Just Third Way", "High Road to Economic Justice" (with its concept of every worker an owner), and "Declaration of Monetary Justice", advocating that the Fed should adopt a two-tier money creation and credit policy which distinguishes between ownership–expanding credit and non-productive speculative uses of credit, but the fiscal implications of doing this are not discussed in detail. The plea for greater employee ownership in the companies they work for is discussed in Chap. 9, which has many similarities to the Employee Stock Ownership Programmes (ESOPS) in the USA, and raises implications for fiscal justice in encouraging people to invest part of their income in the ownership of the companies for which they work.

13.3 Questions for New Economic Thinking

In this section we summarize the key issues discussed in Value Economics and the related questions for new economic thinking.

1. *Economics as a Moral Science*. Key issue: economics as a contributor to "human well-being". Question: "How does the theory and practice of economics contribute to 'human well-being' in terms of analyzing and measuring the creation of economic value, and proposing policies for the distribution and allocation of scarce economic resources?"
2. *Cooperation and Facilitation*. Key issue: understanding the needs, wants and values of the "Other". Question: "What are the requirements, procedures and standards for relating to the 'Other' in terms of empathy for different self-interests, beliefs and objectives?"

3. *Money*. Key issue: money as encapsulated freedom of choice. Question: "How do we manage the supply of money in satisfying consumer preferences, and reconcile the conflicts of greed and altruism in its use?"

4. *The Moneyed Society*. Key issues: the quantity of money, liquidity management, and control of public debt. Question: "How do we manage the supply of money, within the context of balancing the needs of consumption, investment and control of private and public debt in a global environment?"

5. *Boom and Bust*. Key issue: the management of business cycles. Question: "What has been the experience of different economies, and of different economic sectors in those economies, during the economic crises of the past twenty years?"

6. *Work and Unemployment*. Key issues: unemployment, income inequality, and employee participation. Questions: "What are 'acceptable' levels of unemployment? How can we resolve the problem of income inequalities? How can employees participate in decision making and ownership?"

7. *Economic Value*. Key issue: the measurement of the economic value of economic enterprises both private and public. Question: "Can economic value as NOPAT less cost of capital become the first metric for measuring the economic value of private and public business enterprises?"

8. *Relating Economic Value to Compensation*. Key issue: the relationship between reward for the creation of short-term and long-term economic value. Question: "How can we relate performance-related compensation to economic value, and enable employees to participate in profitability and ownership?"

9. *Regulation*. Key issue: the regulation and control of solvency and economic value. Question: "How do we combine capital solidity with measures of economic value?"

10. *Corporate Social Responsibility*. Key issue: combining economic, social and environmental responsibilities. Question: "How does CSR contribute to the creation of economic, social and environmental value?"

11. *Economic Philosophy and Business Ethics*. Key issues: business as a nonprivative, shared value and indeterminate activity. Questions; "what are the implications of these issues for a philosophy of economics, and how can we design codes of business ethics which contribute to controlling unethical business behavior?"

12. *New Economic Thinking and Economic Justice.* Key issue; rational principles of economic justice. Question: "How can we define economic justice in combining 'profits, "value" and 'ethics'?"

Answers to these questions could strengthen the legitimacy of business in the eyes of the general public represented by the man on the famous Clapham Omnibus, as participators in the creation of economic and social wealth, and to recreate that confidence and trust in the financial "system", which was damaged, if not lost, during the last financial crisis. Are things really going to change in the way that economic operators, advisors and regulators behave in managing businesses and the economy? They are also questions which could be put to the opponents of modern capitalism in opening a rational debate with those who may risk throwing the baby out with the bathwater, when it comes to proposing new models of economic justice for modern capitalism.

13.4 Private and Public Business Cycle Management

To answer the questions posed in section 13.2, we need more research which can provide information for new economic thinking.

Such research would analyse the nature of the financial crises of the last twenty five years, and the effects which they have had on specific economic sectors and individual businesses. The results of this research would also provide "hard-fact" information to answering the five strategic questions for new economic thinking proposed at the end of this section.

Analysing Financial Crises
We need understand the causes and outcomes of boom–bust conditions which occur during business cycles, taking as examples the various crises which have arisen in the world economy over the past twenty five years.

1. Black Wednesday of 1992.
2. Default of Mexican debt in 1994.

3. Asian devaluation and banking crises in 1997.
4. Russian financial crisis in 1998, repeated in 2014.
5. Argentine economic crisis 1999–2002.
6. Iceland financial crisis 2008.
7. The dot-com bubble of 2001.
8. Global financial crisis 2007–2008.
9. European sovereign debt crisis of 2010.

Economists need to explain why these crises occurred, why econometric predictive techniques were often unable to forecast them, and how economic theory has changed as a result. This might take the form of a specific research project undertaken by the Bank of England in conjunction with institutions such as the London School of Economics and the Institute for New Economic Thinking in Oxford. Such a research project would also need to involve institutions, such as, the Fed, the IMF, and the BCE, but would need a project sponsor. Could this be the Bank of England as the "kick-starter" of such a "business cycle" research project?.

Analysis of Crises by Economic Sector and Individual Businesses
General "after the event" analysis of these global financial crises could benefit from an analysis of how individual businesses were affected by these crises, perhaps taking the global financial crisis 2007–2008 as a specific case. How did this crisis impact on different economic sectors, and on the economic and market values of individual companies? What actions did they take to survive, and what assistance did they receive from the government? A possible sample of companies drawn from 16 economic sectors is given below.

1. *Retailing*: Wal-Mart and Tesco.
2. *Oil*: Exxon and Royal Dutch Shell, and possibly China National Petroleum.
3. *Computing*: Apple and Microsoft.
4. *Motor*: General Motors and Volkswagen.
5. *Airspace*: Boeing and Airbus.
6. *Chemicals*: DuPont and ICI.

7. *Pharmaceuticals*: Pfizer and Astra Zeneca, and possibly Sinopec for the Chinese experience.
8. *Engineering*: GE and Siemens.
9. *Food*: Kraft and Nestlé.
10. *Beverages*: Coca Cola and Heineken.
11. *Metal*: Arcelor Mittal and Nippon Steel, and possibly TATA for Indian experience.
12. *Electrical*: Sony and Philips.
13. *Banking*: J.P. Morgan Chase and Société Générale.
14. *Insurance*: AXA and Allianz.
15. *Diversified*: Berkshire Hathaway and Black Rock.
16. *Trading*: Glencore and Mitsubishi Corporation

The list above is not intended to be exhaustive, and is provided to stimulate discussion, as to how such research could be conducted, and by whom. An "experience" research project of this kind could help to identify the "successful" and the "less successful" experiences of individual businesses during financial crisis. Such research could also provide economic planners with a realistic basis for setting sectoral economic assumptions for the future, and designing appropriate financial and fiscal incentives, if necessary by economic sector.

The possible sample of sectors and companies above only concerns activities in the private sector, and makes no mention of the public sector, whose experience would be necessary for a more complete economic analysis. We should like to see public services, as economic enterprises in their own right, included in this research, if only as an experiment in analysing the experiences of public sector enterprises as economic operators, subject, like any private business, to investment constraints and the return on investment (ROI) on those investments, and to the disciplines of income and expense budgets, and cost–benefit analysis. In considering public service enterprises we could perhaps start with two public sector "guinea pigs": health and education. Such research could have the advantage of analyzing the economic value of public enterprises in terms of "Triple Bottom Line Accounting" (TBL).

Such research would need to involve the authorities and institutions suggested for the financial crises research, but would need to be extended to the representatives of capital and labour, which for the UK would include the CBI and the TUC.

Strategic Questions for New Economic Thinking

With the results of these two research projects, and the "hard fact" findings arising from the experiences of individual companies within specific economic sectors, we could formulate the kind of strategic questions that new economic thinking needs to answer in identifying, planning and managing business cycles. The findings of the two research projects described above could also have the added advantage of providing a data base for economists and businessmen in setting the assumptions for econometric predictive modelling.

The five strategic questions would cover the following aspects of economic activity, all of which relate to the creation or destruction of economic value.

1. What is the correlation between the creation of economic value and the key performance indicators (KPI) of growth, productivity, inflation, investment, debt, and currency values, and how do these correlations change during business cycles and boom–bust market conditions? It would be useful to have a six-point matrix composed of these factors to highlight how each impacts on the others in light of the sectoral "business experiences" gained from the research above, and their implications for economic value.

2. How do we measure competitiveness in national and global markets, and how does productivity and competitiveness vary between national economies and between economic sectors in those individual market economies?

3. How are capital and liquidity to be provided for the private and public sectors of national economies, and in what form, covering, equity financing, bonds (government, corporate and project), other debt instruments, including securitization and derivatives, credit, mortgages and consumer finance?

4. What are the standards and procedures required for managing and controlling sovereign debt levels, using the economic criteria identified by answers to the three questions above, and how should sovereign

debt be categorized between private and public debt, and quantified in terms of "Triple Bottom Line Accounting," covering economic, social and environmental investment and expenditure?

5. How do we define economic justice in a way which combines business efficiency with ethics and the need to realise the social and environmental requirements of present-day business and a global economy?

None of the answers to the five questions posed above can avoid taking a position on what we mean by economic value and how it can be created. In other words, "value creation" needs to become the basic criterion for planning and measuring economic activity nationally and globally. The final question for any businessman (and the same applies to the economist, banker, regulator and government policy maker) has to be: "What contribution are my economic decisions making to the creation of economic, social and environmental value?"

Who might be the sponsors for a project to answer these questions? At the UK level it could be the same organizations as for the research projects described above, if it was decided to use the UK as a pilot project before going international. An international project would require the sponsorship of the other national banking institutions, including the ECB, and international institutions, like the World Bank, the WTA and the OECD.

13.5 Economic Value and Justice

One of the conclusions of *Value Economics* is that it is rational to see business as a participative, non-privative, "shared value" activity, rather than as a zero-sum game with too much emphasis on the maximization of profit for the shareholders. This concept, while respecting the ethical principles of equity, fairness and equality, still has to answer the question of whether or not it will create greater economic value for economic enterprises (KPI). Here the key issue is business efficiency in terms of the cost–benefit results which result in the profitability which will ensure the future sustainability of the enterprise. The importance of the economic value metric proposed is that it provides a uniformity, clarity and transparency regarding the value of a business, which can contribute to more informed decision making when deciding how the cooperators' surplus can be distributed between all the stakeholders. Decision making based on economic value reporting can also contribute to developing a greater sense of "shared value" on the part of shareholders and employees in particular.

It is a lack of participation on the part of many "wage" earners, and a sense that they often do not have the opportunity to participate in the profitability of a company (if there are no profit-sharing schemes in operation), which can produce a passive acceptance of the "wage" relationship without any strong sense of participation. There are many examples of more active participation, where the experience of a John Lewis in the UK, Luxotica in Italy, or the greater degree of employee involvement in the Japanese or Chinese forms of capitalism, can result in a greater understanding of how economic value is being created and distributed.

The increasing gap in the inequality of incomes is still an unresolved problem for modern capitalism and an question to economic justice. To address this aspect of economic justice, *Value Economics* makes a strong plea for linking compensation at all levels to economic value, and expressing levels of compensation, particularly those that are performance-related, to the economic value which has been created. This may highlight inequalities of income, but it will enable people to understand how much is being paid out to reward the achievement of higher economic value. Participation of this kind is related closely to the concept of the non-privative nature of business, where performance-related compensation may reduce total shareholder return (TSR), and more so when it is related to allocation of shares in the form of stock options, deferred or restricted shares. *Value Economics* also suggests that the allocation of shares be extended to a greater number of, if not all, employees to enable them to participate in the ownership of the firm for which they work. This would also emphasize the concept of "shared value", which is closely linked to the non-privative concept of business.

All these possible incentive compensation systems would reflect the participative, non-privative and "shared value" nature of business, and relative to the economic justice of the way in which business creates and distributives economic value. Equity, fairness and equality are all aspects of economic justice, but they have to be realised in the context of viable business enterprises. A failed business is by its nature an example of economic injustice for all its stakeholders.

The non-privative concept also emphasizes the "giving back", that is, the philanthropic, principle of business where successful economic operators express a freedom of choice to dispose of personal wealth in a way which benefits the society, from which it has been derived is another aspect of economic justice discussed in Chap. 12.

Finally these reflections on the connection between economic value and economic justice, raise important questions for the interface between the private and public sectors. The "Private good, State bad" mentality that often characterizes capitalist economic thinking has produced a conflictual attitude on the part of many citizens towards the State, which, apart from being irrational, leads to a breakdown of a cooperative spirit between the two. In terms of justice, both economic and general, the State needs to be held accountable for the value it is creating for society—for example, what is the economic and social value of the NHS? *Value Economics* proposes an analytical experiment to define and analyse the economic value of the NHS to see if we can establish clearer "value" standards for public enterprises. This links with the concept of the entrepreneurial State discussed in Chap. 5. One might argue that the NHS has a social rather than an economic value. This is not rational because public social "economic" enterprises have economic costs, which, in terms of ethical transparency and accountability, would benefit from an estimate of their economic value in terms of "Triple Bottom Line Accounting" (TBL).

Fiscal contributions are a complex and often contentious for economic justice, as they reduce economic value and the income available for the payee whether a business or the individual tax payer. However, even if taxes are often seen as a burden on the payee, they are a participative contribution to society, and contribute to the economic value of the state. This has implications for the civic sense on the part of companies and individual citizen which Rawls called "civility", and which Jeffrey Sachs refers to as "civic virtue" discussed in Chap. 12. The concept of "civics"emphasises the role of citizens as social as well as political animals in Aristotle's sense of the word, where both words are interchangeable. Fiscal justice is part of economic justice, which requires rational criteria for deciding what levels of taxation should be, and accounting for the efficiency in which these state income resources are used.. Fiscal justice becomes more complex in a global economic environment where different rates of corporate taxation exist leading to the direction of funds into "tax haven" or lower tax economies. Global tax harminisation remains an unresolved issue for economic justice in a world where corporate taxation rates range from 16% in Germany to 20% in the UK, to 25% in China to 35% in the USA.

In concluding the chapter with these considerations on the relationship between economic value and economic justice, we stress the participative, non-privative, and "shared value" nature of business, the importance of basing the interface between the private and public sectors on cooperation rather than the conflict inherent in the frame of mind "Private Good, State Bad", and the need for greater transparency in the communication of private and public wealth.

The publication of tax returns (both corporate and individual), which distinguish between gross and net income, could assist in reinforcing the "giving back" aspect of philanthropy and donational activities in economics by revealing how monetary wealth at both the private and public level is not only being created but also distributed. A national balance sheet of private and corporate "giving" would be a good thing, if it starts with a statement first of gross income received and tax paid, and then how net income is being used for philanthropic and social giving in the distribution of private and corporate net wealth. Better transparency in this sense thus becomes an important principle of economic justice and an ethic of economic activity whether private or public, profit or non-profit.

References

Arrow KJ. Collected papers of Kenneth J. Arrow, Volume 1: social choice and justice. Cambridge, MA: Belknap; 1984.

Center for Economic and Social Justice (CESJ) "Just Third Way" and "Declaration of Monetary Justice".

Durlauf SN, Blume LE, editors. The new Palgrave dictionary of economics. Basingstoke: Palgrave Macmillan; 2008.

Dworkin R. Sovereign virtue: the theory and practice of equality. Cambridge, MA: Harvard University Press; 2002.

Kelso and Adler. The Capitalist Manifesto, Random House, 1958.

Locke J. An essay concerning human understanding. London: Penguin; 1997.

Mill JS. On liberty. New York: Cosimo; 2005.

Rawls J. A theory of justice. Cambridge, MA: Harvard University Press; 1999.

Rescher N. Distributive justice: a constructive critique of the utilitarian theory of distribution. London: Macmillan; 1966.

Sen A. Equity and justice. In: Sen AK, editor. Collective choice and social welfare. Edinburgh: Oliver & Boyd; 1971.

Tax Justice Network, Report of the "UK All Party Parliamentary Group on Tax."

Zalta Edward N, editor. See, "Philosophy of Economics" (Daniel Hausman, September 12, 2013), and "Economics at Economic" Justice (Marc Fleurbaey, May 28, 2004). The Stanford encyclopedia of philosophy. Stanford: Stanford University.

Index

Note: The page numbers followed by 'n' refers to footnote.

© The Editor(s) (if applicable) and The Author(s) 2016
M.R. Griffiths, J.R. Lucas, *Value Economics*,
DOI 10.1057/978-1-137-54187-1